FROM THE BOARDROOM TO THE WAR ROOM

America's Corporate Liberals and FDR's Preparedness Program

Richard E. Holl

UNIVERSITY OF ROCHESTER PRESS

First published 2005

University of Rochester Press
668 Mt. Hope Avenue, Rochester, NY 14620, USA
www.urpress.com
and of Boydell & Brewer Limited
PO Box 9, Woodbridge, Suffolk IP12 3DF, UK
www.boydellandbrewer.com

ISBN: 1–58046–192–1

Library of Congress Cataloging-in-Publication Data
Holl, Richard E., 1960-
  From the boardroom to the war room: America's corporate liberals and
FDR's preparedness program/Richard E. Holl.
    p. cm.
  Includes bibliographical references and index.
  ISBN 1–58046–192–1 (hardcover: alk. paper)
  1. Industrial policy–United States–History–20th century. 2. Corporate
state–United States–History–20th century. 3. Business and
politics–United States–History–20th century. 4. United States–Economic
policy–1933–1945. I. Title.
  HD3616.U46H65 2005
  338.973′009′043–dc22   2005007245

A catalogue record for this title is available from the British Library.

This publication is printed on acid-free paper.
Printed in the United States of America.

To Jody, with enduring affection

Contents

Illustrations

Acknowledgments

This book has been so many years in the making that I find it almost embarrassing. In 1989, I selected the corporate liberals and American preparedness for World War II as the topic for my doctoral dissertation at the University of Kentucky. Young and naïve back then, I underestimated the complexity of the subject and consequently spent many more years on it than I had anticipated trying to get it right. Teaching five classes a semester at Lees College along the way did not make the task any easier. Doubts about whether or not I would ever finish crept into my mind. Final approval of the dissertation in 1996 (and acquisition of the Ph.D.) brought both relief and satisfaction. Tired of the corporate liberals at that point, and much too close to them to have any real objectivity, I put the manuscript aside for a half-dozen years until my good friend Keith Harper persuaded me to dust it off, make revisions, and seek out a publisher.

As one might expect, given such an elongated path to publication, I owe numerous debts. The History Department at the University of Kentucky provided me with financial aid from 1986 to 1990. President Charles M. Derrickson and Dean Kathy Smoot of Lees College helped me secure a Mellon Fellowship for the 1994–1995 academic year. Dorothy Graddy, then director of the U.K. Faculty Scholars Program, always took time to encourage me. Tim Madigan, editorial director of the University of Rochester Press, liked the manuscript topic from the beginning, and it has been a pleasure to work with him. An anonymous reviewer for the University of Rochester Press provided a valuable critique of the entire work, which resulted in more than a few improvements. I thank each of them.

Three professors deserve special mention. Dr. Keith W. Olson, my thesis advisor at the University of Maryland, introduced me to the historical profession. Under Dr. Olson's guidance, I began to think historically and became a better writer. I remember Dr. Olson most, however, for his decency, integrity, and many small kindnesses. Dr. George Herring, a member of my graduate committee at the University of Kentucky, challenged me to be the best historian I could be. Dr. Herring also gave me editorial assistance and kind words when I was down. Dr. David Hamilton, my dissertation director at U.K., lent me his great expertise throughout my doctoral program. His comments on successive drafts of my dissertation made the final product much better than it would have been otherwise.

Friends contributed significantly to this project. Anna Lois Puffer, my word processor and confidant, has always performed her duties with cheerfulness and dispatch. Bob Hilton, Cathy Branson, and Donna Collins, the Lees library crew, have gone above and beyond the call of duty to secure books and other information for me; their professionalism and good natures are deeply appreciated. Linda Cornett, George Ellenberg, Todd Estes, the late Joyce Hardyman, Dan Lykins, Art Mielke, Alice Reagan, and Leila Sandlin Smith heard more than they ever wanted to about the trials and tribulations of writing a dissertation/book. Their understanding and patience have been remarkable. Robert Hodges, Andy McIntire, and Rick Smoot read and commented on part or all of the manuscript before publication; they pronounced the themes and prose clear enough and the publication effort worthwhile. Of course, this book would not have appeared at all if it had not been for Keith Harper's persistent cajoling. Any remaining errors in the book are therefore Keith's responsibility, not mine.

My last and greatest thanks are reserved for my family. Doug and Mike have always been good brothers, except when they locked me in a kitchen cabinet and would not let me out. God blessed me with the best grandparents a little kid (or a big one) could ever have. Mom and Dad taught me the value of education and have always been supportive of my life choices. My wife, Jody, has been extraordinarily forgiving of her moody, sometimes illtempered husband and the dedication at the front is for her.

R. E. H.
April, 2005

Introduction

War is almost always an agent of tremendous social change, and World War II proved no exception. Much attention has been devoted to the role of American women in defense plants and to the stimulus that the war provided to the civil rights movement, to name just two examples, but other changes were also important. Indeed, the conjunction of the Great Depression, the late New Deal, and European war fundamentally altered the contours of the modern American state, while U.S. entry into the conflict itself consolidated these changes.

The personnel and structure of the U.S. state was transformed even before the Japanese attack on Pearl Harbor. During the period from 1939 to 1941, a small band of visionary businessmen accepted key positions within the federal government; they chose cooperation with the Roosevelt administration rather than joining mainstream capitalists in opposition to the reform-minded New Deal. Known collectively as corporate liberals, these businessmen-bureaucrats helped strengthen the United States' national defense during a time of weakness. In the process, the U.S. state grew larger and more powerful, developing a greater planning capacity than ever before in its history. By December 7, 1941, a modified American state had emerged, wherein corporate liberals had effectively substituted their version of state building for that advocated by ardent New Dealers and organized labor. The resultant institutional configuration ensured ample provisions for the military, while big businessmen received better treatment than any other group within U.S. society.

This general state of affairs persisted throughout World War II. Whereas the military lacked weapons up to August 1939, it possessed a multitude of arms and munitions by 1942 and even more thereafter. Allied nations also benefited from American plenty. By December 7, 1942, the United States alone outproduced all Axis nations combined. Given economic realities and the time frame, this result would have been impossible without corporate liberal exertions during the preparedness period. Even after World War II ended, the military-industrial complex and big business dominance of the political economy remained fixtures of American life.

Corporate liberalism, however, did not arrive full blown in 1939 or 1941; it is a strain of enlightened business thinking that has been influential throughout the twentieth century. This philosophy holds that corporate capitalism is the best economic system ever conceived, but it is not perfect, and must therefore be reformed from time to time. Advocates of corporate liberalism—the corporate liberals—view reform as a means to sustain and strengthen the existing business regime. Reform, in this light, undercuts radical critics and furthers goals of prosperity and fairness for all.

Historians and social scientists have treated corporate liberalism and its practitioners in widely divergent ways. Martin Sklar, James Weinstein, and other neo-leftist revisionists depict corporate liberals as crafty, even devious conservatives whose reforms perpetuated capitalism, a rotten system, and were therefore negative. William Appleman Williams, Ronald Radosh, and Murray Rothbard continued in this vein, insisting that corporate liberals had fashioned a pernicious corporate system that "carried the [American people] well onto the threshold of a gentle totalitarianism." G. William Domhoff views the corporate liberals as "sophisticated conservatives," who occasionally sponsored semi-enlightened measures as a means of heading off more far-reaching objectives of labor, farmers, and consumers for true social justice. As Howell John Harris observes, corporate liberals "were not unduly perturbed by the recent increases in power of unions and the federal government." Organizational historians have resisted sweeping generalizations of this sort. They emphasize the complexity of the modern political economy and search for ways to better understand the interstices between the public and private sectors.

From the organizational perspective, corporate liberals appear to be agents of a modern, more rational capitalist order. Disdainful of internecine struggles among business firms and businessmen, indeed repulsed by the counterproductive battles between a variety of American special-interest groups, corporate liberals strove to bring about compromise, cooperation, stability, and progress. Ellis W. Hawley notes that they abhorred "Balkanization" and constantly sought "corporative structures . . . to discipline such impulses and achieve coordination through enlightened concerts of recognized interests." Similarly, Kim McQuaid asserts that corporate liberals emphasized "re-ordering of inter- and intra-industry competition" and "intelligent collaboration" between business, labor, and the state.

The interpretative framework of the organizational school is more useful than that of the New Left for the purpose of my study, so long as it is understood that business-led associationalism and corporate liberal efforts to secure a more rational world do not automatically preclude pluralistic conflict or humanitarian motivations. Business fought with other special interests, and within itself, despite corporatist undertakings. Corporate liberals exhibited a high degree of self-interest on some occasions and impressive human sympathies on others. It is also wise to heed Gerald Berk's admonition that "corporate elites do not automatically discover their interests in reform or easily realize their advantage in politics."[1]

Even taking Berk's caution into account, corporate liberal ideology has attracted some of the most talented businessmen around, who have displayed substantial flexibility. Although it is true that corporate liberals have never deviated from certain bedrock beliefs (such as the predominant role private enterprise should play in a capitalistic system, the importance of extensive managerial autonomy, or the pivotal nature of profit as an incentive to production), their views on many subjects have evolved to keep pace with changing economic, political, and diplomatic conditions.[2]

Nowhere is this process of adjustment more evident than when it comes to their conception of the state. Early on, corporate liberals abandoned the doctrinaire laissez-faire of mainstream businessmen; they envisioned a supporting role for government in the private economy. During the 1920s, corporate liberals pursued private, company-specific solutions for the ailments and inequities bred by capitalism while simultaneously exploring associational prescriptions. In the 1930s, more extensive contacts with government were established. Many corporate liberals took leave from their companies, entering public service in order to combat Depression. Still later, efforts to restore prosperity necessarily yielded to preparations for war. Once again, corporate liberals cooperated with the state, civil servants, and politicians.

During the New Era, corporate liberals such as Henry Dennison helped construct a public–private system designed to achieve their goals of economic stability and growth. This system required appropriate action on the part of individual firms and the state. Corporate liberals implored firms to adopt "welfare capitalism": an innovative program of non-wage benefits for their employees.[3] They asked the state to back up business by discouraging destructive competition and by encouraging socially responsible behaviors.

The logic was impeccable. Grant workers non-wage benefits as a supplement to their pay in order to maximize job satisfaction, regularize production, and insure the well-being of all persons with a stake in corporate capitalism. Have the state stand behind privately arranged standards and norms so that companies would be less likely to depart from them for selfish reasons. In this way, according to the corporate liberals, a new economic order slowly emerged during the 1920s, characterized by greater rationality, order, and progress. Here private interests took the lead, performing public functions such as maintenance of employment, stabilization of the business cycle, and achievement of prosperity, with the state lending its assistance whenever asked. Corporatism, rather than pluralism, suffused this structure.[4]

The combination of Hooverian associationalism and welfare capitalism operated well enough for a while, despite criticism from planners, free marketers, and trade unionists.[5] Advocates of stronger government planning, including cartelistic arrangements, deemed associationalism too weak to cure sick industries or prevent cyclical contractions. Proponents of laissez-faire wished to return to natural market forces, rather than rely on the loose web of government agencies, trade associations, corporations, scientific management societies, and social science research councils that Secretary of Commerce Herbert Hoover helped assemble.[6] Trade unionists and class-conscious workers preferred more powerful industrial unions to employer paternalism.[7] Yet the "new capitalism" seemed to work. Welfare capitalism did provide a cushion for companies and their workers during recessions in 1920–1921 and 1927. Many workmen did view non-wage benefits as protection against economic vagaries. Best of all, New Era prosperity reasserted itself after the downturns and the dream of everlasting progress remained intact.

Unfortunately, the Great Depression proved that the corporate liberals had greatly exaggerated the potential of this public–private matrix for lasting systemic reform. Most firms that had instituted welfare capitalistic programs simply could not cope with such a treacherous economy: a lack of funds rendered private unemployment insurance reserves, and other benefit schemes, insolvent.[8] Associationalism fared no better. President Hoover called on allied corporations, trade associations, and other organizations to counteract adverse forces at work in the economy. He asked businesses to have confidence, to maintain employment and wages, and to invest. He urged trade associations to spread optimism among firms in their industries. They should also spur construction.[9] After their initial exertions of 1929–1930 brought little relief, corporations and trade associations became dispirited. By 1931, pessimism reigned, and companies responded to depression in the traditional manner, by retrenching. Wages were slashed, layoffs mounted, investment dropped to almost nothing. The Great Depression intensified.

With the rout of the "new capitalism," corporate liberals looked elsewhere. Henry Dennison of Dennison Manufacturing Company, Gerard Swope of General Electric, Marion Folsom of Eastman Kodak Company, and others chose to link hands with the incoming Franklin D. Roosevelt administration, accepting the necessity of an expanded role for the federal government. Dennison and Swope reaffirmed their belief in public–private cooperation, which deepened. Folsom concluded, rather ruefully, that large-scale government intervention in the economy was unavoidable and that negotiation, compromise, and partnership between federal authorities and enlightened businessmen was preferable to other alternatives. Their final object remained the same: preservation of corporate capitalism, with all its attendant virtues, through implementation of sensible reforms.

From 1933 through the New Deal, the preparedness period, and war, corporate liberals favored "intelligent collaboration" between business and government.[10] They appeared in a variety of agencies, and although their influence fluctuated up to 1938, it grew steadily thereafter. Corporate liberals played a fundamental role in the National Recovery Administration (NRA). They lent significant support to the Social Security Act of 1935, whose benefits conformed rather nicely to those offered by welfare capitalist companies prior to the Depression. But when the Supreme Court declared NRA unconstitutional, corporate liberal influence waned—in a period that coincided with the time of greatest hostility between Roosevelt and mainstream businessmen. The winter of 1938–1939 saw corporate liberal clout increase again. FDR listened to their appeals for aid to business, naming Harry Hopkins as Secretary of Commerce and spearhead of a major new economic recovery bid based around the traditional concept of building business confidence.

Far greater strides toward improved business–government relations were made after the outbreak of European war in September 1939. Conflict abroad necessitated an American defense-preparedness campaign, since the condition of the U.S. military was unacceptable. President Roosevelt opted to bring corporate liberals into government to help him upgrade the United States' defense. He relied on the corporate liberals specifically, and the business community generally, to supply him with expertise, plant, and equipment available nowhere else. In essence, the state joined private resources to the existing organizational structure to perform a vital public service.

Roosevelt thought this approach best. Though other alternatives might have been pursued, such as a market-driven system, a New Deal–national security state equipped with enhanced regulatory powers, or a government-run munitions complex, he settled on a type of cooperative undertaking along the lines of the World War I War Industries Board and the National Recovery Administration. Tradition, of course, was on this side, as well as expediency. Other options would have required more faith in a relatively unvarnished capitalism or more drastic change in the system as it actually existed, and were therefore ruled out.

Preparedness required a major exercise in state building. According to Theda Skocpol and Stephen Skowronek, among others, the American state passed into the twentieth century a relative weakling compared to other advanced industrial nations. The state structure was characterized by fragmentation and divided against itself. Although the New Deal did result in substantial enlargement of government's ability to provide goods and services, infighting between executive branch and legislative branch agencies performing nearly identical functions was institutionalized. On the eve of World War II, Roosevelt discovered that the state did not have the wherewithal to carry out industrial mobilization. Alan Brinkley correctly asserts that the federal authority, even taking into consideration "its considerable expansion during the 1930s, still lacked anything approaching sufficient bureaucratic capacity for managing a mobilization effort." This being the case, Roosevelt turned to the corporate liberals, who helped overcome the state's semi-dysfunctional nature.[11]

More specifically, Roosevelt and the corporate liberals set up a hybrid organization that borrowed heavily from what Ellis Hawley has described as the "business commonwealth" and "emergency state" formulations. Under the "business commonwealth" idea, business institutions were encouraged by government to develop innovative planning and welfare programs. Government, in effect, acted as a midwife, giving birth to private programs and services available to the citizenry. In this way, business might develop a social conscience and social machinery, while potentially harmful government growth did not occur. The "emergency state" idea postulated the existence of some "crisis," which alone justified the construction of a temporary, emergency administration that coexisted with permanent organs of government. One the "crisis" passed, the emergency form of the administrative state would be dismantled. Again, government was restrained and individual autonomy protected. The preparedness organization Roosevelt ultimately established drew from both models, emphasizing the importance of business initiative, business-led corporatism, crisis management, and dissolution once the European war ended. As Hawley shows us, antibureaucratic impulses have informed American state-building efforts, and this case proved no exception.[12]

From August 1939 through December 7, 1941, corporate liberals Edward R. Stettinius Jr. of United States Steel Corporation, William S. Knudsen of General Motors, and Donald Marr Nelson of Sears, Roebuck and Company ran the emergency-preparedness agencies that set about rearming the nation. They dominated the 1939 War Resources Board, the 1940 National Defense Advisory Commission, and the 1941 Office of Production Management. Holdovers from the New Deal period, such as Marion Folsom and Averell Harriman of the Union Pacific Railroad, assisted them. New men entered the equation. In the process, these businessmen imparted much needed coordination to the evolving federal establishment, creating a structure more and more like the World War I War Industries Board model. Highly visible figures, Stettinius, Knudsen, Nelson, and their colleagues constituted a managerial-technocratic elite pressing Roosevelt's ends in a shadowy but significant area connecting the public and private spheres.

Contrary to the prevailing historiographical assessment, Stettinius, Knudsen, Nelson, and the other corporate liberals performed their work more than well enough. Rather than being the "failures" and "weaklings" so often described in standard accounts, they carried out a difficult task successfully.[13] Interacting with civil authorities, the military, businessmen of all types, and labor, frequently mediating disputes between these groups, the corporate liberals made uneven but significant headway. Relying heavily on persuasion, compromise, and conciliation, partly as a result of a lack of statutory authority during the preparedness period and partly because that was the way they preferred to operate, the corporate liberals helped amass raw materials and stimulated military production in myriad ways. Confronted by a daunting array of constraints, among them President Roosevelt's disdain for both administrative clarity and delegation of power, isolationist opposition to even modest preparations for the possibility of war, lingering hostility between the New Deal state and most businessmen, and military intransigence of a high order, they persevered. Corporate liberal exertions paid off handsomely despite all the discord, adversity, and criticism, pushing industrial mobilization to the mass production stage or beyond by the time Japanese bombs rained down on Pearl Harbor.

The corporate liberals influenced President Roosevelt's attitude toward business. Through bad times and good, they stuck with him. The president and the corporate liberals were united by their common desire to strengthen capitalism and spread its rewards more evenly. They might disagree on specifics, but not on these general goals. Corporate liberal efforts to win FDR over to the broader business community ultimately paid dividends.

Roosevelt's public pronouncements illustrate his conversion. With NRA's demise and the approach of the 1936 presidential election, he had turned against business and it against him. FDR denounced industrialists as "entrenched greed," "money changers," and "economic royalists."[14] He portrayed them as foes of "the needy," "the weak," and "the people's liberties."[15] His rhetoric was such that the majority of businessmen took offense. *Nation's Business* spoke for them, saying businessmen knew full well that Roosevelt's "imputation of [their] arrogant indifference to the common welfare is as undeserved as it is gratuitous."[16] After winning reelection, FDR gradually softened his stance, seeking to placate businessmen, then to entice them. The business aid program of 1938–1939 materialized. By 1940, Roosevelt told corporate liberal Averell Harriman that a "bridge between business and government . . . is indispensable to the effective functioning of our system."[17] In 1944, he congratulated businessmen for playing "a vital part in this war," alluding to "the miracle of [defense] production here at home."[18] He praised them for displaying the "highest type of patriotism by their devotion, their industry, their ingenuity, their cooperation with their government."[19] Roosevelt's turnabout was profound, signaling as it did business' reintegration into the highest public policy circles under Democratic party leadership.

America's corporate liberals, in short, tied the burgeoning public and private sectors together into a more harmonious collectivity. Along the way, they proved themselves trustworthy subordinates of the president; pursued their corporatist vision through a variety of reincarnations; guided preparedness from the outbreak of European war to Pearl Harbor, seeing to it that U.S. soldiers would have their weapons; facilitated construction of the great arsenal of democracy; hastened the demise of totalitarianism; and helped renegotiate business–government partnership. By World War II's end, corporate liberals had done much to restore business power and prestige, bequeathing to oligopoly capital a far greater say in public policy formation than that which prevailed before 1939.

Chapter 1

Meet the New Era Corporate Liberals

Supporters of Welfare Capitalism and Hooverian Associationalism

One important characteristic of corporate liberalism has always been its inventiveness. Corporate liberals have understood the importance of adapting their business practices to changing economic and political conditions—they have been proactive, not reactive. Throughout the 1920s, corporate liberals constantly devised and revised various welfare capitalistic schemes, and the widespread, lasting prosperity of that era convinced them that these programs were working exceedingly well. As company welfare proliferated, its proponents made lavish claims about the benefits this approach conferred on individual firms and the economy as a whole.

The concept of business–government interaction, though less well entrenched in the thinking of corporate liberals, also attracted considerable attention and experimentation in the 1920s. On this issue, however, a split occurred: some corporate liberals favored limited contact between business groups and various agencies of the federal government, whereas others deemed such contact unnecessary or even counterproductive. Support among corporate liberals for welfare-capitalist formulations remained strong until the advent of the Great Depression; although a certain ambivalence about associationalism existed, it did not preclude study of such ideas and even action.

Corporate liberals devoted themselves to creating a more rational, modern economy, one that would be largely liberated from strikes, recessions, and depressions. They sought greater stability for business enterprise and ways to sustain prosperity for major stakeholders: corporate executives, stockholders, and workers. Corporate liberals insisted on business control over the economy and tended to see government and labor as occupying subordinate but supportive positions. The economy they envisioned could be achieved through expansion of company welfare or, perhaps, by application of modest associational prescriptions. Some New Era corporate liberals, such as Gerard Swope or Marion Folsom, emphasized private welfarism while shying away from interaction with the state. Others, such as Henry Dennison, viewed company welfare and associationalism as parts of an integrated whole. All corporate liberals, however, pursued some brand of economic rationalization designed to improve the overall performance of corporate capitalism.

Gerard Swope, Marion Folsom, Averell Harriman, Edward Stettinius, and other like-minded individuals recognized capitalism's flaws and countered them by offering private solutions. In this view, labor got a fair deal through long-term employment and welfare-capitalist packages that included bonuses, profit sharing, group insurance, pensions, and even unemployment insurance. Employers benefited because these programs helped attract and keep workers, while inducing them to work harder.[1] Although union leaders decried these practices as paternalistic and demanded a much greater say in the operation of business, corporate liberals considered this type of thinking unrealistic. Even the establishment of benefit programs often occurred only after overcoming substantial adverse sentiment within a firm's executive ranks. According to enlightened businessmen, workers ought to embrace welfarism, which was certainly better than nothing at all. In this way, of course, management—not labor or the government—handled company problems.

Gerard Swope certainly thought along these lines. Swope insisted that reformed corporate capitalism offered something for everyone: a fair wage and supplementary benefits for the worker; more goods and a larger selection, at lower prices, for the consumer; a salary commensurate with responsibility for management; and satisfactory dividends for the stockholder. As the 1920s passed and the economy continued to run relatively smoothly, Swope's views remained unchanged. Up to 1929, he continued to emphasize private-sector responses to the minor upsets he saw within the capitalist regime.

Swope was born in St. Louis, Missouri, in 1872. An 1895 graduate of the Massachusetts Institute of Technology, he started his career as an engineer and ultimately became a manager-administrator. He originally worked for Western Electric, then moved to General Electric. Lacking family connections, he advanced by dint of merit. One promotion after another led him to the presidency of GE in 1922. Owen Young captured Swope's essence: he "is like a spring under tension always, never spent and never relaxed."[2]

A trip to Europe for Western Electric stimulated Swope's initial interest in welfare. He was particularly struck by the provisions for unemployment, sickness, and old-age insurance that he found in the state-run welfare systems of England and Germany.[3] Because Swope already believed that American businessmen must do something about the rough edges of corporate capitalism, including poverty and unemployment, European welfare schemes intrigued him. Perhaps they could be adapted to circumstances at home. Swope did not yet advocate government welfare programs for the

United States, but he did think seriously about the benefits that would accrue to a private corporation that provided its employees with a cushion against joblessness, illness, and advancing years.

After assuming the presidency at GE, Swope added his own ideas to the welfare-capitalist mix that already existed there. He augmented the employee pension plan, collective-bargaining agreement, and group life and disability insurance plan with high-yield corporate bonds for workers, a profit-sharing plan for supervisory personnel, and an employee suggestion system. The special corporate bonds guaranteed a 6 percent return per year plus 2 percent contributed by GE itself as long as the worker retained his bonds. The profit-sharing plan for supervisors gave them an incentive to work harder and more efficiently. The suggestion system rewarded good ideas with money.

Swope meant these non-wage benefits to bolster hourly pay; he never intended them as a substitute for sustained employment. Indeed, he worked tremendously hard to add more employees to the payroll. Shrewd managerial decisions, such as GE's move into the household electrical appliance field, resulted in increased sales and more hiring. GE's sales of $200 million in 1922 more than doubled to $415 million in 1929. Over the same period, the average number of employees rose from 61,600 to 87,900, and their compensation obviously improved. Profits and dividends were up. Just as Swope and the other welfare capitalists had foreseen, everyone benefited.[4]

Marion Folsom's views about welfare capitalism resembled those of Dennison and Swope. A pragmatist at heart, Folsom concluded that non-wage benefits resulted in a net gain for business firms rather than the loss that most executives expected. Bonuses, pensions, group insurance, and similar offerings certainly cost money, but Folsom figured that the returns more than justified the expenditure. Contented workers typically did not join unions or strike. Old-age pensions induced elderly, inefficient workers to retire rather than hang on to their jobs; as a result, younger, more vigorous employees could be hired years earlier, and productivity would rise. The advent of unemployment insurance forced managers to find ways to retain employees so that jobless benefits would never have to be paid. Folsom's analytical, sophisticated approach to business, coupled with an understated but genuine concern for the needs of workers, helps to explain his devotion to company welfare.

Marion Bayard Folsom was born in 1893 in McRae, Georgia, received his AB from the University of Georgia in 1912 and earned his Master of Business Administration degree from Harvard in 1914. Later that same year, he joined the Eastman Kodak Company, maker of cameras and film, and so began a long and fruitful association with that concern.

Although Folsom's temperament predisposed him toward welfare capitalism, he might never have made the move away from orthodox business practice had it not been for his exposure to two extraordinary individuals at Eastman Kodak. Company founder and president George Eastman and general manager Frank Lovejoy strongly influenced both the general course of Folsom's career and his conversion from rugged individualism to support for corporate welfare.

Folsom started working at Eastman Kodak some fifteen years after George Eastman began his own experiments with welfare capitalism. As early as 1898, Eastman had reorganized his Kodak holdings in Europe, generating a $1 million profit. He then divided up one-third of this money among his employees. By 1910, he had established a formal profit-sharing program. Savings and loan plans, stock options, and a pension program materialized as well.

Eastman's largesse did not stop there. He became a civic leader in Rochester and gave away vast sums of money. The Rochester Red Cross and Community Chest, to name just two examples, benefited from his vision and leadership. He sent millions of dollars to the University of Rochester, the Massachusetts Institute of Technology, Tuskegee Institute, and other institutions of higher learning. Because of his patronage, the celebrated Eastman-Rochester School of Music made its appearance.

George Eastman's sense of corporate and social responsibility helped shape the managerial culture of Eastman Kodak Company. Innovations, whether in camera and film technology, labor–management relations, or the civic and social realms, were taken seriously and evaluated on their merits. George Eastman's reputation as an autocrat notwithstanding, Eastman Kodak Company seemed remarkably open to new ideas.

Frank Lovejoy certainly fit well within this framework. Lovejoy started his career at Eastman Kodak in the last years of the nineteenth century. Hired as a chemist by George Eastman, Lovejoy found a way to produce long rolls of black-and-white motion picture film. Later he moved into management and advanced to the top of the firm. After experiencing success within his job, Lovejoy followed Eastman's lead, serving as president of the Social Welfare League of Rochester from 1921 to 1923 and becoming well known as a humanitarian.

Marion Folsom benefited tremendously from his relationships with George Eastman and Frank Lovejoy. Eastman interviewed Folsom in October 1914 and hired him. During his first three years on the job, Folsom was assigned to Lovejoy and worked in the general manager's office. With Lovejoy as his mentor, Folsom absorbed the administrative and financial intricacies of Eastman Kodak. After serving with the U.S. Army during World War I, he continued his ascent. Named statistical secretary in 1920, he built Kodak's first statistical department and executed cost-benefit analyses. By 1921, Folsom had become assistant to President Eastman and, in this capacity, came to embrace welfare-capitalist schemes. A quiet, reflective man, Folsom convinced himself that non-wage benefits for employees did indeed bring sizable—if not always quantifiable—returns, and were therefore well worth offering.[5]

Welfare-capitalist spokesmen urged businessmen everywhere to adopt employee benefit programs as a means of maintaining a stable workforce, taming the business cycle, and dispersing the rewards to be had from the American economy. Folsom agreed, endorsing Eastman Kodak's profit-sharing plan and spearheading the drive within his company for group insurance and unemployment insurance. He noted that "profit-sharing is a very desirable and effective method of bringing about better cooperation between the workers, the management, and the stockholders."[6] He fought hard for group insurance and unemployment insurance, taking on conservative interests within his firm who objected to them. Kodak's group insurance plan, which commenced on January 1, 1929, made a combination of life insurance, retirement annuities, and permanent disability available to workers. Unfortunately, Folsom's unemployment insurance schemes of 1921 and 1927 were defeated, falling victim to the opposition of plant managers and to the brevity of the recessions.[7] Yet Folsom carried on. "The important factor to keep in mind in considering unemployment benefit plans," he wrote, "is that the adoption of such a plan . . . will give the same incentive to stabilize and thereby reduce unemployment that Workmen's Compensation gave to the reduction of industrial accidents."[8] Arguments like these highlighted his commitment to worker security, the efficient performance of his firm, and the ultimate stability of corporate capitalism.

Like Swope and Folsom, Averell Harriman knew the value of gainful employment and harmonious labor–management relations. Harriman urged each businessman "to develop his nation's resources along sound lines and thus provide useful, remunerative employment to as many breadwinners as possible."[9] He also believed that employers and employees needed to get along if economic progress was to occur. As an important player with the Union Pacific Railroad for decades, Harriman did his part to see that men found jobs and received fair treatment.

Son of the great railroader E. H. Harriman, William Averell Harriman was born in New York City in 1891. He attended Groton and then Yale University, from which he graduated in 1913. By the time of his graduation, young Averell had already begun working with the Union Pacific. Because his family possessed a dominant interest, he moved quickly to the top, becoming director of purchases in 1913 and vice president in charge of purchases by 1914. In 1918, Harriman left the Union Pacific and tried his hand at a variety of entrepreneurial ventures. He returned to full-time work with the railroad in 1932, this time as chairman of the board. He was a shrewd man, motivated by a deeply ingrained sense of noblesse oblige.[10]

Harriman's labor policy reflected his view that workers should be well treated. Not surprisingly, then, he believed in welfare capitalism. Union

Pacific workers received an impressive array of non-wage benefits, including free transportation on the line, a safety organization designed to minimize accidents, a hospitalization plan, retirement pensions, and old timers' clubs such as the Union Pacific Retired Employees Association.[11] Special Representative G. O. Brophy of the company's Department of Public Relations emphasized that "these advantages which we enjoy are not given us for services performed, but because in the Union Pacific Railroad there is a humane spirit which runs through the entire organization. . . ."[12] Brophy added that the "Union Pacific system did not copyright 'Goodwill' but it extended it to its [employees] and the employees passed it on to the traveling and shipping public, to whom they were indebted in the final analysis, for their salaries."[13]

Edward R. Stettinius Jr., another corporate liberal and a high-ranking official at General Motors in the late 1920s, explained welfare-capitalist ideology better than most. Rejecting Karl Marx's theory of class struggle and management–labor conflict, Stettinius emphasized harmony at the workplace and the mutual interests of labor and management. The basic idea of welfare capitalism, he said, is "that the goal of production shall not be profit alone, but material, social and spiritual betterment of all groups" with a stake in the corporation and in the economic system.[14]

On this score, Henry Dennison concurred, noting that business should act ethically, moving constantly "towards the fullest use and growth of each man's powers in the service of his fellows. . . ."[15] Along these lines, Dennison extolled the many virtues of company welfare. Not content to stop there, he moved beyond Swope, Folsom, Harriman, Stettinius, and many other New Era corporate liberals by openly embracing associational strategies.

Son of a well-to-do manufacturer, Henry Sturgis Dennison grew to adulthood in and around Boston, Massachusetts, where he received his education and vocational training. After studying the classics at the exclusive Roxbury Latin School, he graduated from Harvard University with an AB in 1899. From there, he entered the lucrative family business, the Dennison Manufacturing Company, which made paper products. Low-level jobs prepared him for advancement into the managerial ranks. In 1901, he became foreman of the sealing wax department, in 1906 works manager, in 1917 president. By then, Dennison's personality and approach had taken shape: "an essentially private man," he was blessed with high intelligence, an organized mind, and a penchant for seeing the "big picture."[16]

Dennison's thinking about the economy became more sophisticated over time as welfare capitalism, then associationalism, drew his attention. By the 1920s, he had combined both into a coherent program for economic advancement.

Like many other corporate liberals, Dennison advocated welfare capitalism throughout the New Era. He believed that employee benefit programs, in combination with an adequate wage, ensured the happiness of workers. Happy workers, in turn, meant a minimum of strikes and other disruptions. Stable production, continued sales, and regular profits and dividends were the result. Within the individual firm, everybody stood to benefit. Furthermore, if every firm within every industry adopted the same general strategy, optimum performance for the national economy might well be the final outcome. Dennison and other corporate liberals sought nothing less than to flatten out the business cycle, sustain income at high levels, and maintain economic good times permanently.

Dennison's conception of welfare capitalism expanded over the years. Attracted by the corporate welfare programs of National Cash Register (NCR) and other leading companies, he instituted numerous industrial reforms. In 1901, Dennison Manufacturing Company implemented a NCR-style suggestion/bonus system.[17] A factory clinic, worker cafeteria, social club, and savings bank followed by 1908. In 1916, Henry Dennison fashioned the first corporate unemployment insurance plan ever seen in the United States. Based on the "assumption that the opportunity to reduce the amount of unemployment rests very largely with the employer," Dennison Manufacturing Company set up an unemployment fund supervised by a labor–management committee.[18] Temporarily discharged workers with dependents were paid 80 percent of regular wages; single unemployed workers 60 percent.[19] In 1919, Dennison created an employees' committee designed specifically "to enable management and employees to work out mutual problems."[20] Profit sharing for non-managerial employees began in 1920. Dennison knew full well that satisfied workers were reliable, productive workers and that welfare capitalism made sense—monetarily and otherwise.

Associationalism interested Dennison, who recognized that state involvement in the private economy was inevitable and could even be helpful. He repeatedly showed a willingness to join hands with government for the benefit of all concerned. Dennison served with the War Industries Board's Central Bureau of Planning and Statistics during World War I. In 1919, he participated in President Woodrow Wilson's Industrial Conferences. In 1921, he played a big part in President Warren G. Harding's Unemployment Conference, which went forward under the direction of Secretary of Commerce Herbert Hoover. By this time, Dennison and Hoover agreed that microeconomic regularization, achieved through rigorous application of welfare-capitalist procedures and by other methods, held out the promise of macroeconomic stabilization.[21]

More than any other single individual, engineer and politician Herbert Hoover was responsible for the establishment of an associational system. As secretary of commerce from 1921 to 1929, Hoover searched for a "middle way" between laissez-faire and statist regimentation. He did not believe that government and business should be totally apart from each other, nor did he think that the state should coerce corporations. Instead, he believed that government might accept requests from business for various kinds of assistance. After all, government agencies were sometimes in a position to funnel useful economic data to businesses. They might see that industries observed their own standards of right conduct. Government could conceivably arbitrate disputes that arose between companies. Most important, Hoover saw business–government association as a means of minimizing fluctuations of the business cycle and, ultimately, as a way of preserving prosperity.[22]

Hoover's Commerce Department became the heart of the associational system, aggressively expanding its authority over other government bodies and entering into agreements with the private sector. The Commerce Department transformed the Labor Department into a "cooperative satellite," while it influenced the Interior Department, the Agriculture Department, the State Department, the Anti-Trust Division of the Justice Department, and the Federal Trade Commission to one degree or another during parts of the 1920s.[23] Additionally, the Commerce Department constructed ties to numerous capitalist institutions—corporations, trade associations, social science research councils, and philanthropic foundations.[24] Hoover expected the resultant associational network to promote healthy economic development while acting as a bulwark against recession and depression.

Henry Dennison's views meshed nicely with Hoover's. Both men believed that private enterprise should play the leading part in American economic development, with the state in a subsidiary role. While corporate executives controlled investment flows, and through them influenced consumption patterns, the state might function as a midwife, coaxing desired responses from corporate actors. Corporate resources, it followed, could be channeled into appropriate avenues. The state might also become a referee, stepping in to put an end to unfair business practices. Associationalism therefore encouraged constructive behavior while discouraging destructive activities.[25]

Dennison, who believed strongly in this approach, immersed himself in it. From 1922 to 1928, he worked for the U.S. Post Office, as Director of Welfare Work. In this position, he helped establish work councils, credit bureaus, and scientific management bodies in the private sector. Here a corporate liberal, working in a state agency, cultivated the development of socioeconomic machinery and social consciousness in corporations.

As a member of the 1928–1929 Committee on Recent Economic Changes, Dennison cooperated with Hoover once more. He emphasized that good corporate management in alliance with a supportive state might well provide for business equilibrium and prosperity well into the future. Dennison also noted that the Federal Trade Commission (FTC) might engage in "business umpiring," upholding industry-wide agreements relating to fair competition, factory conditions, conservation of resources, and codes of ethics. The FTC might even move beyond this point, "to exempt certain industries from such negative restrictions as are found, for example, in the anti-trust laws, to demand reports which would give the Commission knowledge of the way such exemptions are used, and finally to advise . . . with due regard for the good of the industry and of the community as a whole."[26] Dennison's welfare-capitalist–associational synthesis brought together private enterprise and government into a more balanced, harmonious collectivity; corporations assumed primary responsibility for investment, production, and labor–management relations, while government acted as a facilitator, guarantor, and umpire.

Business stabilization, economic prosperity, and progress were the goals of associational planners such as Hoover, Dennison, Owen Young of GE, and Lincoln and Edward Filene of Filene Department Stores. Like Dennison, Young and the Filenes advocated a mix of welfare-capitalist schemes and associationalism.

While serving as chairman of the board at GE, Owen Young acted on his beliefs, sponsoring numerous non-wage benefits for employees. These measures included group life and disability insurance, a pension plan, and bonuses of various sorts. He also linked up with government periodically, for example when he chaired the Business Cycle Committee that emerged out of the 1921 Unemployment Conference. The Business Cycle Committee determined that private unemployment insurance and wage maintenance might well minimize downswings in consumer spending, while strategic release of construction reserves could buoy investment. In addition, timely monetary policies had the potential to offset shortages of capital, and exports might make up for the lack of domestic demand. These actions, together, promised to moderate the business cycle and sustain employment at high levels.

Brothers Lincoln and Edward Filene, who ran the Boston-based Filene Department Stores, gave workers medical and social services as well as a say in management. The Filenes believed that business must interact with the state and that this course was one of opportunity, not ruin. The Filenes, Dennison, Young, and certain other corporate liberals cooperated with government; they viewed public–private planning along associational lines as a complement to welfarism, asserting that the "new capitalism" produced more order, efficiency, and progress than the old.[27]

Mainstream businessmen rejected associational planning, maligned government officials, and refused to implement welfare-capitalist programs. To them, associationalism reeked of socialism. At a minimum, government intrusion into the private economy threatened autonomous individualism. Government regulation, according to Chamber of Commerce member Merle Thorpe, resulted "in danger of decreasing the benefits we can get from private ownership." Bureaucrats and politicians, from this perspective, were incompetent or dangerous. Dr. Gus W. Dyer of the National Association of Manufacturers (NAM), underscoring the great expertise of corporate executives, found it ludicrous that any political board should determine their actions. This outcome, in his view, was like telling "a doctor what he shall do in the process of performing a surgical operation." As for welfare capitalism, it was either too bothersome to implement or too costly.[28]

Even some corporate liberals voiced ambivalence about government, or proved so leery of it that they avoided involvement. The members of the Business Cycle Committee thought government bureaucrats "tended inherently toward irrationality and wastefulness."[29] Throughout the 1920s, Eastman Kodak's Marion Folsom opposed state welfare, which he predicted would degenerate into a mere dole.[30] Gerard Swope, Folsom, Averell Harriman, and Edward R. Stettinius Jr. were among those corporate liberals who sidestepped New Era statism but were friendly toward welfare capitalism.

Throughout the 1920s, corporate liberals supported welfare capitalism and, to a lesser extent, associationalism. Dennison, Swope, Folsom, Harriman, and Stettinius expressed their approval of welfare capitalist offerings, either because they were cost-effective or out of humanitarianism. Dennison concluded that all firms should phase in the "insurance principle in one or another of its many forms" as a hedge against joblessness and other uncertainties.[31] Folsom concurred, saying that Eastman Kodak's "philosophy is that if it is good business for us . . . it ought to be good for business generally."[32] U.S. Steel's Stettinius not only extolled the virtues of corporate welfare and "good will," he described the factory as a "social organism" where all interests must be balanced in a harmonious fashion.[33] Dennison, Young, and the Filenes pushed well beyond privatism, encouraging government supervision of the private economy as a corrective to reckless competition, a means of acquiring helpful data, and a boon to more comprehensive planning.

The welfare-capitalist–associational synthesis appeared to work well. Corporate liberals watched with satisfaction as welfare capitalism spread, becoming fairly widely developed by the mid-1920s. Medium and small firms tended to adopt bits and pieces of the available slate of non-wage benefits, while some large companies took up almost the whole range of choices. As a result, according to corporate liberals, employee morale rose appreciably and production was regularized.

Gains from associational endeavor seemed equally obvious. The Commerce Department–led system secured an agreement from the steel industry to abide by the eight-hour day. Safety and factory standards were established in the wake of delicate negotiations between the government and concerned industries. Formulation of 100 standardization and conservation agreements occurred, each designed to stimulate mass-consumption industry or to eliminate the waste of resources. After consultation between the FTC and industry representatives, more than fifty trade practice codes emerged, making explicit unfair trade practices and defining ethical behavior on the part of businesses. The U.S. Chamber of Commerce also contributed, putting out a national business ethics code. Meanwhile, the Commerce Department and other government agencies dispensed information, including statistics, to corporations that requested such data. Most important, the national economy was experiencing considerable growth; many opportunities existed to get ahead. Little wonder that corporate liberals attributed 1920s prosperity to the innovative managerial techniques and cooperative mechanisms they had pioneered.[34]

Then the Great Depression struck. Welfare-capitalist and associational formulations faced their greatest test and were found wanting. Massive long-term unemployment incapacitated welfare capitalism. As joblessness increased from 1930 to 1933, topping out at 25 percent of the workforce, unemployment insurance claims rose and payments into unemployment insurance funds plummeted. The inevitable occurred: many companies watched helplessly as their unemployment insurance reserves were drained. Other non-wage programs were liquidated in order to cut costs. President Hoover fell back on the associational bulwark he had done so much to construct, confident that it would counteract the latest slump as it had earlier recessions. But associationalism failed him and its other adherents.

Small and medium-sized firms daring enough to adopt welfare capitalism in the first place fared worst. The fate of Dennison Manufacturing Company—the great pioneer in the field—proved typical. Sales of Dennison paper products slumped beginning in 1929, necessitating a 15 percent reduction in its factory workforce by mid-1930.[35] Yet as late as May 1931, Henry Dennison remained bullish, reaffirming his confidence in the company unemployment insurance fund, which he predicted would "insure the continuance and intensification of our efforts to regularize employment."[36] Shortly thereafter, company layoffs mounted toward a high of 50 percent, the unemployment fund dried up completely, and the fund ceased to make any outlays at all.[37] In response to writer Ida Tarbell's query about the company pension system, an honest but chagrined Dennison admitted that "it hasn't worked out and it hasn't stood up."[38]

Dennison Manufacturing Company was not alone. Under the Rochester Plan of 1931, fourteen firms in Rochester, New York, agreed to provide unemployment insurance to their workers should they be laid off. Workers who lost their jobs reported to the Rochester Public Employment Center, where an attempt was made to find them new employment. Because state government and various philanthropic organizations supplied 90 percent of the Employment Center's budget—in essence linking up with the companies— this plan amounted to a classic exercise in associationalism. Unhappily, six of the fourteen firms "simply couldn't stand the gaff during 1932 and 1933 and had to give the plan up. . . ."[39] These firms lacked the capital of Eastman Kodak, Bausch & Lomb, and the other survivors. In general, smaller firms with limited financial resources simply could not continue to make unemployment insurance payments in the face of such horrendous business conditions.

The real problem, of course, was not that a few undercapitalized firms had signed on to the Rochester Plan or other, similar plans and had failed. The true roadblock lay in the fact that most firms in Rochester—and throughout the United States—refused to try unemployment insurance at all. By 1931, just twenty-nine companies nationwide, with a total of 176,000 workers, had adopted private unemployment insurance. Far too many companies, and the vast majority of workers, were not covered at all. By 1934, more companies were abandoning unemployment insurance than were joining up.[40]

The largest corporations did better. Eastman Kodak, the Union Pacific, General Electric, and other giants managed to keep their welfare funds solvent. Under the Rochester Plan, Eastman Kodak met each and every obligation to its unemployed workers. Benefit payments to Kodak's old employees amounted to approximately $21,000 in 1933, $5,000 in 1934, and $150 in 1935. By 1936, camera and film sales had picked up enough that layoffs ended and unemployment insurance payouts ceased. Profit sharing occurred in every year but 1934. In 1938 alone, a total of $2.9 million was funneled from Kodak management to employees.[41] The Union Pacific dispatched old-age pension checks right up to 1937, then switched over to the federal system under provisions of the Railroad Retirement Acts of 1935 and 1937.[42] All other non-wage programs continued as well. GE handed out "nearly $4,000,000 in benefits and $1,000,000 in loans in the five and one-half years between . . . inception [of private unemployment insurance] and the institution of Social Security."[43] Disbursements for retirement, life insurance, disability, profit sharing, and helpful suggestions remained. Big, capital-intensive corporations normally discharged their responsibilities despite the Depression; welfare capitalism never died out completely, but limped along in an attenuated form for a number of years.[44]

The success of some prominent corporations could not hide the truth. The depth and duration of the Great Depression forced upon corporate liberals the painful realization that their idyllic welfare-capitalist vision was no panacea. Welfare capitalism had promised economic stability, employee security, and the good life, but after 1929, it did not deliver them. Instead, volatility gripped the national economy; uncertainty plagued the nation's workers; and a rich nation became poor almost overnight. Corporate capitalism itself was in some jeopardy, given its dismal performance. Surveying the carnage, Marion Folsom admitted that "private relief failed."[45]

Associationalism was also tested. President Hoover called on the associational network as an antidote to depression. After executive branch officials and trade association representatives met at the White House in the autumn of 1929, some action occurred. The National Business Survey Conference (NBSC), affiliated with the U.S. Chamber of Commerce, established a committee that spoke for roughly 170 trade associations. The NBSC committee returned to the advice of the 1921 Business Cycle Committee, underlining the need for employer confidence, wage maintenance, and new investment. The National Building Survey Conference, another body that relied on trade organizations, emphasized the importance of construction projects as a means of engineering an economic turnaround. A recently created Commerce Department Division of Public Construction pushed other government agencies to accelerate their building projects and tried to ensure that states and municipalities honored their outstanding pledges to carry out public works. Not content to rest here, Hoover asked labor to cooperate with business in all these endeavors.[46]

Other measures augmented associational prescriptions. Hoover induced the Federal Reserve Board to increase the money supply. At the president's urging, Congress provided a tax cut and bolstered public works through a $400 million appropriation. Hoover also set up the Reconstruction Finance Corporation, which loaned money to banks, savings and loans, and railroads.[47] Although he did more than previous presidents to reorder the economy, these moves did not achieve the desired effect. As the Great Depression deepened, corporate liberals scrambled to find a workable alternative to welfare capitalism and associationalism.

Chapter 2

Bad Times and a New Deal
The Corporate Liberals Accede to Sustained Business–Government Collaboration

The onset of the Great Depression forced the corporate liberals to change their modus operandi. As the welfare-capitalist–associational amalgam proved incapable of effectively addressing unemployment and resultant dislocation, the corporate liberals—reluctantly at first, then with greater enthusiasm—increasingly turned to the federal government for help. The new emphasis on extensive collaboration between big business and big government was a means to a familiar end: corporate liberals still wanted to achieve order, efficiency, and prosperity within the framework of a modified, strengthened corporate capitalism, while retaining maximum managerial autonomy. The difference was the resort to constant, sustained interaction with the state, rather than sporadic, rather informal approaches. Although corporate liberals recognized that the expanding federal authority might become oppressive, they considered this unlikely and were therefore willing to join hands.

The corporate liberals' conception of government's place crystallized in the period from 1930 to 1933, as the national economy continued to deteriorate despite their best efforts to stop it. Government, they said, should endorse and promote industrial self-regulation. Government might also provide money for infrastructural improvements, institutional development, and reemployment. A public–private welfare system became a distinct possibility. This formulation required that government respect the primacy of free enterprise and private property while simultaneously providing assistance in several crucial respects. Unless government and business acted in concert, corporate liberals reasoned, recovery would be delayed—with increasing danger to the capitalist system.

Gerard Swope now viewed trade associationalism as the proper means of bringing about industrial self-regulation. The Swope Plan of September 1931 proposed the establishment of trade associations in every industry. After that, a super trade association, or national economic council, would be formed, and exchange of information among all organizations would be encouraged. Once analysis of supply-and-demand conditions was completed, excessive competition could be eliminated and a prosperous stability fostered through establishment of production quotas, market sharing, and price fixing. Antitrust laws that got in the way were to be suspended.

Swope intended that business dominate the process, but he allowed a place for labor and a mechanism to safeguard the public. Workers were to receive expanded company welfare benefits, including unemployment insurance, old-age pensions, and life and disability insurance. Although the Swope Plan made no direct mention of a role for independent trade unions, it did include a general assertion that execution of the plan should be "by the joint participation and joint administration of management and employees." To protect the public welfare, a "federal supervisory council" would oversee the entire structure and would blow the whistle on any abuses. Firms that deviated from the plan risked government coercion to force them into compliance. Swope, Stettinius, and Harriman, among others, believed government should prod intransigents into line, acting in effect as a "regulatory umpire." The Swope Plan envisioned creation of an elaborate, interlocking network of national economic planning reminiscent of the World War I War Industries Board model. Corporate liberals eschewed nationalization of industry or other "socialistic" solutions in favor of a "cooperative capitalism" wherein the federal authority backed up business.[1]

The U.S. Chamber of Commerce, headed by utilities executive Henry I. Harriman, offered its own plan for industrial self-regulation, which differed from Swope's in two significant respects. First, the Chamber of Commerce plan started with creation of a national economic council and then added industrial trade associations, rather than the other way around. Second, and more important, the Chamber plan "made no provision for regulation or review" by the federal government. According to the Chamber of Commerce, government ought to stay out of the economic sphere. Swope had invited the state in to enforce industrial agreements and standards arrived at in the first instance by private firms. He also wanted government to shelter special interests weaker than big business, such as workers and consumers, and he undoubtedly hoped that this action would head off government edicts promulgated without business input or assent. The Chamber of Commerce showed less concern for non-business interests.[2]

Spurred by the ever worsening economy, the corporate liberal definition of permissible government activity expanded. Unlike the Chamber of Commerce, corporate liberals urged the Hoover administration to involve itself more heavily in the private economy. During September 1930, Swope called for a $1 billion government bond issue to finance desperately needed roads, electrify railroad terminals, and construct schools, hospitals, jails, and refuse disposal plants.[3] The Swope plan followed soon thereafter. More daring still, Swope advocated federal housing, suggesting that moderately priced homes be built.[4] Dennison also supported public works. Given a large enough volume and a steady flow of useful construction projects, the economy as a whole might turn around and business cycle swings could be minimized. Folsom, like Swope and Dennison, advocated a public works program. Furthermore, incomplete or nonexistent company benefit packages for workers convinced him that a federal welfare system had become a necessity. In 1932, motivated by a desire to see universal coverage, he accepted the need for a "state-compelled, state-run unemployment insurance system."[5]

President Herbert Hoover repudiated the corporate liberal design. Wedded to a less extensive type of associationalism and voluntarism, he rejected the Swope plan, which he viewed as unnecessarily coercive, even "fascistic." The relatively benign Chamber of Commerce proposal did not suit him either. He profoundly disliked cartelization, nor did vigorous government enforcement of private arrangements appeal to him.[6] He preferred to let business work out its own disagreements without the application of government force. Hoover also disregarded Swope's bond proposal and rejected government unemployment insurance, though he did move forward with a public works program and endorsement of Walter Teagle's Share-the-Work campaign.[7] By winter 1932, the views of the corporate liberals more closely resembled those of New York governor Franklin D. Roosevelt than those of either Hoover or mainstream businessmen.

President-elect Roosevelt and the corporate liberals approached the economy from the same basic angle, and, although their views were not always synchronized, they shared much in common. Corporate capitalism, according to Roosevelt, required reform, so that more Americans could partake of its benefits and radical detractors could be silenced. Corporate liberals concurred, recognizing full well the value of constructive revision. Cooperation with the state offered potential benefits that outweighed the slim risk of statist regimentation.

Roosevelt's original domestic agenda, though subject to continual modification, included industrial self-regulation and agricultural subsidies. He placed only very slight emphasis on public ownership, viewed public works as a means to jump-start the economy, and supported collective bargaining and a balanced budget.

Swope, like many other corporate liberals, favored his own form of industrial self-regulation. He also devised a production-control plan for farmers that featured establishment of local and state farm cooperatives, as well as a National Association to be guided by the Department of Agriculture. The "Swope plan for farmers," formulated in early 1933, viewed extensive organizational linkages between agriculture and government as the proper means to institute crop quotas and secure higher prices for corn, wheat, cotton, and other commodities. Corporate liberals were not fearful of farmers and could sometimes be persuaded that federal assistance to the latter would be beneficial to economic regeneration.[8]

Common ground existed elsewhere, too. FDR's rejection of extensive public ownership reassured corporate liberals that government intended no real harm to free enterprise or private decision making. Dennison inclined more and more toward public works, ultimately favoring up to "10 billions of dollars worth of useful projects in which we can furnish governmental employment to the precise extent that the Private Enterprise Machine at any moment finds it impossible to provide jobs."[9] Corporate liberals had voiced support for labor–management negotiations since the 1920s. A balanced federal budget appealed to them, too, as it did to virtually every businessman. Dennison even persuaded himself of the value of underbalanced and overbalanced budgets—foreshadowing Roosevelt's later reliance on deficit spending.[10] As a group, the corporate liberals found much of Roosevelt's early program to their liking, and an impressive convergence of interest occurred.

Most businessmen repudiated the line of reasoning which united corporate liberals and Roosevelt, arguing that government was big enough already and that the economy would bounce back on its own. At best, big government led to burdensome rules and regulations, duplication of services, federal competition with private enterprise, and other inefficiencies that impeded economic rejuvenation. At worst, statist regimentation might end in the loss of precious American freedoms. From this perspective, public works constituted mere "make work," with little sustained benefit to the national economy, while collective bargaining threatened managerial control, cost containment, and profits. Roosevelt's balanced-budget pledge was fine, but would he keep it? In 1932–1933, the average businessman—if such a creature existed—wanted government to exercise restraint and let time do its job.

The National Association of Manufacturers (NAM) and the Chamber of Commerce endorsed this type of thinking. The antidote to the Great Depression, in their view, was not bigger government but self-help. In 1930, NAM President John Edgerton sounded this theme, which would be repeated over and over again in the following years. Edgerton found "too many who are trying to escape individual responsibility for the full and proper use of their opportunities."[11] Government, they thought, would bail them out, but this was not the way it should be. Edgerton emphasized the need for greater individual initiative and focused on the destructive effects of government assistance on self-reliance.

Julius Barnes, past president and current chairman of the board of the Chamber of Commerce, outdid Edgerton. In December 1930, he blamed government for "manifest evils" such as unfair taxation and unwise regulation of utilities, concluding that these policies caused "the present undermined welfare of all peoples."[12] As late as December 1932, *Nation's Business* enthusiastically reported Roosevelt's "instinctive preference . . . for a minimum of coercive action by government."[13] The National Association of Manufacturers, the Chamber of Commerce, and their leaders preached caution; they did not consider the expansion of government powers and functions advisable.

Roosevelt, once elected president, was not disposed to wait. The state he inherited from Hoover required quick bolstering if economic deterioration was to be arrested. New agencies, additional support staff, and greater funding were obvious requirements. Of even greater significance, government needed to find skilled personnel who possessed both an overarching view of the economy and specific, detailed knowledge of industry and industrial processes. In this way, the state might counter its lack of industrial expertise and experience.

FDR paused briefly to weigh his state-building options, then moved. Industrial self-regulation was only one of many alternatives open to him. Central planners stressed the need they saw for independent federal administrative control over the economic order and its resources. Proponents of an "interest group commonwealth," too, called for expansion of the state's administrative powers while insisting that civil servants remain answerable to politicians and interest-group leaders. Trust-busters argued for more vigorous use of the Sherman Anti-Trust Act in hopes of restoring atomistic competition. Ironically, even this formulation, which was intended to free the people from the clutches of "robber barons," necessitated growth of state power in the form of an enlarged Justice Department. Roosevelt bestowed initial favor upon the corporate liberal version of state building (i.e., a form of business-propelled corporatism in which private experts and administrative resources were drafted for public purposes) while holding the other models in reserve.[14]

Integration of business and government required construction of appropriate avenues for communication. Corporate liberals found the necessary channels within the National Recovery Administration, the Business Advisory Council of the Department of Commerce, and various Social Security agencies. They pursued their "cooperationist" vision through these bodies, promoting industrial self-regulation, innovative recovery schemes, and public–private welfare.

Swope, Dennison, Edward Stettinius, and Averell Harriman supported the National Recovery Administration.[15] Each man accepted NRA "codes of fair competition," which typically included maximum hours, minimum wages, collective bargaining for employees, and a means to determine output for each industry involved. Swope used his position as chairman of the Business Advisory Council to supply NRA with executive personnel. Dennison served as chairman of NRA's Industrial Advisory Board (IAB) during 1934. Around that time, he also helped to frame the code for the tag industry and was influential in other areas.[16] Stettinius acted as liaison between the NRA, IAB, and the greater business community. He saw to it that "every affected industrial group is fully and adequately represented in an advisory capacity."[17] Harriman rose further than the others, advancing from the New York NRA to national headquarters in Washington, DC, where he became deputy administrator in charge of heavy goods production, "Special Assistant Administrator," and finally "Chief Administrative Officer." All agreed with NRA's first boss, General Hugh Johnson, that NRA codes for industry would "eliminate eye-gouging and knee-groining and ear-chewing in business."[18] When conflict gave way to collaboration and consensus, and efficiency prevailed, then recovery must occur.

Industrial self-regulation, NRA-style, surged ahead. The first major code, submitted originally by the Cotton Textile Institute for the cotton textile industry, and duly amended, received Roosevelt's approval on July 9, 1933. The shipbuilding, woolens, electrical, and garment industries followed in rapid succession. The last of the nation's big ten industries, bituminous coal, came on board on September 18.[19] In just three months, Johnson had brought the commanding heights of the U.S. economy under federal supervision, substantially enlarging the scope of government action in the areas of resource distribution, production, and labor–management relations.

Corporate liberals accepted federal direction because it was non-threatening. The NRA leadership, including Johnson and counsel Donald Richberg, proved to be pro-business.[20] The Industrial Advisory Board exercised considerably more sway in the code-making process than either the Labor Advisory Board or Consumer Advisory Board. Section 7(a) of the National Industrial Recovery Act, the collective-bargaining provision, proved sufficiently elastic to accommodate many views on the subject. Under these circumstances, company unionism and proportional representation schemes competed well against majority representation.

After NRA codes went into effect, trade associations managed them with virtually no instruction from government. Trade association officials, who benefited from the suspension of antitrust laws, used their newfound clout to orchestrate market sharing and output restriction. Higher prices for a host of commodities in dozens of major industries occurred. Large, oligopolistic corporations reaped the largest reward from the changed conditions, which promoted order, regularity, and higher profits. The NRA clearly functioned along lines amenable to the corporate liberals.

Kinks existed, but they could be straightened out. The new system of industrial self-regulation gave government a bit too much power, at least in theory. Additionally, workers needed welfare benefits, otherwise complaints might arise. Swope, for one, questioned Roosevelt's ability to revise NRA codes at will and to refuse individual industries a necessary license. The regulatory umpire might not be so easily checked given these powers.[21]

Unemployment insurance for workers, and old-age pensions for retirees, should be provided—especially given the high rate of joblessness, the likelihood that it would linger, and prevalent dissatisfaction with corporate capitalism. Corporate liberals thought these defects correctable, with time.

Time, however, was not on NRA's side. Critics of industrial self-regulation abounded, the economy remained poor, and the Supreme Court stepped in. Small business, particularly in the South, thought itself victimized by NRA's minimum wages and maximum hours, which increased costs and limited flexibility. Large businesses rebelled when NRA staff economists proposed to limit price controls to the short run. Later, in 1934–1935, threats to abolish price fixing angered them further. Labor and consumers resented capital's say. John L. Lewis rebuked industrial self-regulation because it contained no real place for mass production workers or "majority representation." Consumers noted the impotence of the Consumer Advisory Board and complained about inflation. Far more damaging, the Depression continued pretty much unabated. Production quotas brought higher prices and dividends but mitigated against reemployment and increased purchasing power. Harriman defended the agency valiantly, saying that NRA hurt only those small businessmen who sweated labor, noting that workers should receive company welfare augmented by national "Social Security," and insisting that the Agency sought a happy medium between cutthroat competition and monopoly. The Supreme Court's Schechter decision of May 1935 ended the debate, declaring the National Industrial Recovery Act unconstitutional. NRA expired shortly thereafter, and Roosevelt swung government away from business-led corporatism toward a more forceful regulatory approach that favored labor and senior citizens.[22]

Corporate liberals did not let NRA's woes deter them for long. They sought other ways to influence public policy and achieve long-standing goals. The Business Advisory Council (BAC) of the Department of Commerce, an organization of businessmen dominated by corporate liberals, pursued its vision of what the political economy should be.

Founded in 1933, the BAC represented the interests of large, progressive-minded, capital-intensive firms more than anything else, giving the corporate liberals a sustained presence within government throughout the New Deal–World War II era. It stressed business control over the national economy, arguing that government should play a supporting role as a fair broker. Government should arrange compromises between feuding companies; it might police privately determined standards; it should not run the economy from on high.[23] Having supported NRA, BAC now chose to float another variation of industrial self-government. A small group within the organization pushed for "social security." Several corporate liberals there showed an affinity for planning. Although the failure of NRA certainly frustrated them, corporate liberals reaffirmed the basic principle of business–government cooperation, including the need for federal supervision of the economy.

American capitalism, and the return of economic prosperity and stability, would be best served in this way.

At this point, Business Advisory Council Chairman Henry Kendall took the lead. In February 1935, Kendall informed Roosevelt of a Council recommendation urging "that Recovery functions of government be separated from ordinary Administration activities."[24] The BAC visualized a "separate emergency organization . . . subdivided into single purpose agencies such as Loans, Housing, Relief, Decentralization of Industry, Federal Highways, Grade-Crossings, Public Health, etc."[25]

The inspiration for Kendall's proposal came from World War I, when temporary, ends-oriented defense agencies existed side by side with permanent organs of civil government. BAC members recalled that the defense agencies had been dismantled soon after Allied victory, and expected that the Depression agencies, once successful, would meet the same fate. As soon as the economy returned to health, the Loan Administration, Housing Administration, and the rest would be retired and government returned to its normal condition. During the interim, business advisory committees would be attached to each freshly minted government body. This approach, from the corporate liberal perspective, promised businessmen an adequate voice during the crisis, the eventual return of prosperity, and protection against the type of government growth that might conceivably endanger autonomous individualism.

The Business Advisory Council recommendation went nowhere. Without the urgency of war, and with some slight improvement in the economy since 1933, the Kendall initiative was easily ignored. One suspects, too, that some members of BAC hoped to forestall the creation of more New Deal agencies with this plan, and that Roosevelt saw through the ploy. NRA's failure also discredited industrial self-regulation, at least for the moment. Statist regulation of business concerns prevailed throughout the mid-1930s, drawing cries of protest from mainstream businessmen, while the corporate liberals continued to work diligently to achieve their ends.

A minority faction within the Business Advisory Council experienced some success. Swope, Folsom, and Standard Oil's Walter Teagle supplied important backing for the Roosevelt administration's social security plan.[26] They provided input through the Advisory Council on Economic Security, an adjunct to Secretary of Labor Frances Perkins's Committee on Economic Security. Harriman and Dennison also supported social security. The result, after much debate and compromise among many groups, was the Social Security Act of 1935.[27]

The Social Security Act provided for old-age pensions and unemployment insurance. The federal government was to run the old-age pension system itself, collecting funds from both employers and employees on an equal basis. Pension benefits were to range from $10 to $85 per month once they began to be dispensed. Unemployment insurance operated differently, each state being required to enact its own law. Companies would certainly bear the greatest share of the burden, but workers might, or might not, be taxed. "Uncle Sam" collected the money raised, then channeled appropriate shares to the individual states for final disbursement to the jobless. The normal unemployment benefit was to be $15 per person per week for a maximum of 16 weeks.

Social security reflected corporate liberal ideology. Both old-age pensions and unemployment insurance received support. Swope described the old-age pension plan "as a great forward-looking and constructive achievement. . . ."[28] Folsom concurred, noting that for Eastman Kodak Company the cost of providing retirement annuities to its workers would be approximately the same after passage of the Social Security Act as before. The old-age tax payments to the federal government would be offset by reduced payments to the Metropolitan Life Insurance Company, which had administered retirement annuities for Kodak prior to 1935. Folsom added only that federal administration of old-age pensions should be along "simple and economical lines" with no build up of a vast reserve fund.[29] Both men viewed unemployment insurance as a boon, but much depended on the details of each state law. They recommended that the states construct statutes stipulating employee contributions as well as employer contributions, and advocated employment stabilization features.[30]

Employment stabilization, in particular, appealed to Swope, Folsom, and other corporate liberals. Employers who did a good job maintaining their labor force should be rewarded with a lower unemployment insurance payroll tax. Conversely, firms that laid off workers in bunches should be taxed more heavily. As it turned out, states like Wisconsin, California, and Washington enacted unemployment laws that met with their approval. But in other states, such as New York, where no distinction was made between employers with good employment records and those with bad employment records, the result was less salutary. Preservation of employment, leading to a more rational and humane workplace, motivated Swope, Folsom, and others like them.[31]

In any event, social security bore an unmistakable resemblance to welfare capitalism. The benefits contemplated for the elderly and unemployed under the federal–state system were comparable to those provided earlier by corporate welfare. Employment stabilization, it was hoped, would be a key feature of both plans. Significantly, coverage was much more complete under the federal program; in effect, the corporate liberals—thwarted on their own—joined forces with the government, compelling businesses that had once resisted private welfare programs to help pay for a federal–state plan. No longer would socially irresponsible firms enjoy a cost advantage over their more conscientious competitors; every firm involved would deal with "the same social burden"; and corporate capitalism would be sounder for it. Even with the regulatory approach in command, the government legislative process, responsive as ever to interest-group pressures, yielded concrete if limited gains for liberal businessmen.[32]

The "social security" breakthrough aside, corporate liberals experienced a good deal more frustration than satisfaction in the period from 1935 to 1938. The National Recovery Administration died. The Business Advisory Council proposal for a separate relief and recovery administration fell by the wayside. Council efforts to resolve a New England textile strike proved abortive; the United Textile Workers Union would have none of it.[33] Swope called for a National Chamber of Commerce and Industry, "a pluralistic form of advisory planning representing already organized economic interests," but it received no hearing.[34] So many rejections generated substantial ambivalence among corporate liberals toward the ideal of business–government partnership. Doubts about the value of the relationship appeared, along with negative feelings. On at least two separate occasions, in July 1935 and again in January 1938, the continued existence of BAC was called into question. In the first instance, members of the Council voted on the issue of disbanding, but decided to continue.[35] In the second, forty out of fifty members "threatened to resign" unless President Roosevelt muzzled vociferous critics of big business within his administration.[36] BAC persevered, as did the corporate liberals, but morale was low. Edward Stettinius remarked that the businessmen-bureaucrats "are discouraged" and perceive that they are "being regarded purely as 'window dressing'. . . ."[37] Corporate liberals found it quite difficult to act as intermediaries between big business and big government during a time of pronounced business–government animosity.

Fundamental ideological disagreements between business and government had resurfaced during the second New Deal. Moderate and conservative businessmen, upset by the tenacity of the Depression and by the proliferation of federal agencies and regulations that seemingly did little good, reiterated their belief in laissez-faire. The Chamber of Commerce and the National Association of Manufacturers beseeched government to refrain from meddling with the free market and the "invisible hand." The demand for smaller government, controlled expenditures, and a balanced budget grew. Big government, according to business critics like Merle Thorpe, was bad government, and quite possibly oppressive government. Roosevelt might even become a dictator, like Adolf Hitler in Germany.

Specific New Deal acts came under fire. Businessmen characterized the Revenue Acts of 1935 and 1936, which created a graduated corporate income tax, an excess-profits tax, and an undistributed profits tax, as soak-the-rich schemes. Utilities magnates viewed the Public Utilities Holding Company Act, which abolished all utilities holding companies of more than two tiers, as a direct threat to their existence. The National Labor Relations Act (NLRA), sponsored by Senator Robert Wagner (D-NY), drew an especially venomous reaction.

The Wagner Act reestablished collective bargaining in the wake of the Schechter decision, endorsed majority representation on the shop floor, and set up a National Labor Relations Board (NLRB), which arbitrated labor–management disputes. Almost all business organizations and businessmen found fault with it. The Chamber of Commerce and NAM vehemently opposed the Wagner Act, as did their constituencies of small and medium-sized businessmen. Together, they strongly disagreed with the concept of federal enforcement of collective bargaining; rejected majority representation because it favored independent trade unions over company unions; and branded the NLRB a biased body, so pro-labor that it amounted to judge, jury, and executioner of business concerns.

Big business leaders disliked the Wagner Act, too. General Motors president William S. Knudsen, for example, claimed that "90 per cent of the grievances" workers brought before his management team were "trumped-up" and that members of the National Labor Relations Board "frankly admit that it is not their business to protect the employer in any way." Even the Business Advisory Council announced itself in opposition, arguing that the Wagner bill would result in "delay," "interminable litigation," "an over-whelming mass of administrative detail," and "strife." Among corporate liberals, only Swope and Teagle gave much support at all, and they did so furtively. Though they believed that the New Deal must inevitably offer benefits to groups other than big business, and Swope thought "labor must have more protection than it has had before," including "consent elections" to determine a single bargaining agent on the shop floor, it was not prudent to speak out. Thus, the National Labor Relations Act met with sweeping condemnation from the business community. The NLRA, combined with the Revenue Acts and the Public Utilities Holding Company Act, caused most businessmen great indignation, and they protested vociferously. A regulatory state that sided with labor against business, and taxed heavily besides, was not at all to their liking.[38]

Differences of opinion between government and business led to a shouting match. The Chamber of Commerce and NAM continued their assault on President Roosevelt and his coterie, seeking to remove from Washington, DC "economic crackpots, social reformers, labor demagogues, and political racketeers."[39] John Jacob Raskob of General Motors warned "that businessmen must stop federal officials from destroying capitalism."[40] New Dealer Tommy Corcoran retaliated, explaining to Raymond Moley that, "Fighting with a businessman is like fighting with a Polack. You can give no quarter."[41] FDR himself waded into the fray, branding certain businessmen economic autocrats out to build an "industrial dictatorship."[42]

Business Week declared that the brief business–government marriage of NRA days had ended up in "divorce court."[43]

In reality, the situation was not quite so clear-cut. The great size and diversity of the business community made unanimity on any subject almost impossible to achieve. Small and medium-sized businesses routinely opposed Roosevelt, but notable exceptions can be found in certain industrial sectors and among certain companies (such as Dennison Manufacturing). The attitude of big business toward the federal government was no less complex. Whereas large, labor-intensive corporations favoring protectionism certainly fought the New Deal, technologically advanced, capital-intensive firms supportive of free trade gravitated toward it. The oil, electricity, telecommunications, and business machine industries, among others, participated in this realignment, along with giant companies such as Standard Oil, General Electric, International Telephone and Telegraph, and International Business Machines. Financiers and bankers made the transition as well. Not coincidentally, internationally oriented corporate liberals such as Teagle (Standard Oil of New Jersey), Swope (GE), and Harriman (Brown Brothers Harriman) remained staunch advocates of business–government partnership and the cooperative arrangements it might promote even in the bleakest of times.[44]

Corporate liberals clearly thought the exchange of harsh words between various businessmen and government officials counterproductive; they kept up efforts to bring the two together. Sears, Roebuck and Company's Donald Nelson explained that neither side really understood the other. Nelson believed, "Many businessmen think of the government as a place where men sit around a table and devise plans for obstructing and harassing businessmen. . . ."[45] By the same token, "many in Washington think of business as a closely-knit conspiracy intent only on profit and amassing wealth."[46] Both views amounted to caricature. Swope, Harriman, Dennison, Folsom, Kendall, Teagle, Stettinius, Nelson, and others like them refused to give up. They sought to reestablish the "business commonwealth," rather than giving in to separation and laissez-faire.

Shifting economic, political, and international currents finally rewarded corporate liberal persistence, touching off an effort to bring about business–government rapprochement. Given the steep recession of 1937–1938, the restoration of business confidence became more important to Roosevelt. If businessmen could be reassured that government truly supported their endeavors, confidence might well return and with it private investment, reemployment, and prosperity. After the Democratic party suffered a reversal at the polls in November 1938, FDR fantasized about adding business votes to the New Deal coalition. Foreign intrigues by Japan and Germany reminded Roosevelt of U.S. military vulnerability and that a thoroughgoing rearmament required the plant, equipment, and expertise only business possessed. These factors compelled FDR to inaugurate a substantial business assistance program during the winter of 1938–1939. Awaiting just such an opportunity, the corporate liberals joined in with enthusiasm.

Secretary of Commerce Harry Hopkins, who had been in office since December 1938, orchestrated the Roosevelt administration business assistance campaign. In an address before the Economic Club of Des Moines, Iowa on February 24, 1939, he defended the New Deal against charges that it had been anti-business and promised immediate succor to the business community. Hopkins emphasized that "the Government is not and has never been opposed to business. It has no desire whatever to harass or punish business. It fully realizes that business must succeed, and must be able to work with Government, if our economic system is to be preserved."[47] The Roosevelt administration not only endorsed the basic tenets of capitalism, including free enterprise and private profit, it wished "to create an environment in which private capital will be encouraged to invest."[48] Hopkins vowed that there would be no "general rise" in federal taxes for 1939. Furthermore, levies that "tend to freeze the necessary flow of capital" could be amended.[49] Additional incentives, such as lower interest rates, became a probability.

Averell Harriman, now Business Advisory Council chairman, lavished praise on Hopkins' speech. Harriman, who had pledged to aid Hopkins' good faith efforts to ensure "re-employment in private enterprise," stressed the Secretary's "understanding of the profit system."[50] The Brown Brothers Harriman–Union Pacific man said Hopkins "talked in terms business men will understand," insisting that the Des Moines address "should be encouraging to every one responsible for the conduct of business."[51] Harriman concluded with the prediction that Hopkins "will be the greatest Secretary of Commerce that we ever have had."[52] What Harriman really wanted to do, of course, was to work through Hopkins to reach Roosevelt. This strategy, designed to bolster business influence and reinvigorate the "business commonwealth" idea, looked quite promising.

Secretary Hopkins' actions suggested that he intended to keep his promises. Hopkins brought corporate liberals into the Commerce Department. He encouraged creativity, welcoming fresh ideas about Commerce Department reorganization and business–government partnership. He urged businesses everywhere to show faith in capitalism by freeing up money for investment in productive enterprise. Years of business–government antipathy and only partly successful pump-priming convinced him that such innovations were worth trying.

Corporate liberals took up important positions in Hopkins's Commerce Department. Edward Noble, Willard Thorp, and Robert Wood were the most prominent. Noble, originally of Lifesavers' Corporation, left his duties as chairman of the Civil Aeronautics Authority to become Undersecretary of

Commerce. His job involved "stimulating business."[53] Dunn and Bradstreet's Thorp wished to restructure the Commerce Department, tying it into industries throughout the national economy. Sears, Roebuck and Company's Wood operated as "first liaison officer to big business."[54] Together, this trio sought to turn the Commerce Department into what Assistant Secretary of Commerce Richard C. Patterson called a "business embassy."[55]

Willard Thorp's program was most intriguing. He asked that the Commerce Department be expanded and reconfigured to give businessmen and bureaucrats greater access to each other, and that the Department truly become an advocate for business. A class of civil servants, termed "traveling salesmen," would function as key intermediaries. In essence, they were industrial liaison officials paid by the Commerce Department to interact with representatives of all major industries. Dozens or hundreds of these positions could be set up, ensuring the necessary public-private linkages. Thorp pictured "traveling salesmen" for the steel industry, oil, coal, textiles, automobiles, even a boot-and-shoe agent.[56] Every "traveling salesman" acted as a contact point, or conduit, between government and business. As a group, they might unclog old lines of communication, open new lines, stimulate dialogue, and build mutual understanding.

Influenced by Thorp, Hopkins pushed for an agency within the Commerce Department called the Bureau of Industrial Economics (BIE). BIE's tasks were to include not only liaison with trade associations and corporations, but also statistics gathering and moderation of the business cycle.[57] Certainly, Hopkins recognized the need for "traveling salesmen," whatever their exact title might be. Information on all facets of enterprise, such as output, inventory, marketing, consumer credit, costs, and prices could be collected and made available to government and businessmen alike. This information, which amounted to economic intelligence, could be used to encourage public and private spending during depressions or restrain production during booms. The potential for economic stabilization and cultivation of prosperity inherent in such an operation was considerable. Business-driven corporatism could be revived and regulatory pressure released.

The Bureau of Industrial Economics found supporters in government and out. Hopkins saw it as the precise mechanism he needed to spend federal money "in ways that will encourage people to gamble private money."[58] Blackwell Smith of Wright, Gordon, Zachry & Parlin, an intimate of Stettinius and other corporate liberals, suggested that the Bureau's proper function was to act as a "triborough bridge" between the Temporary National Economic Committee, the Department of Commerce with its Business Advisory Council, and industry.[59] Roosevelt liked the idea too, inquiring into its practicality.[60] BIE offered government and business a way to communicate, an intelligence-gathering apparatus, and the possibility of economic regeneration and stable expansion. This type of intelligent collaboration between business and government held out the appetizing prospect of achievement of all goals once connected with the associational system of the 1920s.

Unfortunately, the Bureau of Industrial Economics never took form. Conservative opposition doomed the Bureau, which seemed too radical to many members of Congress. New Dealers, too, were divided. Acting on his own authority, Hopkins created a Division of Industrial Economics within the Commerce Department, but it quickly departed from a business advocacy-advisory role, veering sharply toward Keynesianism with a decided stress on national income analysis. The corporate liberal coterie within the Commerce Department therefore engineered little real change; business planning stalled, compensatory fiscal policy took hold, and a more complete integration of business and government awaited World War II.[61]

Gains were achieved in some areas. The Securities and Exchange Commission eased its restrictions on short selling of stocks, facilitating private investment.[62] The Reconstruction Finance Corporation, under banker Jesse Jones, lowered interest rates on its loans.[63] Tax and social security legislation, which originated in the Executive Branch, reached Congress. Perhaps even more might have been accomplished, but Administration point man Hopkins was hit by a mysterious gastrointestinal malady that often kept him at home, thereby reducing his effectiveness and restricting Harriman's access to Roosevelt.[64]

Tax revision, more than any other subject, came to dominate the Roosevelt administration's business assistance drive. Again, a businessman-bureaucrat played a key role. Corporate liberal John W. Hanes, Undersecretary of the Treasury, framed the original proposal. On March 10, 1939, Hanes called for the elimination of all existing corporation levies, such as the undistributed-profits tax, the excess-profits tax, and the capital-stock tax, and the substitution for them of a single flat tax of 22 percent on corporate incomes.[65] Hanes's plan was not intended to reduce total revenue to government, only to revamp the tax structure so as to remove business "deterrents" and induce more private investment. The bothersome Revenue Acts of 1935 and 1936 were his chief targets.

After much legislative wrangling, lasting through June, the Revenue Act of 1939 resulted. It established a flat tax rate of 18 percent on large-earning corporations, defined as those with incomes above $25,000 per annum. The undistributed-profits tax was set to expire as of December 31, 1939. Corporations received authorization to increase capital-stock valuations for 1939 and 1940 as a means of offsetting excess-profits taxation. A two-year loss carryover allowed them to write off their loss of one year by subtracting from profits in the next. The Revenue Act, in sum, simplified the tax code, improving the overall tax position of corporate America. The psychological boost businessmen received proved even more valuable than the actual stimulus provided to the economy.[66]

The Social Security Act Amendments of 1939 contained even greater savings for businessmen. On March 27, 1939, Roosevelt proposed that the payroll tax for old-age pensions remain at 1 percent throughout 1940 rather than rise automatically to 1.5 percent.[67] In early August 1939, the Senate passed the final package, which was even more generous. The payroll tax on employers not only stayed at 1 percent, but the step-up to 1.5 percent was postponed until 1943. The anticipated $47 billion old-age pension reserve fund was replaced by a contingent reserve system with a cap set at $7.752 billion, a figure that was not to be exceeded through 1954.[68] Marion Folsom applauded this provision, which made it less likely that politicians would be tempted to use the money for other than the original purpose.[69] Another feature of the law permitted states with adequate unemployment insurance reserves to reduce unemployment insurance taxes collected from employers if they so chose.[70] Folsom, Swope, and other corporate liberals lauded this measure, which could be used to reward firms that maintained their workforce by granting them a lower tax than the one paid by less socially responsible competitors. One authority notes that the "administration's concessions represented a giant step for the business legislative program—a billion dollar tax cut. . . ."[71]

Passage of the Social Security Act Amendments brought the Roosevelt administration's business assistance campaign to a close. Although the business legislative program brought neither instant economic recovery nor many business votes to Roosevelt in 1940, it did yield tax reform and clear a new evolutionary path for Social Security. Far more important, the partnership between FDR and the corporate liberals opened up the real possibility of a rapprochement between the federal government and orthodox businessmen.

Roosevelt, certain key subordinates, and the corporate liberals were responsible for the improvement in business–government relations. FDR told outgoing BAC chairman Averell Harriman that business and government must keep in touch so that capitalism could be effectively preserved and enhanced.[72] According to Secretary of Commerce Hopkins, government needed to do everything possible to promote "the confidence, success and . . . profits of legitimate business enterprise."[73] George Mead, a BAC member, reciprocated, saying that business now accepted "constructive regulation" from government.[74] Swope, Folsom, Stettinius, and Nelson were gratified; cooperation between industry and politics had advanced and might well deepen.

Even the mainstream business community took note. *Nation's Business*— once seemingly incapable of mustering a kind word for the Roosevelt administration—gave in, admitting the positive nature of the Revenue Act and the Social Security Act Amendments.[75] *Business Week* exulted, describing the recent "boost to business" as "far more extensive than business men dared dream."[76] By August 1939, business–government interaction increasingly emphasized conciliation and accommodation. This constructive attitude, which certainly made restoration of the "business commonwealth" more likely, carried over from the late New Deal into the preparedness period and World War.

Chapter 3

The Unready State

Throughout the 1930s, corporate liberals had devoted themselves to problems related to the Great Depression. Returning stability and profitability to the national economy, reemployment, social security, taxation, and reorganization of government ranked highest among their interests. Even before the corporate liberals' job was done, however, events abroad nagged at them and increasingly captured their attention, time, and energy. After July 1939, their focus gradually shifted from depression at home to war in Asia and Europe. Many corporate liberals, including Edward Stettinius, Robert Wood, and Averell Harriman, changed positions in government, moving from domestic agencies concerned with employment, income, and welfare matters, to defense-preparedness bodies.

The march of totalitarianism was responsible for this transition. Corporate liberals watched—uneasily at first, then with growing dismay—as militarist and fascist regimes victimized weak neighbors. Japan invaded Manchuria, establishing the puppet state of Manchukuo in 1931, and later attacked adjoining areas of northern China. Italy took over Ethiopia in 1935, as Benito Mussolini's planes and tanks wreaked havoc on tribal warriors. Under Adolf Hitler, Nazi Germany repudiated the Versailles Treaty, remilitarized the Rhineland, engineered the Anschluss, and swallowed Czechoslovakia by March 1939. People in the United States, including the corporate liberals, fretted about fighting in Asia, the prospect of European war, and the unappetizing possibility of U.S. involvement. In this uncertain, dangerous environment, the decrepit state of American national defense provoked substantial adverse comment, and the call went out to fix it.

Corporate liberals knew that the United States was unprepared to meet the challenges posed by an increasingly unfriendly world. From their vantage point, three interrelated factors stood out most prominently. First, and most obvious, the U.S. military establishment suffered from disorganization and an appalling shortage of arms and munitions. The country lacked the equipment, particularly the weapons, with which to fight. Second, the federal government operated only a very small and inefficient arsenal. This pitiful munitions establishment could supply no more than a fraction of the guns, ammunition, ships, planes, and other implements necessary for national security. Finally, American industry was not well equipped to take up the burden of defense production. Twenty years of peace, with little opportunity to turn a profit, had rendered the private munitions industry nearly defunct.

The U.S. Armed Services were in extremely poor condition on the eve of European war, with all branches of the military plagued by a scarcity of some weapons, a complete absence of others, and a shortage of related goods. Obsolescence was yet another problem. The U.S. Army and air forces compared especially badly to the German Wehrmacht and Luftwaffe, the National Guard was a laughingstock, and even the American Navy needed upgrading.

The U.S. Army was ranked seventeenth in the world in terms of overall effectiveness in 1939, just behind such non-powers as Poland and Rumania.[1] The Army as a whole was painfully small, its divisions were chronically under strength, and, most troubling of all, it lacked materiel. Counting forces at home and overseas, the Army numbered about 200,000 troops.[2] As of July 1, three organized infantry divisions and six partially organized divisions occupied U.S. soil. Not a single one of these divisions was operating at full strength; indeed, none was close to its combat complement.[3] Two cavalry divisions were functioning at something under half strength, totaling fewer than 2,500 men.[4] The Army had not yet formed a true armored division. Tank units existed, but were dispersed and manned by fewer than 1,500 soldiers. In stark contrast, Germany had deployed 60 infantry divisions and 14 mechanized and motorized divisions against the Polish border alone.[5] Although the U.S. Army was clearly emaciated, there was not enough equipment to go around. Chief of Staff George C. Marshall warned that American soldiers desperately needed more small arms, field artillery pieces, antiaircraft guns, and tanks.[6] The list went on and on. There was not enough small-arms ammunition, shells, demolition bombs, or gas masks, either.[7] Military authorities and other experts concluded that the Army was very inadequate, especially in light of the threat posed by fascism.

The American air forces were not consolidated in a separate branch but were divided among the various services, including the Army and the Navy. In 1939, the U.S. military as a whole controlled just 5,100 planes.[8] Of this paltry sum, the Army Air Corps possessed 1,700 aircraft—most of them obsolete—and the rest were scattered elsewhere.[9] Bombers and fighter planes, too, were in short supply; indeed, the Military Intelligence Division of the Army General Staff credited the United States with just 301 bombers and a correspondingly low number of fighters.[10] Germany and Italy, by comparison, possessed 14,000 first-line craft, including 4,269 medium and heavy bombers, and these planes were of superior quality relative to their American counterparts.[11]

A complicating factor was that the U.S. aircraft industry could not be expected to close the gap any time soon. Through 1938, the Army Air Corps received fewer than 90 airplanes a month from its production sources.[12] Military planners expected "present [airplane] manufacturing schedules . . . to be expanded three to four times," but that type of growth required time, and still might not be sufficient.[13] Even after President Franklin Roosevelt called for "Airplanes now—and lots of them!" in late 1938, nothing much happened.[14]

The root problem remained. Without a separate and distinct U.S. Air Force, air power took a back seat to ground and sea power. Meanwhile, the Army and Navy failed to define adequately their respective air defense and reconnaissance responsibilities. Confusion about the precise duties of each service with regard to air power persisted up to the very moment of the attack on Pearl Harbor.[15]

The National Guard was in even worse shape than the Army and air forces. During 1939–1940, the Guard used "World War I tents, webbing, shoes, and blankets in various stages of decay."[16] Weapons were antiquated, and trucks with "tank" painted on both sides were deployed for training purposes.[17] Professional soldiers looked down on the amateurs, because the Guard did not get comparable training. Guardsmen, on average, practiced marching and handled their weapons only 48 nights a year. Additionally, they left their jobs and participated in two weeks of full-time field duty over the same interval.[18] Army regulars deemed this commitment to soldiering insufficient. State control over National Guard units also mitigated against proper training and coordination of forces; political influences and entrenched localism further divided and weakened them.

War games held in Plattsburgh, New York, in August 1939 highlighted these defects and others. Fifty thousand soldiers of the First Army participated, 68 percent of them National Guard.[19] These maneuvers constituted "the biggest peacetime war games in the country's history" to that time.[20] The results were disappointing, to say the least. The National Guardsmen at Plattsburgh testified to the inadequacy of their ragtag army. One soldier declared, "we didn't have adequate transportation for men or supplies, we didn't have the proper weapons or field equipment. . . ."[21] *Fortune* reported that "Good Humor trucks in the 'war' area had to be camouflaged with mud by orders from G.H.Q. because they were a dead giveaway of troop concentrations and could be spotted by enemy reconnaissance planes."[22] National Guard units from different states lost their bearings, wandering around in circles or bumping into one another. As newspaper criticism of the "mock war" reached a crescendo, one Guardsman asked why journalists did not focus greater attention on "Guard officers that get their jobs through political pull instead of military knowledge or brains?"[23] To some observers, the Plattsburgh maneuvers were a farce; to others, a warning. The U.S. military—in particular the National Guard—lacked adequate funding and necessary equipment, including firearms; it also lacked the vital element of cohesion.

The Navy fared somewhat better than the other services in the period immediately preceding the European war. Widely recognized as the United States' "first line of defense," it was "continually prepared. . . ."[24] Roosevelt, perhaps recalling his service as assistant secretary of the navy under Woodrow Wilson, made the Navy a priority from the earliest days of his presidency. The Naval Expansion Act of 1938, which called for construction of new battleships, aircraft carriers, and other vessels, provided a foundation on which to build. Under this legislation, Congress authorized a navy of 1,577,480 tons.[25] In 1939 and 1940, granted some delays in shipbuilding, the U.S. Navy still amounted to well over one million tons. A year later, as of January 1, 1941, Germany and Italy possessed only 850,000 tons between them.[26]

Even so, the U.S. fleet needed to remedy significant shortcomings. Most important, it was not large enough to operate effectively in the Atlantic Ocean and the Pacific Ocean simultaneously. To dramatize this vulnerability, one critic compared the notion of the fleet "shuttling back and forth between the Atlantic and Pacific" to "the elaborate arguments conclusively demonstrating that the Nazis could never hope to break the Maginot Line."[27] Other drawbacks were almost as obvious: just six aircraft carriers were in operation; the majority of battleships, destroyers, and submarines were over age; Japanese heavy cruisers came equipped with torpedo tubes whereas American heavy cruisers did not; and many ships, though "serviceable," were "slow in speed."[28] Although the Navy looked good in comparison to the Army, air forces, and National Guard, it required additional bolstering and modernization to fulfill its rapidly expanding strategic mission.

A shortage of ordinary, everyday items existed, too, in all branches of the military. Soldiers, airmen, and sailors must have weapons, but they also need uniforms appropriate to various weather conditions, drinkable water, and edible food. In 1939, the Army, air forces, and Navy lacked many such essentials, including tropical apparel, water purifiers, food containers, and cooking ranges.[29] The National Guard and regular Army solders who had trained at Plattsburgh complained often about the absence of "fresh beef," and about bologna, "which is practically all we've had since the first day."[30]

The upshot was dramatic and shocking: the U.S. military, taken in its entirety, was pathetic. Certainly, the military was not ready for a modern war. In a time of peace and international stability, this situation had been overlooked, even praised, but it could not be tolerated any longer. Totalitarian aggression demanded that American military deficiencies be redressed, if only as a possible deterrent to further hostile moves by Germany, Italy, and Japan and as protection for the Western Hemisphere.

The American civilian state, like the military, found itself ill prepared to meet the fascist challenge. A traditional American distrust of state power stood in the way of preparedness. If the state grew too strong, especially militarily, it could deprive the American people of hard-won freedoms, and that had never been acceptable. Not surprisingly, given this kind of apprehension and the American aversion to socialism, the United States possessed no sizable government munitions industry. The absence of a specialized preparedness agency capable of reaching outside government to tap the resources of the private sector also hampered industrial mobilization.[31]

The peculiar historical development of the American state, coupled with the basic psychology of U.S. citizens, mitigated against easy construction and maintenance of a powerful military machine. From the first days of the Republic, Americans distrusted centralized power and a standing army, viewing them as threats to individual liberties. In order to protect freedom, Americans relied on constitutional safeguards, including checks and balances between the executive, legislative, and judicial branches of the federal government, and division of power between federal, state, and local authorities. Under these conditions, the growth of the federal establishment was restrained, concern for comprehensive planning was virtually absent, and the Army and Navy operated as mere "frontier" forces. Among the founders, men such as Thomas Jefferson viewed perpetuation of a small, amateur military as a blessing rather than a curse, and this feeling lingered for a very long time indeed.[32]

Forces of individualism and localism remained powerful throughout the eighteenth century and into the nineteenth and twentieth centuries. Up to the Progressive Era, certainly, the United States had been dominated by a "state of courts and parties."[33] Citizens expected the legal system to resolve conflicts between them, especially those involving property rights and violence. They looked to the two-party system for patronage and settlement of contentious political issues. They insisted that the federal government remain small and unobtrusive, and that states, localities, and individuals solve their own problems whenever possible, without the intervention of a heavy-handed central authority. Preservation of the people's rights took precedence over a strong peacetime military.

During the New Deal, the federal government expanded, assuming more functions and responsibilities than before. It provided many goods and services to diverse special interests. Unfortunately, comprehensive planning, emphasizing coordination and efficiency, did not always accompany Roosevelt's agencies. The National Resources Planning Board and regional planning authorities such as the Tennessee Valley Authority provided insufficient direction. Planning went forward in only a partial, piecemeal fashion: a multitude of agencies "carried on more or less independently of central control. . . ."[34] The result, from the perspective of 1939, was unsettling: although autonomous individualism flourished, planned efficiency had been badly neglected, and the weak American state would be hard-pressed to carry out quick, effective industrial mobilization.[35]

Traditional constraints on state power, alone, do not adequately explain the United States' military backwardness. Suspicion of excessive central authority, which might conceivably be used to oppress the citizenry, defined only the broad parameters within which the New Deal state operated. Within those confines, many other factors intermixed. Revulsion toward war, isolationist sentiment, the New Era illusion of international stability, and depression economies all contributed their share to a limited state capacity for preparedness.

During the 1920s and 1930s, Americans fervently wished to avoid war. Pacifists, of course, pushed harder for preservation of peace than anyone else. Americans certainly did not want to sacrifice their youth—or the young men of other nations—on the altar of another Great War. An "altruistic spirit" swept the United States, demanding replacement of the existing "war system" with a "peace system" lest civilization "go down to ruin in the holocaust of the Next War."[36]

Isolationists, for their part, rejected "very large military preparations" as well as entangling European alliances.[37] They believed that the United States need only defend the Western Hemisphere, nowhere else. A navy or air force capable of projecting power over vast distances was unnecessary, indeed counterproductive, because it made U.S. involvement in a conflict more likely. A modest army was all that was necessary. A stronger military only invited profiteering by bankers, shipbuilders, and munitions makers, as Senator Gerald P. Nye's Munitions Investigation of 1934 to 1936 had pointed out. European alliances were to be avoided in order to further minimize the chances of dispute. This approach, so isolationists argued, maintained peace while sustaining national security at a level that was acceptable but not provocative.

Another segment of American public opinion differed markedly from the thinking of the pacifists and isolationists. This group, which existed through the 1920s and into the early 1930s, failed to discern any reason for real concern over the state of foreign affairs. They believed that the international system was stable enough, and the absence of obvious enemies generated in them a "lack of any apparent urgency."[38] The proponents of New Era international stability argued that the presence of the Atlantic and Pacific Oceans shielded the United States from European and Asian problems. Like the isolationists, they saw European problems as Europe's alone. Unlike the isolationists, however, they did not worry that the U.S. government would allow itself to be drawn into foreign hostilities.[39]

This ideological climate, characterized by abhorrence of war, pronounced pacifism, a powerful isolationism, and considerable naïveté, worked against proper upkeep of the military. Under the influences of these forces, the military was suffering from manpower and equipment shortages long before the onset of the Great Depression. When the Depression did come, funding for the Army, Navy, and air forces was further restrained by budgetary considerations. While Hitler propelled Germany on the path of rapid rearmament, Roosevelt faced a public not favorably disposed toward massive military spending. Not surprisingly, U.S. military expenditures from 1933 to 1938 amounted to only 1,175 million pounds compared to Germany's 2,868 million pounds.[40] Financial woes, on top of a mind-set already ill disposed to militarism, make more explicable U.S. military weaknesses of all types.

It follows logically enough that the United States made do with a puny federal munitions establishment. After the end of World War I, the Wilson administration had demolished all government-owned powder plants and left the art of weapons-making to a few War Department installations. Altogether, the government controlled only six army ordnance arsenals, an army chemical warfare arsenal, a navy gun factory, and the odd, scattered navy yard.[41] One expert, Burnham Finney of the *American Machinist,* estimated that in wartime "they could turn out less than 10 percent of the munitions needed."[42] Another, Colonel Harry K. Rutherford of the Army Ordnance Department, noted that the "productive capacity of these arsenals is of little account in war when mass production is the rule."[43]

Authorities pointed out that the equipment in government weapons facilities was antiquated, and much of it required rehabilitation.[44] A February 1939 survey indicated that "85 percent of the machinery [in the arsenals] was over ten years old, that much of it predated this century, and that some of it was installed before the Civil War."[45] Outdated equipment needed to be junked, aging but salvageable equipment fixed, and new equipment brought in. Although government arsenals would not produce a significant volume of weapons during war, they might "help to fill the breach in the early months of [an] emergency before the large converted commercial plants can begin production" and "serve as yardsticks with which to compare methods and costs in private establishments."[46] The state-sponsored munitions complex, all told, was fragile, ill connected, and rudimentary at best.

The lack of an emergency preparedness agency similar to the 1917–1918 War Industries Board (WIB), was another major concern. In the absence of such an agency, the state was operating without the precise mechanism necessary to bring together civilian authorities, military leaders, corporate executives, and other parties interested in upgrading national security. This state of affairs might not have prevailed at all, except that permanent government organs having to do with industrial mobilization were inadequate. The Office of the Assistant Secretary of War (OASW), which carried out mobilization planning, and the Army-Navy Munitions Board (ANMB), which coordinated the supply needs of the two most important military services, faced chronic shortages of personnel and money throughout the 1920s and 1930s. They also lacked prestige as a result of the fact that mobilization planning was a relatively new function of the War Department and military services and was not yet fully accepted. Just as crippling, OASW and ANMB lacked permanent, well-established connections to business leaders and their corporations. In 1939, the War Department expected that 90 percent of its arms and munitions would come from private sources should there ever be a major war, yet OASW and ANMB did not know which firms were best suited to certain types of defense production or which executives would cooperate. Under these circumstances, Army and Navy distribution of contracts to corporate America would probably be a highly inefficient proposition, perhaps even a disaster. Bernard Baruch contended that the War Department was "not organized to place business" and that only the establishment of an agency like the WIB, under firm civilian control, would get the job done. He argued that the hazardous munitions shortfall could not be addressed and eliminated until an emergency-preparedness agency appeared.[47]

Bureaucratic incapacity, as much as the actual scarcity of arms and munitions, stood in the way of an adequate American preparedness campaign. The state lacked enough plant, equipment, and expertise to make the necessary quantity of rifles, tanks, bombers, and aircraft carriers. It functioned without sufficient connections to the private sector. This situation, though increasingly hazardous, was predictable in a freedom-loving country with a tradition of rugged individualism, private enterprise, and weak government. Even more to the point, domestic and foreign conditions after World War I had created little need for a large defense establishment and had engendered some opposition to it from sources such as the Nye Committee.

The private munitions industry was in bad shape, too. Two decades of neglect had left their mark. By 1939, the munitions business had become a small-scale operation that confronted formidable obstacles in its quest for growth. Although the "building blocks" for expansion were available, they required considerable assembling.

During World War I, corporate America had focused its attention on large-scale production of weapons and related goods. By November 11, 1918, U.S. companies were producing more than enough of some articles and in certain categories verged on mass production. Quartermaster goods were plentiful, and light munitions appeared in adequate numbers. Heavier munitions did not, though 1919 would have seen significant output. U.S. industry, for example, could not supply the American Expeditionary Force with even one tank in the short time it had before the Armistice was signed. The War Department contracted for 10,000 75 mm guns, and only 143 made their way to France. Of necessity, U.S. troops fought using certain types of French and British weapons. On the whole, the U.S. industrial effort was spotty, but American allies filled in the gaps and mobilization succeeded. Unfortunately, the munitions industry the United States did have fell apart once the fighting stopped and operated at minimal levels thereafter.[48]

After Armistice Day, the Wilson administration preferred to return to civilian life as quickly as possible. It terminated the activities of the various industrial mobilization agencies and notified defense contractors that their services were no longer required. Paradoxically, the government did not remove the wartime excess-profits tax. Thus, munitions business dried up, opportunities for contracts and profits decreased, and most companies got out. Bethlehem Steel, to cite a typical example, closed its defense plants and scrapped the equipment rather than pay heavy taxes—but only after Uncle Sam refused to take the machinery![49] Under these adverse conditions, it made sense for private companies to switch back to civilian goods, and the World War I munitions capacity was almost lost.

The Great Depression also hurt the private munitions industry. As defense expenditure shrank from fiscal year 1931 through fiscal year 1934, fewer and fewer companies obtained defense contracts. By 1939, despite modest gains from 1935 on, the quartermaster and ordnance departments of the armed services were interacting with only a small number of firms.[50] Regular defense business was minuscule. Even educational orders, designed to acquaint firms just breaking into the defense business with the various ins and outs of defense production, were scarce.

The emaciated condition of the private munitions industry caused consternation. U.S. businesses could make cars, washing machines, and radios by the tens of thousands, yet lacked the ability to construct tanks and other weapons in large numbers. The requisite machinery was not yet in place, and specialized managerial experience was scant. In addition, Senator Nye's "merchants of death" thesis—that World War I weapons makers had preferred war-induced profits to the lives of American boys—discouraged firms from taking defense contracts, making it more difficult to resuscitate the private munitions industry and catch up to the Germans.[51]

The German munitions industry, by contrast, was better adapted to prevailing conditions. Germany possessed machine tools, assembly-line techniques, and specifications for countless defense items. This equipment and information was not immediately at hand in the United States. Indeed, U.S. companies possessed specialized machine tools that oftentimes could not be converted to armaments production, whereas German firms employed universal machines that were readily redesigned for weapons manufacture.[52]

American unreadiness, then, included military deficiencies, bureaucratic shortcomings, and industrial inexperience. Shortages of weapons, or even the utter unavailability of certain types, represented only the most glaring defect. A far more deeply embedded problem was the inherited predisposition toward a divided, fragmented civil government and a small, skeletonized military. Nor was the private sector prepared to pick up the slack: the moribund munitions industry could not supply an immediate fix.

President Roosevelt was aware of the conditions that hindered any successful American preparedness effort. He knew that the government arsenal was understocked and that the private munitions industry was tiny. He recognized that military power in the modern age rested on a foundation of industrial supply, and that the American foundation was shaky. The New Deal state, disjointed as it was, required alterations in order to facilitate preparedness. Changes were in order.

Roosevelt considered three broad state-building options. A state-run munitions industry was one. A market-driven system was another. The third alternative, government–business cooperation, was the approach ultimately selected.

Resort to a state-run munitions complex appealed to New Deal stalwarts. Secretary of the Interior Harold Ickes, allied with certain other cabinet members and younger, more aggressive New Dealers, advocated the incorporation of defense-preparedness powers and responsibilities into an expanded New Deal state.[53] In this manner, industrial mobilization and military readiness could be ensured, along with preservation of New Deal reforms that were beneficial to labor, the unemployed, the elderly, and others.[54] Big business power, too, might be restrained and channeled in appropriate directions.

Roosevelt, though sympathetic to this line of argument, was not convinced. The American antibureaucratic tradition mitigated against creation of such a powerful state.[55] Earlier, the Nye Committee had proposed nationalization of the munitions industry—with industrial managers excused—but this plan had been rejected.[56] The Executive Reorganization plan of 1938, which proposed major structural changes in the U.S. government, had been watered down by Congress and resulted only in minor revisions.[57] If these efforts met with little success, FDR recognized that a sweeping redesign of the state in the midst of a crisis was even less likely to bring positive results.

Drastic change of the type ardent New Dealers preferred would not be helpful. It was sure to bring down charges of dictatorship and socialism against the administration. Delay stemming from the revamping of corporate capitalism to fit a new pattern would surely result. Most of all, Roosevelt could not be certain that the federal bureaucracy even possessed the capacity to take on such an immense task.[58] Although state growth during the 1930s put the government in a better position than it had been in 1916–1917, it was reasonable to question the ability of the state itself to carry out rearmament. A highly centralized preparedness campaign, conducted in the teeth of business opposition, was not an appetizing prospect for the president. American suspicion of state power, doubts about the capability of bureaucracy and bureaucrats, an aversion to nationalization of industry, and political expediency all combined to lead Roosevelt away from creation of a European-style, state-run munitions industry.

Reliance on a market-driven system was another possibility. In theory, at least, escalating demand for weapons and related goods, in combination with lucrative profits, would have brought about reallocation of private resources toward production of the necessary arms and munitions. The workings of the "invisible hand" made the shift from civilian production to defense production likely, and it could happen without state intervention. The essential considerations here, of course, were time and control. In 1939–1940, many industries (including steel and automobiles) wished to capitalize on returning economic vitality by making their traditional products and supplying their traditional customers.[59] Under these circumstances, the move to large-scale defense production might well have been postponed until 1942 or 1943, a delay that was not acceptable to the administration. In Roosevelt's eyes, moreover, dependence on market mechanisms meant forfeiting his authority to corporate executives. Though inclined now to conciliate big business, FDR was not about to give it carte blanche.[60] In any preparedness scenario, Roosevelt believed in government supervision of defense business. Regulation of prevailing market forces, and redirection of them whenever advantageous, was a must.

Government–business cooperation therefore prevailed. Roosevelt, having earlier offered business an olive branch in the form of the business assistance program, now moved to further solidify the relationship. As the European crisis intensified, eventually spawning war, he established temporary emergency agencies one by one. Corporate liberals dominated the most important of them. An "emergency form of administrative state" materialized, combining public and private resources.[61] Because this edifice was to be dismantled at the satisfactory conclusion of the conflict, and the status quo ante bellum restored, the antibureaucratic streak in the American temperament was appeased. The continuing emphasis on private enterprise, albeit more closely monitored than before, headed off allegations of socialism. Government-sponsored cartelism required relatively little tinkering with the economy when compared to alterations that would have been mandated by a state-run munitions industry; thus, delay was minimized. Cartelism, too, might draw from the War Industries Board/National Recovery Administration experience.[62] Of greatest import, the temporary employment of private-sector human capital and other resources promised a quick and relatively painless solution to the problem of bureaucratic incapacity.

Having decided to go forward with a public–private preparedness system, Roosevelt called on the corporate liberals once again. They responded as they had so often in the past, lending FDR their unique managerial talents. Edward Stettinius Jr. came forward first, followed by William S. Knudsen and Donald

M. Nelson, among others. They lent FDR the precise "administrative resources of information, analysis, and expertise" that the state increasingly required.[63] Without the corporate liberals, the New Deal state lacked the size and skills to perform "large tasks" such as industrial mobilization.[64] With them, government acquired substantial industrial acumen, almost limitless connections to the best business minds outside government, the ability to borrow corporate personnel, and access to private plant and equipment. Given these assets, defense preparedness became an arduous but manageable proposition.

Of the many motivations that inspired Stettinius, Knudsen, Nelson, and the other corporate liberals to join Roosevelt, three stand out most prominently. First, the corporate liberals sincerely wanted to help the president. Second, they grew increasingly aware of the United States' national security liabilities and the need to address them. Finally, they were motivated by the probability of exerting greater influence over public policy.[65]

Having served Roosevelt previously, certain corporate liberals had developed a heartfelt loyalty toward him; others were flattered by his attention. Edward Stettinius Jr. fit into both categories. Stettinius's support of basic New Deal economic and social policies, including various recovery schemes and assistance for labor, the unemployed, and the elderly, was well known, as was his willingness to work hard for FDR whenever the call came.[66] Even after rumors circulated among ultraconservative businessmen that Stettinius had become an out-and-out New Dealer and therefore a turncoat, he remained with the administration in one capacity or another.[67] He carried out orders with dispatch, proved himself a capable administrator, and developed a high regard for Roosevelt, Secretary of State Cordell Hull, and many other New Dealers.[68]

William Knudsen also developed feelings for the president. Back in 1933, as a member of the National Automobile Chamber of Commerce, Knudsen had played a part in formulating the National Recovery Administration's automobile code. Later, Knudsen sometimes acted as General Motors' representative at meetings of the NRA's National Labor Board.[69] Although he was no Stettinius, these occasional contacts with the New Deal government differentiated him from those corporate executives who swore they would have nothing to do with the federal authority at all. Knudsen did exhibit periodic resentment toward the New Deal, but he knew that the state was ignored only at one's peril, and he was never associated with the hard-line conservative position.[70] Additionally, he could be stroked. During the fall of 1940, the Washington press reported that Knudsen would step down from his position with the National Defense Advisory Commission and would back Republican Wendell Willkie in the upcoming presidential election. Knudsen vehemently denied the rumor, saying: "Me resign? Me quit the President? Why—why, he calls me Bill!"[71] Knudsen stayed on.

Donald Nelson, at least in this regard, was not all that different from the other two. He touched bases with government during the New Deal, then joined on a full-time basis from 1940 on. In 1944, after "sweating out" multitudinous defense-related problems, Nelson left Washington, DC—but only when Roosevelt relieved him.[72] Even at that, Nelson reported that "the President and I parted congenially and as good friends, which I think we always were."[73] Stettinius, Knudsen, and Nelson established an attachment to Roosevelt that had to do partly with the aura that surrounds any chief executive, partly with the president's magnetic personality, and partly with the international emergency.

Although European crisis did not greatly concern corporate liberals at first, the magnitude of events was such that none could escape their implications for long. Mindful of General Motors' German operations, which produced over 50 percent of the cars sold in that country during 1935, Knudsen had displayed "tactful goodwill" toward the Nazis.[74] Up to mid-1939, Nelson was only "vaguely disturbed" by the predatory actions of totalitarian nations.[75] Stettinius, like many other corporate liberals, concentrated his attention primarily on domestic business, showing only occasional interest in foreign affairs. German moves in 1939 and 1940, however, led to war and brought harsh reality home. Corporate liberals came to the uncomfortable realization that what was happening in Europe profoundly affected them. Knudsen had four sisters who lived in Denmark, only a short distance from Germany and ultimately a war zone.[76] U.S. corporations such as General Motors, General Electric, and Standard Oil had European subsidiaries, connections to European corporations, and a desire to retain European markets.[77] Brought into the preparedness program by Roosevelt, Stettinius, Knudsen, and Nelson were more quickly sensitized to the United States' national security shortcomings than were mainstream businessmen. If corporate liberals were somewhat distracted from European affairs in the beginning, or cautious not to offend Germany, their attitude was to change dramatically. Increasingly alarmed by totalitarian aggression, they committed themselves in an intense, passionate way to the American preparedness campaign.

American national security weaknesses ultimately drew condemnation from the corporate liberals. They understood that the U.S. military paled by comparison to Germany's. They knew that the state-operated arsenal was not even worthy of the name. Better than anyone else in government, they recognized the inadequacies of the private munitions industry.

Donald Nelson labeled the U.S. Armed Forces of 1939 our "Disarmed Forces."[78] Echoing Chief of Staff George Marshall, Nelson recalled that "we didn't have a large and well-equipped Army."[79] In a hostile world, 200,000 soldiers were simply not enough. The equipment situation was even worse. The average U.S. infantryman still carried a 1903 Springfield rifle, with powder that might well be decades old, and the field artillery depended on

World War I–vintage 75 mm howitzers rather than a state-of-the-art weapon.[80] Nelson lamented that "our 500 or so tanks seemed a pitiably small corporal's guard to be sent against the armored divisions of almost any other major military force."[81] As late as January 1940, he reported that the United States could manufacture only 2,000 warplanes a year.[82] Stettinius remarked that even this small figure was misleading, because many planes made in 1939 were actually trainers, not full-fledged combat aircraft at all.[83] Even more startling, the U.S. Army Air Corps did not have "a single dive bomber and had not even approved a model for production."[84] Nelson noted, too, that the National Guard trained with wooden guns and that Guardsmen "fired" field pieces that had stovepipes for barrels.[85]

Germany's military machine, by contrast, dwarfed the American one. Germany possessed a well-trained, battle-tested army of several million men. There soldiers employed cutting-edge weapons, including the Mark III and Mark IV Panzer tanks. The Luftwaffe used the Ju-87 Stuka dive bomber. What is more, German industry had reached a far greater current capacity for making weapons than American industry. Having witnessed the sorry Louisiana war games of May 1940, which were not that much of an improvement over the Plattsburgh games of the previous year, *Time* magazine conjured up the awful specter of total war in Europe, saying that "the U.S. Army looked like a few nice boys with BB guns."[86]

Corporate liberals accepted the prevailing wisdom regarding the federal arsenal: it was not up to twentieth-century standards and therefore could not be counted on to close the weapons gap or to fight a modern, total war. Nelson characterized the American munitions operation, especially when compared to that of the Germans, as "a pigmy."[87] He bemoaned the fact that the United States "had no Krupp or Vickers."[88] The state by itself simply could not manufacture the implements of war that were missing, let alone guarantee defense production over and above that should future circumstances dictate.

The private munitions industry, like the U.S. military and the government arsenal, was underdeveloped. Nelson stated that American industry "knew all about mass production, but nothing about war or the instruments of war."[89] He exaggerated a bit here, but he was closer to the mark when he wrote that German weapons "were designed primarily for mass production" whereas American weapons were not.[90] Stettinius pointed out that industrialists had had to build a munitions industry almost from scratch while the load increased terrifically month by month from mid-1939 on.[91] Recovery of the munitions business from its post–World War I, Depression-induced slump required existing firms to expand their business tremendously while newcomers were enticed to enter the field.

Corporate liberal awareness of U.S. military and industrial weaknesses was obvious, but the situation did not depress them. They saw through all the troubles to a better day ahead. Nelson, Robert Wood of Sears, Roebuck and

Company, and others emphasized American "economic potential for war." Although the United States "had nothing that would have been recognized in Europe as a going munitions industry," Nelson was sure that "we did have the makings of the greatest powerhouse of munitions production in the world."[92] The raw materials, labor, and managerial talent existed to do the job. Wood thought "that the [future] capacity of this country to produce the machinery of war is perhaps its greatest weapon of defense."[93] Corporate liberal faith in the ability of U.S. industry to make weapons in colossal numbers proved unwavering. They did ask for time in which to "practice," and for public support and appreciation for the enormity of their task.[94]

Participation in the defense-preparedness program, of course, opened the way for corporate liberals to shape public policy in ways beneficial to corporate America. As always, Stettinius, Nelson, Knudsen, and others like them fought to preserve maximum business autonomy. Likewise, they guarded against efforts to use the defense emergency as a pretext to expand central planning or increase state authority over business.[95] Industrial self-regulation remained their objective, based on the WIB-NRA precedent. This approach left business the maximum amount of room to maneuver while still acknowledging the undeniable reality of greater state authority. Oligopolistic stability and profit making were other major considerations.[96] Nor did these goals necessarily conflict with the provision of national security. If anything, the World War I experience seemed to indicate otherwise. Corporate liberals, in short, skillfully exploited their strategic positions within the evolving mobilization structure to gradually restore and extend their vision of the "business commonwealth."[97]

One point stood out more sharply than the others: the "unready state" could no longer be tolerated. German, Italian, and Japanese adventurism called for an appropriate institutional response from the United States. Patriotism combined with self-interest to bring the corporate liberals into the mix. After Hitler's Czechoslovakian seizure, American Telephone and Telegraph's Walter Gifford reiterated his plea for reactivation of the Great War's National Defense Advisory Commission. According to Gifford, trouble in Central Europe and Asia made it imperative to reconstitute the Advisory Commission "as a peacetime planning agency for coordinating national resources. . . ."[98] Wood and Stettinius supported a move of this type. Wood, though an ardent isolationist, insisted on a stronger U.S. military presence in the Western Hemisphere to deter aggressors and thereby preserve the peace.[99] From his perspective, establishment of an industrial mobilization agency made sense. Stettinius saw a need for an agency similar to Baruch's old War Industries Board. Not surprisingly, given their views, Gifford, Wood, and Stettinius were among those who agreed to sit on President Roosevelt's newly created War Resources Board.

Figure 1. **Henry S. Dennison, president of Dennison Manufacturing Company, Framingham, Massachusetts.** Courtesy of Framingham Historical Society.

Figure 2. **Eastman Kodak Management Advisory Committee (1926).** Marion B. Folsom is the young man pictured at center, standing. Seated directly in front of Folsom is the legendary George Eastman, founder of Eastman Kodak Company and chairman of the board. To the right of Eastman (seated) is Frank Lovejoy, vice president and general manager. Eastman and Lovejoy helped advance Folsom's career at Eastman Kodak, contributing significantly to his business ideology. Courtesy of Rochester Public Library Local History Division, Rochester, New York.

Figure 3. **Key Roosevelt advisor Harry Hopkins (right) with Colonel McDonough at a Boston Works Progress Administration meeting on June 17, 1938.** Photo courtesy of Franklin D. Roosevelt Library, Hyde Park, New York.

Figure 4. **Secretary of the Interior Harold Ickes, a long-time critic of the corporate liberals.** Photo by Maurice Constant. Photo courtesy of Franklin D. Roosevelt Library, Hyde Park, New York.

Figure 5. **William S. Knudsen, president of General Motors Company, bows to President Roosevelt.** Knudsen was in Washington, D.C. for the first meeting of the National Defense Advisory Commission. May 30, 1940. UPI (ACME) Photo courtesy of Franklin D. Roosevelt Library, Hyde Park, New York.

Figure 6. **Assistant Attorney General Thurman Arnold, head of the Anti-Trust Division of the Justice Department.** Photo courtesy of Franklin D. Roosevelt Library, Hyde Park, New York.

Figure 7. **United Automobile Workers executives Walter Reuther and R. J. Thomas (left) confer with government officials Sidney Hillman (center) and William S. Knudsen.** General Electric's Charles E. Wilson (far right) is also involved. The topic of discussion is conversion of automobile plants to production of fighter planes. January 5, 1941. Photo courtesy of Franklin D. Roosevelt Library, Hyde Park, New York.

Figure 8. **Major participants of a lend-lease conference of the Office of Production Management on August 19, 1941.** Left to right: John Lord O'Brian, General Counsel, OPM; Edward Stettinius, Jr., Director of Priorities, OPM; Lord Beaverbrook, British Minister of Supply; William Knudsen, Director General, OPM; and Averell Harriman, Lend-Lease Administrator in London. Photo courtesy of Franklin D. Roosevelt Library, Hyde Park, New York.

Figure 9. **Under Secretary of War Robert P. Patterson tries out a light machine gun at Fort Leonard Wood, Missouri, August 21, 1942.** Patterson and the corporate liberal leadership of the industrial mobilization agencies did not always see eye to eye. Photo courtesy of Franklin D. Roosevelt Library, Hyde Park, New York.

Figure 10. **President Roosevelt and Mrs. Roosevelt inspect an automobile plant that has been converted to war production.** Kenneth T. Keller, president of Chrysler Corporation, talks while FDR listens. War Production Board chief Donald Nelson (far right) is also involved in the conversation. September 18, 1942. Official U.S. Navy photo. Photo courtesy of Franklin D. Roosevelt Library, Hyde Park, New York.

Figure 11. **Edward R. Stettinius, Jr., converses with President Franklin D. Roosevelt, December 11, 1942.** Stettinius served Roosevelt in many capacities during the New Deal and World War II, moving from the chairmanship of the War Resources Board through high-ranking positions with the National Defense Advisory Commission and the Office of Production Management. In 1944, Roosevelt made Stettinius Secretary of State. Photo courtesy of Franklin D. Roosevelt Library, Hyde Park, New York.

Figure 12. **Lieutenant General Brehon Somervell (right), head Army Services of Supply, with Lord Louis Mountbatten in January 1943.** Somervell's bullheadedness and inflexibility earned him the epithets of New Dealers and corporate liberals alike. Photo courtesy of Franklin D. Roosevelt Library, Hyde Park, New York.

Chapter 4

The Corporate Liberals, the War Resources Board, and Industrial Mobilization Planning

President Roosevelt set up the War Resources Board (WRB) to study mobilization of American industry for war. FDR recognized that, should war come, production of arms and munitions by private firms for supply to fighting men would be every bit as important as military strategy and tactics.[1] It followed logically that industrialists and manufacturers, as well as generals and admirals, needed to be consulted about contingency planning. Roosevelt responded to bureaucratic incapacity—more precisely, a lack of governmental knowledge about intricate, hands-on production matters—by drafting business experts who could be expected to fill this void. The loyalty and availability of the corporate liberals, who had been with FDR from the start of his first term, went without question. Although Roosevelt positively wished to avoid war, he had to be prepared for any eventuality, and WRB's corporate liberals would help him.

The War Resources Board was the emergency-preparedness agency that corporate liberals such as Walter Gifford had awaited for so long. WRB's presence provoked an important debate about the proper way to organize the preparedness campaign. Corporate liberals had urged that mobilization functions be vested in temporary, emergency agencies. They favored the use of ad hoc emergency powers. Because corporate liberals rejected any permanent accretions to federal bureaucracy, their thinking about preparedness state building was in some sense antibureaucratic. Their distrust of state bureaucracies and state management led them in this direction, as did the realization that business might more readily shape public policy through this type of framework than an expansion of the New Deal state. This approach clashed with that of ardent New Dealers, who thought a more powerful New Deal state should be constructed to discharge extraordinary defense-related responsibilities and safeguard earlier liberal reforms. By allying itself with the military and interested segments of the business community, corporate liberals put forward a formidable claim for preference from Roosevelt.[2]

Corporate liberals dominated the War Resources Board. Aware that American industry was the most productive in the world, they also knew that U.S. manufacturers were not used to making weapons. To combat this lack of familiarity, WRB's corporate liberals emphasized the need for the military to place "educational orders" with business concerns. Where necessary, conversion of existing private plant to defense production was recommended, and other, more far-reaching steps might be taken as European and Asian circumstances dictated.

The War Resources Board sought increasing coherence for industrial mobilization as time passed. Rationalization necessitated an overarching planning effort calculated to better unify the disjointed U.S. government, strengthen the military, and reinvigorate the private munitions business. Thus, WRB concerned itself with every major facet of economic mobilization, from raw materials through production to distribution, as well as with liaison between the public and private sectors. The Board looked far beyond simple procurement of weapons for U.S. soldiers, surveying the United States' vast "economic potential for war" and searching for ways to translate it into reality.[3]

The origins of the War Resources Board stretch back to the National Defense Act of 1920. It vested responsibility for industrial mobilization planning in the hands of the assistant secretary of war.[4] Almost two decades later, in August 1939, Assistant Secretary of War Louis Johnson used his authority under this statute to establish the WRB. Roosevelt permitted Assistant Secretary Johnson to go forward, even over the objections of Secretary of War Harry Woodring, disturbed New Dealers, and isolationists. As the European crisis worsened, FDR recognized the growing need for defense preparedness. He determined to proceed, albeit cautiously. The war scare influenced his decision more than any other factor.

After consultation with FDR, Johnson chose Edward Stettinius to be chairman of the War Resources Board. Stettinius then acted as "confidential intermediary in selecting the (other) members."[5] As he had during New Deal days, the president depended on the youthful steel man to lay down a line of communication between government and business.

Son of a wealthy businessman, Edward Reilly Stettinius Jr. was born in Chicago, Illinois, on October 22, 1900. Stettinius attended the University of Virginia from 1919 to 1924, but never graduated. His lackluster academic career did not prevent him from making a great many friends and engaging in a host of extracurricular activities. "Stett," as he was affectionately known on the Charlottesville grounds, revived the struggling campus YMCA, participated in Bible groups and missionary outreach activities, and set up a job placement bureau designed to help poorer students raise money for tuition and other essentials. An earnest, idealistic young fellow, he was strongly committed to bettering the society in which he lived.[6]

Like many other young men just out of college, Stettinius did not know what he wanted to do. For a while, he thought seriously of becoming an Episcopalian minister. But his influential father would have none of that idea.

The elder Stettinius nudged his son toward the tried-and-true path of business, arranging a personal interview with John Lee Pratt, a vice president of General Motors. Pratt convinced the young Stettinius to join GM; he pointed to the possibilities for useful work in industrial and public relations and promised an eventual "congregation" of thousands of workers.[7]

Stettinius took up his new duties late in 1924 and rose quickly through the ranks. Beginning as a stockroom clerk with the Hyatt roller bearing division of GM, he became, successively, employment manager, assistant to Pratt, assistant to President Alfred P. Sloan Jr., and, by 1930, vice president of public and industrial relations. In 1934, Stettinius left GM for a position as vice chairman of the finance committee at the U.S. Steel Corporation. Two years later, he was made chairman of the finance committee and eventually, in April 1938, chairman of the board. Just thirty-seven years old, he ran one of the largest companies in the United States. Family connections, an inherent likability, a striking appearance, hard work, and good fortune accounted for his phenomenal success.[8]

Along the way, Stettinius advanced the cause of his employees by pursuing classic welfare capitalist formulations. He followed the pattern of enlightened industrial leadership already visible in Dennison Manufacturing Company, General Electric, Eastman Kodak, the Union Pacific, and likeminded concerns. His most notable achievement at General Motors came with implementation of the 1928 group insurance plan, which covered over 200,000 employees, making each eligible for a life insurance policy of $2,000 and sickness and accident benefits of $15 per week. This plan constituted the largest group insurance policy ever written up to its time, with an aggregated value of $450 million.[9] At U.S. Steel, he urged then-chairman Myron Taylor to enter into delicate negotiations with the Congress of Industrial Organizations that led to company acceptance of a collective-bargaining agreement.[10] This agreement, permitting union organization of much of the steel industry, represented a great stride forward for the American labor movement. Stettinius's concern for the welfare of his workers, the flock he had originally sought in his first conversations with Pratt, was readily apparent.

With the onslaught of the Great Depression and the decline of welfare capitalism, Stettinius—like Dennison and the others—accepted the need for intelligent collaboration with government. A veteran of the National Recovery Administration and the Business Advisory Council (BAC), he believed in maximum hours, minimum wages, collective bargaining, old-age pensions, and unemployment insurance, among other liberal measures. In August 1939, at the time of his appointment to the WRB, he continued with the New Deal as a member of the executive committee of BAC and a member of the Advisory Council on Social Security.[11]

With the white-haired, handsome Stettinius acting in his familiar capacity as middleman, Johnson, Acting Secretary of the Navy Charles

Edison, Army Chief of Staff Marshall, and two senior members of the Office of the Assistant Secretary of War (OASW) picked the other members of the War Resources Board.[12] Robert Wood, who had returned to Sears, Roebuck and Company after his stint with the Commerce Department, Gifford of AT&T, Pratt of GM, Karl T. Compton, president of the Massachusetts Institute of Technology, and Harold G. Moulton, head man at the Brookings Institution, joined Stettinius. A seventh member, John Hancock of the New York Stock Exchange, was added in September.[13] Stettinius, Wood, Gifford, Pratt, and Hancock represented industry and finance; in general, they fit the welfare capitalist–corporate liberal mold. Compton and Moulton gave the academy a voice. Labor, agriculture, and consumers were excluded. Roosevelt was most interested in acquiring the businessman's perspective about the industrial mobilization planning of the military. With a European war likely by this time, he had in mind tighter integration of the Executive Branch, the armed services, and industry.

Among the members of the WRB—with the exception of Stettinius—Robert Elkington Wood best illustrates the corporate liberal response to Roosevelt, the New Deal, and preparedness. Throughout the 1930s, Wood supported the president and his administration in the fight against the Great Depression. In 1939, when war clouds darkened Europe, Wood proved equally willing to do what he could to shore up American national defense.

Born in Kansas City, Missouri, in 1879, Wood graduated from the U.S. Military Academy at West Point in 1900. Army life took him to the Philippines and later to Panama. In 1915, having retired from the Army, Wood took a job with DuPont, where he got his first taste of business. A short interval as assistant to the president of the General Asphalt Company followed. When World War I intervened, he returned to uniform. A colonel and then a brigadier general, he put his earlier managerial and administrative experiences to good use, rising to become acting quartermaster general of the U.S. Army. In this capacity, he bought and distributed all manner of goods, including food, clothing, and equipment, for 4 million American soldiers. In 1919, he left the Army again, having acquired a knowledge of mass buying and mass distribution almost perfectly tailored to the successful operation of a large mail-order business.[14]

Not surprisingly, Wood secured employment with Montgomery Ward. He became a vice-president. During a five-year run, which lasted until 1924, he pushed for expansion and achieved it. To cite just one example, the tire business increased ten-fold, from 100,000 casings a year to more than 1,000,000.[15] Montgomery Ward even began to close the retail gap on Sears, Roebuck and Company.

Not to be outdone, Sears lured Wood away—taking advantage of a personality conflict between the General and new Montgomery Ward president

Theodore Merseles. With Sears, Roebuck and Company, Wood began as vice-president, becoming president in 1928 and chairman of the board in 1939. During these last 15 years, he exhibited the usual corporate liberal commitment to welfare capitalism, arguing that Sears' Savings and Profit-Sharing Pension Plan "helps to avoid labor unrest and strikes, and gives the employee a feeling of greater security and unity of interest with the employer."[16] A constant-wage plan for seasonal workers and sickness and vacation allowances also received his blessing.[17]

Wood's behavior was unusual. A big businessman, and a Republican, he voted for Democrat Franklin D. Roosevelt in 1932 and 1936 while supporting the New Deal.[18] Though Wood disliked unbalanced budgets, excessive outlays for relief, and a sometimes too solicitous attitude on the part of government toward labor unions, he praised Roosevelt and the New Deal for such measures as the Civilian Conservation Corps, the Agricultural Adjustment Act, and the Social Security Act of 1935.[19] In typical no-nonsense fashion, he asserted that the Social Security Act "was demanded by modern industrial civilization and should have been put into effect long ago."[20] He favored all such constructive government regulation, crediting Roosevelt with doing "a great deal to arouse the social conscience of employers."[21] Wood's corporate liberalism clearly separated him from the prevailing business orthodoxy of his day.

Wood was with the government from time to time, too, moving in and out of Washington. Like Dennison, Swope, Folsom, Harriman, and Stettinius, he served with the Business Advisory Council. As noted earlier, he accepted a position with the Commerce Department during the 1938–1939 Roosevelt administration business recovery drive. He did what he could, consistent with his duties at Sears, Roebuck and Company, to stimulate business confidence and bring about recovery. A good capitalist, though of liberal proclivities, Wood announced to his business colleagues that he did not think that "the charge of socialism, communism, or regimentation should be hurled at every new proposal or reform."[22] He insisted that the "hate talks" between business and government end.[23]

When disaster threatened Europe in August 1939, Wood was all for American preparedness. Again, he believed FDR deserved some credit, this time for upgrading national defense. The Chief Executive, according to Wood, had taken positive steps during his time in office to partially overcome "the parsimony of Coolidge and the pacifism of Hoover. . . ."[24] Defense expenditures were higher since 1935; national defense was moving up from the depths of its descent. Wood, though an isolationist, was a former military man who appreciated this progression. He desired a strong hemispheric defense, which would discourage any would-be invader from attacking the U.S. and thereby sustain peace. Wood did oppose any new American Expeditionary Force—American soldiers should not be sent to Europe.[25]

Within these parameters, then, Wood's devotion to preparedness was firm and he accepted his assignment with the War Resources Board unhesitatingly.

The first meeting of the WRB occurred on August 17, 1939. Chairman Stettinius presided. Discussion went on behind closed doors. Afterwards, Stettinius met with the press and released a statement. He said it "will be the duty of the War Resources Board to assist the War and Navy Departments in perfecting their plans for national defense."[26] Seeking to defuse any isolationist charges of war mongering, he explained that the Board hoped that the U.S. "will never again be drawn into war. It is our belief that one way to prevent this is to be fully prepared."[27] Stettinius also let it be known that the military, business organizations, and individual businessmen would work together, with the WRB as a go-between, to see that "all of our major industries lined up."[28] Significantly, no mention was made of New Dealers or the enhanced New Deal state.

These announcements revealed something of the general character of the War Resources Board, and its modus operandi. Owing its very existence and continued life to the European crisis, the Board was an emergency agency designed to examine and coordinate planning for industrial mobilization in the event of war. While the military always retained primary responsibility for national defense, the Board helped wherever possible, especially as a conduit between branches of the armed services, corporations, and other business organizations. From the beginning, too, WRB wished to "maximize business discretionary input" and objected to "permanent expansions in independent government authority."[29] The construction of temporary, emergency agencies to aid industrial mobilization appealed to it because these agencies could be staffed with businessmen rather than New Dealers, and might impart an additional increment of direction to preparedness. Furthermore, once the crisis passed the agencies would be phased out and the growth of government curtailed. In essence, WRB's corporate liberals expected that the fundamental structure of the preparedness state would be shaped primarily by anti-bureaucratic impulses.

Specifically, Board members were asked to render a verdict as to whether or not the War Department industrial mobilization plan would work in practice. On paper it looked fine, but what about in the factories where the arms and munitions were to be produced? And what of the thousands of details that might go wrong? Real life, after all, often confounds theory and America's national defense could not be allowed to fail the people in the face of totalitarian barbarity. Roosevelt tapped the "real life" experience of the businessmen-bureaucrats, hoping that WRB would add coherence to American mobilization planning. He also sought to build on the gains of the business appeasement campaign, perhaps further conciliating a powerful special interest from which he had been estranged at a time when fate put a special premium on its services.

Additional meetings of the War Resources Board were held in late August and September. Members read over the various industrial mobilization plans prepared by the Army-Navy Munitions Board during the 1930s. The Industrial Mobilization Plan (IMP) of 1939, the latest in this line, naturally attracted the most scrutiny. The corporate liberals withheld immediate comment, preferring to solicit outside experts before going further, but it soon became apparent that they liked what they saw.

Stettinius and the others asked veterans of the World War I preparedness experience to share their wisdom. The response was encouraging. "Elder statesmen" such as Bernard Baruch, Frank Scott, and Hugh Johnson found the IMP to be a valuable document. Baruch, chief of the old War Industries Board, declared that the 1939 variant "meets generally with my approval," suggesting only relatively minor changes.[30] He implied that implementation of the Industrial Mobilization Plan would markedly improve the condition of the Army and Navy.

Every industrial mobilization plan shared certain basic characteristics. Each "blueprint" featured a War Resources Administration (WRA), one-man leadership, and a commodity committee-war service committee organizational structure. The War Resources Administration functioned only after declaration of hostilities between the U.S. and another nation. A temporary, emergency super-agency, above all others and outranked only by the president, WRA would be surrounded by additional agencies as circumstances dictated. A single "Administrator" was to determine the basic policies for the utilization of American national resources with an eye toward victory. The economic integration of the military and industry would be accomplished through a commodity committee-war service committee system. WRA commodity committees (examples might be for steel or aircraft) were expected to interact with their private, civilian war service committee counterparts. In this way, Army and Navy requirements for weapons and other essential goods would be transmitted to those businessmen and firms best able to meet them. Overall, military-industrial coordination was to vanquish inefficiencies of all types, contributing substantially to final American triumph in case of a major war.[31]

The 1939 Industrial Mobilization Plan contained all the basic elements of its predecessors: the WRA, the "Administrator," the commodity committee-war service committee arrangement. Simpler than the others, more closely modeled after the Great War's War Industries Board, this revision gave the military somewhat less influence over civilian agencies but retained the cardinal principle of military-industrial dominance over any wartime economy.[32] The War and Navy Departments made explicit their desire that the personnel of the War Resources Administration come "from the patriotic business leaders of the nation."[33] WRB members concurred, playing up the importance of recruiting "senior executives" who "have won the confidence of their associates in industry" and who are "good team-workers."[34] The "Administrator" would obviously be an influential capitalist. Semi-private war service committees were "proposed as valuable points of contact between emergency coordinating agencies and industry. They would afford the best possible means of presenting to industry national needs and requirements and of informing the emergency administrations of industry's prospective ability to meet those requirements."[35]

Having scanned Baruch's critique, and the remarks of the other "elders," a process which did not delay them long, the War Resources Board endorsed the major features of the 1939 IMP. WRB viewed the War Resources Administration in much the same manner as it did the venerable War Industries Board, as an impermanent, ends-oriented agency which existed only as long as war raged and whose job it was to insure that American economic might be brought to bear against an enemy with maximum effect. The corporate liberals sanctioned this degree of extra centralization, and planned efficiency, but no more. One-man rule seemed commonsensical to Stettinius, Wood, and their colleagues, coming as most did from corporations run by a single individual. The WRA commodity committee-war service committee mechanism translated into the standard corporate liberal refrain for industrial self-regulation. In effect, businessmen in War Resources Administration commodity committees would give advice to businessmen in war service committees (often members of trade associations) who would pass it on to businessmen in their respective industries and factories. The commodity committee-war service committee interlock allowed corporate executives to exercise considerable control over defense production while simultaneously offering them a platform from which to jump up and "infiltrate" higher councils of public policy.[36]

WRB clearly thought the Industrial Mobilization Plan of 1939 transferable from theory to real life. Military planners and corporate liberals advocated a type of mixed planning that would allow business to regulate its own affairs during war subject only to broad presidential policy and obvious military need. An unwritten assumption here was that labor would do what it was told without complaint. When war ended—with victory secure—the "abnormal concentration of power in central agencies" and "extraordinary powers" of the state, "which involve the encroachment on individual liberty," would be terminated automatically and a beneficial status quo restored.[37]

The War Resources Board interpreted its mission quite broadly. WRB advice covered not only industrial mobilization planning in general and the 1939 Industrial Mobilization Plan specifically, but also inputs, production, finished commodities, and distribution. Liaison between the public and private sectors fascinated it.

All public agencies that touched on industrial mobilization fell within the Board's purview. WRB reached out to the armed services, to be sure, but also to the Maritime Commission, the Labor Department, the Justice Department, the Treasury, and more. Links were strengthened between WRB's corporate liberals and those still working in the Commerce Department. Stettinius, for example, requested that Moulton confer with Willard Thorp about the "state of inventories of various industries."[38] In an informal way, at least, Thorp had carried on with his "traveling salesman" concept and therefore possessed crucial information about raw materials, stockpiles, factory capacities, and the like which WRB proposed to put to good use. Establishment of the WRB-Commerce Department connection shows the attempt at rationalization underway.

Stettinius touched base with the private sphere as well. He postponed immediate establishment of "war service committees to represent trade associations," content for the time being to talk with prominent businessmen and the larger business organizations.[39] Soon, he secured the support of many corporate executives, the United States Chamber of Commerce, and the National Association of Manufacturers.[40] Business was positioning itself behind the efforts of the corporate liberal-dominated WRB, even as that agency sought to widen its mandate.

Stettinius assigned his associates tasks related to their areas of specialization. Colonel Harry K. Rutherford, secretary to the board and Army liaison, undertook an inventory of raw materials used in defense production.[41] Pratt and Compton, in conjunction with Commissioner of Labor Statistics Isador Lubin, investigated ways "to increase supply of skilled personnel available to industry in war emergency."[42] Moulton suggested steps to contain inflation, which normally afflicted the country when war broke out. Gifford focused on transportation and communication. Wood took charge of distribution. Hancock, who became increasingly significant over time, dealt with the organizational structure of the War Resources Board. His task was to prepare "detailed organization charts," including efficient arrangement of "industrial groupings."[43] As for the chair, Stettinius handled all top-level coordination and liaison activities, meeting with Roosevelt on occasion, as well as with Secretaries Johnson and Edison, Chief of Staff Marshall, Rear Admiral Emory S. Land of the Maritime Commission, and others.

Many government officials, the press, and the public assumed that the War Resources Board would metamorphose into the powerful War Resources Administration upon a declaration of war. The extent of WRB's activities, broad as they were, lent credence to this assumption. Stettinius and his colleagues often thought along these lines themselves. Hancock, for instance, devised organizational charts that presumed U.S. involvement in the European war and establishment of WRA. His prospective Service Industries Division, War Resources Administration included sections A (Power and Fuel) and B (Transport).[44] Within each of the two sections were several units. Hancock went so far as to suggest names of prominent industrialists who might serve. His chart mentioned Stettinius and Harriman, predictably enough, but also Wendell Willkie of Commonwealth and Southern Corporation (Power and Fuel) and Sewell L. Avery of Montgomery Ward (Transport)![45]

Given the composition of the War Resources Board, its ambition, and the chance it might actually become the WRA, critics abounded. Charges were hurled from many different directions. Some critics repudiated the WRA idea entirely, depicting an agency that did not yet exist as "fascistic" because it would involve a stronger state, business–government cooperation, and perhaps cartelization. Others, alarmed by the vast potential powers of WRA, labeled Stettinius a "dictator." Nor did the presence of Roosevelt comfort them, especially in light of the recent debate on Supreme Court "packing." Given Stettinius's almost obsequious nature and Roosevelt's regard for democratic politics, cries of dictatorship were strained, but some believed them. More serious objections emerged, too, emanating from suspicious New Dealers, representatives of labor and agriculture, and isolationists.

Certain New Dealers rejected any resort to ad hoc emergency powers and employment of temporary emergency agencies. Older, ideologically inclined cabinet members, desirous of upholding their own authority and sustaining New Deal social advances, fell into this camp. They, in turn, aligned themselves with younger, aggressive New Dealers who wished to make forceful use of the state to regulate corporate capitalism and big business. Whereas corporate liberals and military planners advocated the antibureaucratic solution, zealous New Dealers preferred to incorporate such wartime powers and agencies as would be needed into permanent, preexisting organs of government. If they succeeded, the resulting New Deal state would be larger and more powerful, capable of preserving New Deal reforms and providing for national security. The organizational direction that preparedness took, it follows, was crucial; concerned New Dealers believed that nothing less than the soul of the administration was at stake.[46]

Security of the Interior Harold Ickes, Secretary of Labor Frances Perkins, and Secretary of Agriculture Henry A. Wallace felt ill disposed toward the War Resources Board. Ickes noted the apprehensions that he and others such as Robert Jackson had about the growing influence of "Wall Streeters and economic royalists" in Washington.[47] Against creation of anything like the World War I War Industries Board, Ickes asked Roosevelt to permit all cabinet members to select their own business advisers. He thought this strategy "would make these business advisers subservient to the Government instead of the Government's being a tail to the businessmen's kite."[48] Perkins insisted that any special preparedness agencies "use existing services rather than creating their own."[49] In the area of labor–management dispute, she explained to Samuel Rosenman that "the Department of Labor has the only existing machinery . . . and that to build up new machinery would be complicated, expensive and full of antagonisms."[50] Up to the attack on Pearl Harbor, she opposed creation of a new war manpower commission. Similarly, Wallace clearly stated his desire that any wartime food administration be placed under the authority of the Department of Agriculture.[51] Indeed, he objected to having WRB handle any agricultural matters at all. Ickes, Perkins, Wallace, and many of their colleagues and subordinates resisted any return to industrial self-regulation. To the extent that business–government cooperation for the sake of mobilization meant retreat from New Deal ideals and abandonment of New Deal social gains, they were against it, imploring Roosevelt to take the route of state capitalism and a state-run munitions complex instead.

The vision of an expanded central state, capable of dealing with peacetime and preparedness problems, appealed to "new" New Dealers as well.[52] This group believed in the "regulatory state" in one form or another. Big government needed to regulate big business, indeed corporate capitalism as a whole. New "New Dealers" included among their ranks second-generation "brain-trusters" such as Benjamin Cohen and Thomas Corcoran, trustbusters such as Thurman Arnold, and Keynesians such as Lauchlin Currie.[53] It was Cohen who gave Ickes the idea that each cabinet officer should pick business advisers, the intent being to establish firm New Deal authority over businessmen in the defense program and to prevent the latter from engaging in collusive activity. Corcoran saw the conflict with the War Resources Board as a "last-ditch" effort to keep big business from exercising undue sway over preparedness.[54] Assistant Attorney General Arnold was determined to resist any pleas from business for suspension of antitrust; he deemed it essential to bring suits against corporations who gouged consumers by foisting on them artificially inflated prices.[55] Arnold's version of statist regulation depended on antitrust prosecutions to induce both efficient production by companies and lower prices for customers. He would not back away, even as corporate liberals, military men, and defense contractors put additional pressure on the Roosevelt administration to place the Sherman Anti-Trust Act on hold. Currie and other New Deal economists influenced by John Maynard Keynes and Alvin Hansen fit into the picture as well, because they wished to restore economic prosperity and full employment by increasing spending on social welfare programs and public works.[56] Corporate liberals insisted on stabilization measures rather than expansion.[57] The "regulatory state," whether of the Arnold type, the Keynesian model, or some other variant, was not in keeping with the version of business–government cooperation envisioned by WRB's corporate liberals.

The exchange between corporate liberals and New Dealers could be rancorous indeed. Their debate soon went public, hitting the airwaves and newspapers.[58] Each side slammed the other, since neither wished to be shut out once Roosevelt made his final decision.

More strident than other New Dealers, Ickes was concerned that "super-agencies" manned by businessmen would interfere with a host of New Deal departments, including his own Interior Department, the Labor Department, the Agriculture Department, the Justice Department, Federal Works, and many more.[59] He declared the War Resources Board a "potential nucleus for an extra-legal autocracy."[60] WRB, according to Interior's head, jeopardized New Deal social gains and democracy itself.[61] In response to this alert, Federal Works Administrator John Carmody contacted Roosevelt in late August, telling the president that the Federal Works Administration was set to "wheel into war preparations."[62]

Corporate liberals Bernard Baruch and John Hancock countered Ickes, Carmody, and the other New Dealers. Baruch, naturally enough, favored the "emergency form of the administrative state." He believed that peacetime departments, such as Agriculture or Labor, ought to be confined to their "usual activities."[63] "I like, in war," he said, "to see all [mobilization] operations in emergency organizations."[64] Moreover, to his mind, greater defense spending meant that expenditures in other areas should be reduced, not increased.[65] WRB as a whole, following the Baruch line, maintained that "maximum efficiency could not be achieved by agencies mainly concerned with peacetime problems and whose personnel had been chosen for peacetime activities."[66] Hancock voiced a different concern, namely that permanent New Deal agencies of the type Ickes ran might try to "fasten sweeping controls on business" from which there would be no escape, even at war's end.[67] Stettinius, for his part, listened to Hancock's complaint, but downplayed it. Stettinius refused to employ the harsh words of Ickes or Hancock; he believed Roosevelt to be a friend of free enterprise and managerial rights; and he continued his relatively quiet pursuit of business–government collaboration, industrial self-regulation, and the appropriate use of ad hoc emergency powers.

Labor and agriculture, seconded by both Perkins and Wallace, were quick to criticize their lack of representation on the War Resources Board.[68] John L. Lewis of the CIO was particularly outspoken in his opposition. At one point, FDR had considered naming Lubin as labor's man, but the president never got around to it.[69] The bias of the board in favor of business brought the predictable protests from less powerful special interests.

Isolationists and pacifists generally depicted the WRB as a troublemaker.[70] For many of them, though not all, fine distinctions were lost between preparedness, which might make war less likely, and war itself. These individuals saw WRB in a negative light; its very existence would bring war, destruction, and the death of American youths closer.

Undeterred by the swirling controversy that surrounded it, the War Resources Board forged on. WRB continued its struggle to inject order and purpose into the evolving national security complex, sometimes succeeding, sometimes not. Mobilization planning remained the chief occupation of the members, but they often strayed beyond planning into the realm of operations. Specific measures designed to counteract industrial inexperience and weapons shortages were required more than ever.

A paucity of munitions know-how among American executives and the need for more and better weapons made the limitations of the small private munitions industry a growing concern, especially after Hitler's invasion of Poland. WRB reacted to European war by recommending that the "volume of 'educational orders' . . . be greatly expanded."[71] Additionally, the board encouraged interested companies to seek defense contracts and convert existing plant and equipment to defense production. In these ways, WRB's corporate liberals helped increase the knowledge base and size of the private munitions industry, enhancing U.S. security while obviating the need for dramatic expansion of the number of government-owned armaments facilities.

"Educational orders" permitted the military and industry to get a feel for each other. The Army or Navy dispatched a small order to an individual business for some vital, noncommercial good. In the process of filling the order, the company learned what adjustments must be made in its assembly-line technique while the service perfected its munitions design and procurement system.[72] Each side cooperated with the other, coordination improved, and integration of military and industry moved ahead.

Congress, recognizing the value of this idea, authorized greater expenditures for educational orders on April 3, 1939. It made available an additional $34.5 million over a three-year period for War Department purchase of weapons and for special instruments such as gauges, dies, and jigs, which were used in the assembly of arms and munitions. Congress also allowed the War Department to buy production studies—in essence, engineering blueprints for future defense production in a particular factory.[73]

WRB supported the educational orders concept fully, backing the Educational Orders Act of 1938, while helping to implement the Educational Orders Act of 1939. The Educational Orders Act of 1938 allocated $2 million to be spent on critical items during fiscal year 1939.[74] Six goods received top priority, and contracts were issued. Winchester Arms won the right to produce the M1 semiautomatic rifle, slotted to replace the antiquated Springfield; forgings for 75 mm shells went to American Forge Company; machining of 75 mm shells to S. A. Woods Machine Company; recoil mechanisms for antiaircraft guns to R. Hoe & Company; gas masks to Goodyear Tire & Rubber; and the 60-inch searchlight to General Electric.[75] The Educational Orders Act of 1939 required much more assistance from industry. Since June 1939, Hancock had served as one of nine industrial representatives on a special War Department educational orders advisory committee.[76] In this capacity, he and the other members, including William Knudsen of

General Motors, participated in a selection process that culminated in the award of many additional educational orders. Contracts were signed for guns, shells, planes, and tanks. From August forward, of course, Hancock made Johnson and other War Department officials aware of WRB's views regarding those corporations best suited to produce weapons prototypes.

Because educational orders consumed only a tiny fraction of total defense appropriations for 1939, Stettinius, Hancock, Wood, and the rest emphasized opportunities for improvement available elsewhere. The aircraft industry looked best, but there were other avenues. Given that the United States had entered 1939 without "a real munitions industry" and was only just developing one, conversion of existing peacetime plant to military uses was one of WRB's more important themes.

WRB pushed conversion, and some progress occurred. Board advice on firms that might do a particular job well, as in the case of educational orders, was given and, not infrequently, taken. When a corporate liberal suggestion matched up with a firm already on the War Department's Allocated Facilities list, chances were extremely good that a contract would be issued.

Some choices were more obvious than others. General Electric easily secured the contract for the 60" searchlight, owing to the company's reputation, War Department familiarity with it, and Gerard Swope's influence. In 1939, GE also made turbines for Navy ships and many other related defense goods.[77] Curtiss-Wright Corporation, United Aircraft Corporation, and several other aeronautical firms got in on the lucrative defense business, too, producing primary training airplanes, airplane engines, and the like.[78] Colt constructed machine guns. Knudsen's GM began to manufacture trucks and tractors having military applications long before Pearl Harbor. York Safe & Lock Company secured work making 3" antiaircraft gun carriages, and on it went.[79]

The case of Scovill Manufacturing Company is particularly revealing. Established in the early nineteenth century, it originally made brass buttons and later diversified, becoming one of the United States' leading metal products makers. During World War I, the company converted entirely to munitions production, dropping all commercial business. Employment, production, and profits soared. When war ended, however, Scovill was left without any sort of saleable product. Government had deserted it, as was the case with Bethlehem Steel and the defense industry in general. Scovill eventually reestablished itself in the commercial market and thrived once again. By the end of 1939, backed by the War Department and War Resources Board, both aware of its great size, immense capacity, and talented personnel, Scovill Manufacturing Company complemented its 300,000 commercial goods with an increasing array of defense items. Scovill made metal gear for uniforms, 75 mm cartridge cases, parts for gas masks, forged fuse bodies, primers and primer parts, center tubes for shell casings, percussion fuses, cups for 30-, 45-, and 50-caliber cartridge cases, and disks from which all types of large shell cases were pressed. It was back in the munitions business in a substantial way, having gone to the point of realigning some equipment, but the lion's share of its 200 buildings in Waterbury, Connecticut, loaded with $20 million worth of modern metal-working equipment, awaited future War Department contracts.[80]

Corporate liberals on the War Resources Board understood that the United States possessed tremendous, unused "economic potential for war." Many firms, such as Scovill Manufacturing Company, stood ready to take on additional defense business, and literally thousands waited for their first defense contract. Stettinius and his colleagues used their influence to funnel defense work to well-known, prosperous companies loaded with the appropriate expertise. They did not take risks.

The War Resources Board downplayed more extreme alternatives to educational orders and conversion of preexisting plant. Although a few firms such as Consolidated Aircraft built wholly new defense plants in 1939, this approach was the exception. WRB's corporate liberals deemed construction of new defense plants useful only "where no counterparts capable of conversion to war work now exist," and they rejected any resort to a European-style, government-owned munitions complex.[81] Measures like these received a lower priority because WRB's members did not yet feel the type of urgency associated with actual U.S. involvement in a shooting war. Additionally, isolationist strength deterred such moves, which could easily be portrayed as provocative. Finally, the corporate liberals' natural aversion to creation of an "overgreat state" ruled out erection of a vast government arsenal. National security demanded prudent action, not daredevil, entrepreneurial ventures that might end in losses or radical departures from standard American practice. Public–private cooperation, together with industrial mobilization keyed by cautious conversion of private plant, remained the order of the day.

Advances occurred nonetheless. Educational orders acquainted roughly three hundred of the most significant businesses in the country with the vagaries of defense production.[82] These firms began tooling up, acquiring experience that would prove invaluable in later years. Ninety facilities accepted War Department payment for production studies of 97 items.[83] Conversion accelerated, spurred by educational orders and other defense business, often related to the airplane industry. WRB's corporate liberals facilitated this entire process, pitching in where they could be of assistance. Private plants, converted to defense work, made the weapons; the armed services let contracts and handled procurement; WRB undertook troubleshooting. Still, these efforts—though strenuous compared to what had gone on before—left much to be accomplished. The United States still faced an ominous weapons deficit.

Corporate liberal planning took into account the United States' "disarmed forces." If European events compelled U.S. entry into war, as had been the case in 1917, a much greater volume of defense production than that which prevailed in September 1939 would become vital. Arms and munitions output must soar. This assumption, that war would necessitate mass production of weapons, underlay WRB's thinking. The questions were simple, the answers difficult. How many articles, of all different types, would be used in a modern, total war? How many plants would be needed to make the weapons and other items? Did the United States possess enough raw materials to do the job? What incentives might government offer business to guarantee defense production?

To further complicate matters, the WRB knew that war had become a much more complex undertaking since 1918. New, more intricate weapons had been developed, and more would have to be designed and constructed. Advancements in other areas, aside from ordnance, made provision of war materiel more difficult and costly. The War Resources Board announced to the nation that it must study more than 10,000 goods essential to the Armed Services in emergency.[84] These goods "include[d] everything from guns, chemicals and aircraft to uniform leggings, canned goods and cigarettes."[85]

Defense production of this magnitude implied involvement of the most important industries and the use of many of their factories. The War Department Allocated Facilities booklet already contained a thick list of businesses in all major industries that had agreed to specific wartime assignments. These businesses were typically large and celebrated, often oligopolistic. WRB, echoing Assistant Secretary of War Johnson, emphasized that there were 20,000 American manufacturing plants that had been surveyed by the Planning Branch, OASW, and the Army-Navy Munitions Board. Of these, more than 10,000 were on "stand by for the manufacture of emergency materials."[86]

Stettinius informed automobile, aircraft, railroad, and other executives of the demands that war would bring, assuring them, too, that the essential core of the civilian economy would be preserved. Detroit's automobile makers were told by WRB's corporate liberals that a wartime scenario called for them to produce light combat tanks, airplane parts, and 75 mm cartridge cases, in addition to trucks. Airplane companies were to convert from commercial craft to training planes, fighters, and bombers. The Pullman Company, famous for its Pullman sleeping cars, learned—amazingly enough—that contingency planners wished it to produce forgings for the 105 mm howitzer, a weapon of great significance for American infantrymen that was regrettably still on the drawing board in the United States![87] WRB industrial mobilization planners assured the American people that U.S. participation in a major conflict would bring General Electric, Winchester, Scovill Manufacturing, and other firms currently participating in defense work plenty of company.

Finished products, of course, require raw materials. Rifles, airplanes, antiaircraft guns, ships, and uniforms cannot be made without these inputs. Stettinius had designated Colonel Rutherford point man on this subject. Rutherford reported back that the natural resources of the United States, though abundant compared to those of most nations, were finite, and that there was cause for worry in certain crucial areas. The United States possessed more than enough cotton textiles for clothing, crude oil, and foodstuffs but might well face shortages of antimony, quinine, rubber, and aluminum.[88] As for steel, that most vital of all substances for modern war, there was no guarantee. Although the United States produced more than twice as much steel as its leading competitor, Germany, Rutherford warned that the "steel industry requires ferromanganese at the rate of about 14 pounds per ton of steel. . . ."[89] Should the sea lanes to America be closed, ferromanganese imports would not get in. Because the country had no usable ferromanganese of its own, this situation would result in the production of lower quality steel, and maybe even a lesser quantity.[90] Rutherford's message was a worthwhile one: raw materials must not be taken for granted; insidious complications associated with a major war might appear unexpectedly and imperil the munitions effort.

In peacetime and wartime, the pursuit of private profit drives a capitalistic economy. Companies must turn a profit in order to survive, and a larger profit still if they are to flourish. WRB's corporate liberals took these simple truths as articles of faith, and therefore sought out means to ensure that corporations made an acceptable return on their investment in defense plant and equipment. Antitrust laws drew their attention, as did the U.S. Army's emerging policy regarding defense contracts.

Stettinius and Hancock met on several occasions with Thurman Arnold, Assistant Attorney General in charge of the Anti-Trust Division of the Justice Department. All parties agreed that the meetings were harmonious and that a cooperative relationship had been established, but this rhetoric obscured very real divisions. The corporate liberals looked toward relaxation of the antitrust laws as encouragement to big business and a way to augment defense production whereas Arnold had in mind scrupulous enforcement and board assurances that business would not use the emergency as an excuse to stretch existing statutes.[91]

Again, the overriding issue was that of state-building. Arnold did not seek to break up all large corporations, only those that behaved irresponsibly. In this way, he encouraged efficient production while restraining prices and protecting consumers. Arnold, it seems clear, was not trying to restore atomistic competition at all. Instead, he wanted to police corporations, expanding the scope and power of the American "regulatory state" in the process. Stettinius, Hancock, other corporate liberals, and business interests in general objected to this philosophy, which they considered unnecessarily coercive and a threat to managerial prerogatives. In their view, industrial self-regulation, accompanied by modest government supervision rather than outright direction, ought to prevail instead. Arnold and the corporate liberals remained far apart throughout the preparedness period, and the antitrust debate would not be resolved until after Pearl Harbor.[92]

In the matter of defense contracts, corporate liberals witnessed a far more salutary outcome. The War Resources Board expressed complete approval of the Army's position that defense contractors be protected against losses. Here was a prime inducement that the military enthusiastically offered to business.

Brigadier General Charles Tillman Harris Jr., Assistant Chief of Ordnance, in charge of Industrial Service, provided details. Speaking at the Industrial Preparedness Round Table sponsored by the Army Ordnance Association in October 1939, he answered a series of questions put to him by leading corporate executives. All Army plans assumed defense production under the capitalistic system. The Army intended "to do everything possible to insure against loss by producers."[93] Competitive bidding, under Section 3709 of the 1920 National Defense Act, would be suspended if the emergency got bad enough, and the Army would issue "negotiated contracts with producers whom they regarded as best suited."[94] Harris dodged "the question as to whether or not different prices would be paid to different suppliers for the same item, but left little doubt that this would be done if necessary to secure needed supplies."[95]

Corporate liberals and New Dealers listened to Harris's remarks with interest. Stettinius hailed Harris's words. He thought it "wholly desirable and even essential that these plans should combine both the civilian and the military viewpoints."[96] The Army, in short, wanted business on its side, needed defense goods in bulk, and was willing to pay the price; greater reassurance for the WRB, the corporate liberals, and prospective defense contractors could not be found. On the other hand, New Dealers like Ickes were appalled by the position of the War Department and military services. Even Leon Henderson, who was sensitive to the need for greater defense production, was ambivalent. Henderson appreciated the importance of more arms and munitions, but he knew full well that big business was about to reap substantial profits and exert a more powerful influence on public policy. Under these circumstances, the future of New Deal reform was cloudy.[97]

WRB exertions in the realm of armament and munitions supply helped make military procurement in 1940 and 1941 easier. Accommodation and cooperation with the War Department, Army, and Navy familiarized an important segment of the business community with overall American requirements for defense goods, defense plants in which to produce them, and the raw material equation. These steps, unlike educational orders or more extensive conversion, did not yield weapons immediately but aided their production down the line. The Army already wooed business by offering exemption from loss—indeed, by guaranteeing "decent profits."[98] Cost-plus contracts and lucrative fixed-price contracts were just around the corner. Furthermore, since General Harris and other high ranking officers preferred to deal with the dominant firms in all major industries, oligopolistic stability was virtually assured. The most lucrative defense contracts would go out to market leaders.[99]

On September 26, 1939, Roosevelt announced that the work of the War Resources Board was nearly done. Thanking its members for "exceedingly good work," FDR declared that the WRB would be disbanded shortly.[100] The WRB report, once completed, would not be made public.

Numerous factors prompted Roosevelt's decision. Ickes, Wallace, Perkins, Jackson, Corcoran, and Cohen kept up their attack, motivated by a common desire that the War Resources Board "be no more than a pale shadow in the future. . . ."[101] Labor and agriculture did not hide their contempt for the board. More significant, isolationists portrayed Stettinius, Pratt, and Gifford as warmongers of the U.S. Steel, GM, Morgan, and DuPont stripe.[102] On a personal level, Roosevelt, weary of press comments about the omnipotence of the proposed War Resources Administration, said that he did not envision "abdicating the presidency" to anyone.[103]

The exact timing of Roosevelt's announcement can be traced to Neutrality Act revision. On September 21, 1939, a special session of Congress convened to consider an urgent administration request for amendment of the 1937 Neutrality Act, which barred U.S. arms sales and loans to belligerent nations. Only five days later, Roosevelt, not wanting "to add a feather of support" to non-interventionists,[104] sacrificed the War Resources Board. "Cash-and-carry" to aid Britain and France against Germany took precedence over Board activities. WRB proved much too controversial to suit Roosevelt's political and foreign policy tastes.

Even then, the War Resources Board lingered. Late September gave way to October, then November and December. A final report was prepared, and enough confusion remained about further work to generate internal discussion about a future Board role.

The War Resources Board completed its final report on October 13, 1939, and copies went to Roosevelt, Johnson, Edison, and a few others. Stettinius and company praised the Industrial Mobilization Plan of 1939, which they described as "a decided advance in the field of national preparedness and adequate plans for defense."[105] They accepted the need, during an emergency, for a War Resources Administration, one-man leadership, and the commodity committee–war service committee structure, all reminiscent of the 1917–1918 War Industries Board experience. One key War Resources Administration objective involved "coordinating industry to meeting requirements of government for war purpose and civilian needs."[106] Surely one-man leadership for the WRA would evolve, for FDR was far too busy to provide constant oversight, let alone daily hands-on management. The "Administrator," almost certain to be a corporate liberal, should rely on "voluntary cooperation" where possible, because this would be the most efficient and least offensive approach, but would be endowed with the "requisite power" to force recalcitrants into line.[107] The commodity committee–war service committee interface permitted WRA to "provide point of contact between government and industry."[108] Hancock and other WRB members recommended one representative of the War Resources Administration for every defense factory.[109] Without a doubt, businessmen turned bureaucrats (corporate liberals) anticipated meeting with factory managers, trade association officials, and other industry representatives to ensure mutual satisfaction.

At least one significant qualification did appear. Under the IMP, the War Resources Administration controlled all economic functions during wartime. Other agencies that arose merely supplemented WRA's work and were clearly subordinate to it. According to the War Resources Board report, the War Resources Administration should not be that dominant. While the WRA would guide industrial mobilization, even to the point of punishing industry "by denying essential elements such as power and fuel, transportation or the importing of essential commodities to those who refuse to cooperate voluntarily," other independent, emergency agencies were to take charge of public relations, selective service, war labor, war finance, food administration, and price control.[110] WRB would cooperate with the other agencies, not dictate to them. Just the same, the War Resources Board retained the IMP's basic blueprint for mobilizing the nation's material resources, even hinting in an ill-concealed way that WRA would be more equal than its companion agencies. These recommendations, of course, ran directly counter to those put forward by proponents of the expanded New Deal state.

With dissemination of the final report, the board entered a period of extreme uncertainty. The membership had received conflicting signals regarding its continued existence. Although FDR had apparently dismissed it, Assistant Secretary of War Johnson and some others within the administration hedged. Addressing Stettinius on November 22, 1939, Hancock complained of "the present lack of decision" and asked for clarification "on some features of the [WRB] plan that would make further work more productive. . . ."[111] Stettinius, in turn, corresponded with Gifford, requesting feedback.[112] Inquiries to executive-branch officials indicated definitively that the board's services were no longer required, and no more discussion was heard after early December.

For many months thereafter, until May 1940, an uneasy quiescence characterized the organizational-institutional scene, paralleling the European military equation. Industrial mobilization plans had been improved but did not yet reach far into the nation's factories. Large-scale conversion, driven by the Industrial Mobilization Plan and War Resources Board report, awaited a later day. Again, the United States limped along without a single highly specialized emergency defense agency capable of translating mere concepts and ideas into decisive action. Having discontinued WRB, Roosevelt played a waiting game. As long as the front between Germany and France held and the lull in the fighting continued, he contented himself with inaction. The American people, for the most part, wanted to stay out of the European mess, making FDR's strategy politically expedient. Roosevelt decided to fall back on the old Advisory Commission to the Council of National Defense only if European conditions deteriorated badly.[113] He knew, too, that he could call on the corporate liberals again should the need arise.

Corporate liberal advocacy of "intelligent collaboration" between business and government remained a constant, as it had since the early 1930s. Increasingly, however, corporate liberalism operated through channels provided by the defense emergency. The use of temporary, emergency agencies appealed tremendously to corporate liberals, particularly as a means of resolving the dilemma between planned efficiency on the one side and autonomous individualism on the other. This way, war planning could go forward expeditiously, while the threat to economic and political freedoms was minimized.

Corporate liberal support for FDR remained strong and, as time passed, became even more meaningful. Edward Stettinius continued as a loyal and trusted subordinate. Stettinius and WRB's other corporate liberals agreed with Harold Moulton's assessment that "we had a bully good time while it lasted."[114] Outside of WRB's ranks, Averell Harriman, Gerard Swope, Marion Folsom, Henry Dennison, and Donald Nelson stood ready to assist the president. These men represented multinational corporations or, at a minimum, had professed their devotion to government-sanctioned private arrangements designed to bring about economic stability and prosperity. Free trade (or cozy international market-sharing agreements brokered by the U.S. government and friendly nations) benefited their corporations, and German economic autarky could not have pleased them. Restoration of peace and of normal domestic and international business conditions (including preexisting market shares), was in their best interest. Foreign developments as well as domestic ones therefore united the corporate liberals and FDR, producing closer ties.[115]

Potential recruits to the corporate liberal cause had been listed by WRB. Some entered the defense establishment down the line, one example being Ralph Budd of the Chicago, Burlington & Quincy Railroad. Others, including Willkie and Avery, most emphatically did not. More corporate liberals waited in the wings. Only a few of the earliest converts to corporate liberalism were to be disqualified from later service; a prominent example was General Wood, damned by his eventual affiliation with the stridently isolationist America First Committee.[116] In any event, corporate liberals certainly deemed cooperation with government far better than ostracism, and redoubled ongoing efforts to persuade mainstream businessmen of the value of conciliation and partnership. Corporate liberal diplomacy, which undergirded the 1938–1939 business appeasement campaign and the empowering War Resources Board experience, coupled with the natural self-interest and patriotism of businessmen, permitted steady improvement of business–government relations into the early 1940s.

Nor were WRB's immediate exertions in vain. WRB granted business's stamp of approval to the twenty years of industrial mobilization planning carried out by the War Department in conjunction with the Army-Navy Munitions Board. Although the War Resources Administration itself never materialized and Stettinius did not become the "Administrator," the ideas they represented remained very much alive. Even as New Deal activists celebrated WRB's demise, corporate liberals and their military allies continued their advocacy of an "emergency form of administrative state." Encouraged by the fate of the War Resources Board and its report, New Dealers thought that "when mobilization began, it would be a New Dealer's mobilization."[117] An enhanced New Deal state capable of performing both peacetime and wartime functions, perhaps even of building on the liberal record of the 1930s, must surely appear. The drift of events, however, soon proved otherwise, favoring the military-industrial combination over New Dealers.

Mounting crisis abroad dictated increasing reliance on large-scale public–private planning in the United States. From mid-1940 on, one temporary, emergency creation after another emerged, each more like the War Resources Administration (and the World War I War Industries Board) then the one before it. The National Defense Advisory Commission, the Office of Production Management, and ultimately the War Production Board followed the War Resources Board. The state-building approach of the corporate liberals and military planners, though temporarily stymied with the eclipse of the WRB, reasserted itself in relatively short order.

Chapter 5

Preparedness Proper
The Corporate Liberals and the National Defense Advisory Commission

The complexion of the European war changed dramatically in the spring of 1940, necessitating an American state-building response. German victories in Scandinavia and the Low Countries compelled President Roosevelt to make a decision that he had put off for many months. After reviewing his options, he returned to the concept of business–government cooperation, reviving the moribund National Defense Advisory Commission (NDAC) in order to spur industrial mobilization. NDAC's most important leadership posts went to corporate liberals, who again supplied their knowledge of production and distribution to the federal government. Under corporate liberal direction, contingency planning yielded to institutional experimentation, and the preparedness period reached a more active stage. National defense gradually improved, despite the intrinsic difficulties surrounding conversion from civilian production to defense production and the loud protests of isolationists and other groups.

The National Defense Advisory Commission, officially known as the Advisory Commission to the Council of National Defense, originated with the Army Appropriation Act of 1916.[1] NDAC's purpose had been to give advice on a wide range of defense matters to the Council of National Defense (CND), a body made up of selected members of the president's cabinet. In practice, NDAC did the work and CND never amounted to much. After World War I ended, NDAC remained on the statute book but quickly passed into disuse.

A massive German offensive, which ended the "phony war" phase of World War II, forced NDAC's recall. On April 9, 1940, German troops landed in Denmark and Norway. Denmark fell in a single short day, Norway in just twenty-three days. On May 10, the second stage of the "blitzkrieg" commenced. Operating in tandem, the Luftwaffe and Wehrmacht hit the Netherlands, Belgium, and Luxembourg. In short order, these nations capitulated. Germany completed the rout by driving into France, forcing that country to surrender after only a little more than a month.

The decisive nature of German triumph prompted U.S. action. On May 26, while French and British forces in France were still reeling under heavy Nazi assault, Roosevelt informed Americans that he intended "calling on men now engaged in private industry to help . . . in carrying out" the defense program, and that the public would "hear more of this in a few days."[2] On May 28, 1940, the president resuscitated the National Defense Advisory Commission.[3]

The National Defense Advisory Commission was a coordinating body designed to assist the U.S. defense program. Roosevelt expected NDAC to "expedite the provision of supplies and munitions to the armed forces. . . ."[4] The Defense Commission did not appreciably increase the size of the federal government, but directed available resources more intelligently than otherwise would have been the case, permitting FDR to work more effectively toward his goals of a 1.2 million man army, 50,000 planes per year, and a two-ocean navy.[5]

Like the War Resources Board, NDAC was non-statist. A temporary, emergency agency, sure to be retired once war ended, it attacked bureaucratic incapacity by harnessing corporate liberal expertise and connections to carry out industrial mobilization. An experiment in public–private planning and intelligent collaboration, NDAC prepared the way for similar but larger and more meaningful efforts after 1940.

NDAC's advantages and the disadvantages inherent in other approaches made it a rather obvious choice. Roosevelt had at least four options open to him as Germany advanced through Western Europe. He might do nothing at all. He might rely on market forces to accomplish industrial mobilization, which in reality was equivalent to the first option. An expanded New Deal state was still a possibility; indeed, ardent New Dealers expected it to materialize given WRB's dismissal. Business–government cooperation, with the federal authority in the lead, constituted the final alternative. The president ruled out the first three options, choosing the fourth. NDAC's reappearance signaled Roosevelt's continuing inclination to employ corporate talents in an "emergency form of the administrative state."[6]

Because Axis advances threatened U.S. national security more and more, Roosevelt rejected the notion of further inaction. He wanted to protect the United States, indeed the Western Hemisphere in its entirety, from attack. Increasingly, he wished to give the British and Chinese whatever assistance was necessary to help them ward off the Germans and Japanese. Freedom of all types—including democracy—was at stake as well. Sitting still was no longer a viable strategy. Circumstances demanded that the U.S. state take all prudent steps to organize itself for the provision of additional arms and munitions to the military services and friendly nations.[7]

Adam Smith's "invisible hand" was not the answer, either. Reliance on supply and demand to bring about an adequate mobilization went against

human nature. To trust such an important task to impersonal market mechanisms, which would then presumably bring about the required economic
adjustments, and to do so without intervention while the Axis powers swallowed country after country, was beyond human endurance.[8] Moreover, this
approach promised to rob Roosevelt of his power. Market forces, not FDR,
would make all significant economic decisions. Naturally, the president
found this prospect unpalatable. Even more relevant, U.S. corporations preferred to supply growing peacetime markets rather than switch to defense
production.[9] Under these conditions, the "invisible hand" did not offer any
guarantee that enough weapons and related goods would be made to rectify
existing deficiencies within a reasonable amount of time.

Politics and expediency mitigated against development of a New Deal
state endowed with the requisite legal power and administrative capacities
to carry out a comprehensive, efficient defense mobilization. With the
1940 presidential election approaching, and conservatism on the rise,
Roosevelt could ill afford the fallout that would result from any effort to
construct a liberal state powerful enough to fully protect the national security of the United States. This path might well lend credence to
Republican and isolationist charges that the president was a warmonger
and an erstwhile dictator, costing him votes in November. It also promised
to alienate business, which any new laws and decrees would presumably
place more firmly under the control of a government run in large part by
its longtime critics. Roosevelt needed the intellectual and material assets of
business too much to take such a big risk. He also understood that the
advantages of private ownership were "difficult [for the state] to override,"
especially when there was no imminent threat of foreign invasion.[10] Better—
in this delicate situation—to follow the antibureaucratic tradition, using ad
hoc emergency powers to create a temporary, emergency agency to do the
preparedness job. The specter of a vast New Deal–national security state
was much too provocative at a time when FDR was pursuing only military
readiness, not war, and when he desired reelection to an unprecedented
third term in office. NDAC permitted Roosevelt to do something, but it
was not an extreme solution; the Defense Commission resulted largely as a
function of the president's relatively limited maneuverability when it came
to state-building.

Seven members sat on the National Defense Advisory Commission, one
each for raw materials (Edward Stettinius), production (William Knudsen),
labor (Sidney Hillman), agriculture (Chester Davis), consumers (Harriet
Elliot), transportation (Ralph Budd), and prices (Leon Henderson).[11] In June
1940, Roosevelt designated Donald Nelson Coordinator of National Defense
Purchases, putting him on a par with the others.[12] Although these individuals
came from many walks of life and represented diverse interests, businessmen-
bureaucrats Knudsen, Stettinius, and Nelson were most significant because

they were best positioned to make use of the assets of corporate America. Knudsen, in particular, played a prominent role within NDAC.

William S. Knudsen was born in Denmark on March 25, 1879. He attended school in Copenhagen, learning to read English and excelling in mathematics. He loved the sea and yearned to become a sailor, but his father pushed him into an apprenticeship at a bicycle shop. There his mechanical abilities asserted themselves, much to his later advantage.[13]

In February 1900, at age 20, Knudsen left Denmark for the United States, where he hoped to find a job in a factory that made bicycle parts. He intended to save some money and then return to his homeland. As fate would have it, he remained in the United States for the rest of his life—excluding short trips abroad—becoming a naturalized citizen in 1914 and a famed industrialist thereafter.[14]

A big, gregarious man, Knudsen owed his initial success to hard work and an unwillingness to give up. He took short-term jobs, first in a shipyard and then on the Erie Railroad. Two and a half years passed. Late in 1902, Knudsen interviewed for a job with the John R. Keim Mills, manufacturer of bicycle parts, and was offered a position. Persistence had finally paid off: he was hired for the type of job he had originally sought.[15]

In 1911, Knudsen's career took a dramatic turn. Ford Motor Company acquired the Keim Mills, compelling him to make the transition from bicycles to cars. After studying the infant auto industry, he started his career with Ford by installing Model T assembly plants in different parts of the country. By World War I's end, Knudsen had become Ford Motor Company production manager and Henry Ford's chief assistant.[16]

Another turning point occurred in 1921. In March of that year, during a steep recession, Knudsen quit his job, unwilling to carry out all the layoffs Ford deemed necessary. General Motors soon came calling, recognizing his production genius. Knudsen began with GM as vice president of Chevrolet, building a new car that outsold the Model T. His reward for exemplary performance was the executive vice presidency of GM in 1933 and the presidency in 1937.[17]

As a top manager, Knudsen dealt often with forces outside his firm. He criticized the New Deal and the labor movement publicly, whereas a Stettinius, Harriman, or Swope would not. The Roosevelt administration approach to the wealthy upset him, as did the National Labor Relations Act and sit-down strikes. After Secretary of the Interior Harold Ickes and Attorney General Robert Jackson questioned his salary of $350,000, Knudsen rebutted them, noting that "Government and charity had gotten 90% of this amount."[18] He also thought that the "idea of having everybody get poor so nobody can get rich is not going to work in the long run."[19] As for the National Labor Relations Board, it "makes no pretense of paying any attention to the employer's side" of a labor–management dispute.[20]

Sit-down strikes were odious in the extreme, going against legitimate managerial authority and violating property rights; the strikers themselves, such as those at the General Motors plants in 1937, were simply "lawless trespassers."[21] Yet Knudsen paid his workers an above-average wage, tolerated welfare capitalist programs such as group insurance, was generally respected by his employees, and gave in to the United Automobile Workers on the collective-bargaining issue. He also joined the Business Advisory Council, and accepted Roosevelt's personal invitation to sign up with the National Defense Advisory Commission.[22] Although Knudsen did not fit the classic profile of a corporate liberal, he can certainly be seen as a "sophisticated conservative."

Industrial mobilization remained NDAC's ultimate objective; it began to position business and other interests in such a way that the military would have the support it needed and therefore be better prepared to defend the United States. As long as the Axis constituted a threat, the commission had a job to do. Knudsen made the task sound easy. "Ed [Stettinius] will bring in the stuff" and I will "cut it up."[23] Labor Commissioner Hillman saw to it that workers entered the national defense program, and he kept watch over labor standards and labor relations.[24] Trying to minimize destructive competition and unnecessary price hikes, Nelson prevented government purchasing agencies from bidding against one another. Price Commissioner Henderson also battled inflation. Consumer Commissioner Elliot guarded the public welfare, including that of individual buyers. Agriculture Commissioner Davis supervised collection of foodstuffs and the use of farm surpluses, since soldiers and civilians had to eat. Transportation Commissioner Budd, another corporate liberal, added that he would see to it that "Mr. Stettinius' raw materials move to Mr. Knudsen's plants. . . ."[25]

Reality was not quite that simple. NDAC operated in a way little understood then or now. A facilitating agency only, it lacked the funding and personnel to do everything by itself. Instead, NDAC commissioners and their recruits reached out to private plants and "operating agencies," which alone possessed the immense resources required to make and purchase weapons and haul them from one place to another. As had been the case during the period immediately before U.S. entry into World War I, a chaotic and disjointed organizational scene greeted those individuals and agencies charged with preparedness, and their struggles to achieve progress yielded "de facto decentralization, a system that helped to coordinate the activities of the primary organizations without actually depriving them of much of their power."[26]

NDAC's design was purposeful; it came with built-in constraints that forced members to work in a prescribed fashion. Defense commissioners possessed advisory powers only; their suggestions might be disregarded. Congress set aside no money for the Defense Commission as of its inaugural meeting on May 30, 1940.[27] Just $1 million was made available during July for the fiscal year ending June 30, 1941.[28] NDAC's support staff numbered 250 at the start, drawn mainly from private-sector dollar-a-year men. These limitations forced NDAC to interact with public- and private-sector organizations. The Commission supplied guidance, including vital information unavailable elsewhere; the operating agencies contributed vast sums of money, manpower, and other essentials.

The Industrial Materials Department (IMD) became the best organized and largest part of NDAC.[29] Stettinius derived IMD's structure from the corporate model and his earlier War Resources Board experience. IMD contained two major units, the Industrial Divisions and the Administrative Divisions. Industrial Divisions dealt with the acquisition of raw materials. Division A handled Mining and Mineral Products; Division B, Agricultural and Forest Products; Division C, Chemical and Allied Products. Industrial Divisions broke down further into two or more commodity groups, each of which concentrated on a single material. Iron and Steel Products Group fell into Division A, Lumber and Timber Products Group into Division B, Petroleum and Natural Gas Products Group into Division C, and so forth. At the request of Stettinius, who employed his well-known amicability and wide industrial acquaintance to good advantage, leading industrialists and trade association officials entered the organization, along with a sprinkling of academics, engineers, and scientists. William L. Batt, president of SKF Industries, took over Mining and Mineral Products; Clarence Francis, president of General Foods Corporation, Agricultural and Forest Products, and Dr. E. R. Weidlein, director of the Mellon Research Institute, Chemical and Allied Products. Big businessmen at the top of this organization interacted with former trade association members further down, who in turn moved through their old trade associations to facilitate economic and political exchanges between individual firms and the IMD leadership. The Administrative Divisions provided support to the Industrial Division, including secretarial assistance, statistics, and legal services. All told, IMD exceeded even the Production Department in size and efficiency.[30]

On June 3, 1940, Stettinius defined IMD's mission. He told his subordinates that we are "a group of business men (who would) . . . make certain that industry has the material . . . to meet the program set up by the Army and Navy."[31] The Industrial Materials Department needed to maintain "a continuous and adequate flow of raw materials from the source to factories and other points of fabrication."[32] Stettinius urged the commodity groups to proceed forthwith, under the assumption that the United States "will be involved in war in another six months. . . ."[33] His declaration, of course, was meant to galvanize the men working under him. It was not intended for public consumption, nor did he have any better idea than anyone else in government about whether or not the United States would become involved in war.

The Industrial Materials Department channeled raw materials to production sites, trying to ensure that the output of arms, munitions, and related goods was not impaired by a shortage of inputs. After July, it moved beyond this point, helping to stockpile raw materials so that future demand could be satisfied. Special attention was devoted to the accumulation of aluminum and rubber.

Typically, IMD located strategic commodities, whether at home or abroad, then passed on the information to an operating agency. The operating agencies, the Reconstruction Finance Corporation (RFC), the Army, the Navy, the Maritime Commission, or others made the actual purchases and transported the goods to the factory. On one occasion, for example, Stettinius learned that a large amount of tungsten and antimony had been discovered in Indo-China. He relayed this information to the RFC, which bought the metals and used the Isthmian Line to haul them home from Haiphong. On another occasion, IMD located 22,000 tons of chrome ore in Turkey. Again, word was passed to RFC, and another purchase resulted, with the Maritime Commission arranging for transportation this time. Vital materials flowed to factories across the country, and stockpiles increased. Without IMD assistance, none of this would have happened.[34]

Increased production of aluminum was crucial, because this metal went into warplanes and many other weapons. Commissioner Stettinius, Deputy Commissioner Batt (who had moved up in the organization), and new Mining and Mineral Products division executive Marion Folsom spearheaded the drive for more aluminum. Given the existing supply of aluminum and rapidly growing demand, Folsom used words such as "tight" and "unsettled" to describe the situation in 1940–1941.

The corporate liberals certainly saw the need to act, even though the Aluminum Company of America (ALCOA) had increased production over the course of the preceding decade to stay ahead of demand and the overall aluminum equation was not quite as bad as critics contended. NDAC persuaded ALCOA to expand its output from 400 million pounds of aluminum in 1940 to an estimated 710 million pounds by 1942. When the Reynolds Metals Company broke ALCOA's monopoly on aluminum, NDAC helped Reynolds obtain electric power from the Tennessee Valley Authority, certifying that this extra "production was necessary to national defense." Another 60 million pounds of aluminum was assured for the period between July 1941 and July 1942. Over time, more and more aluminum became available.

Despite upward revision of military aircraft requirements, and no estimate at all in the beginning for the amount of aluminum needed to satisfy other military requirements, NDAC's efforts to expand the capacity of the American aluminum industry ended successfully enough. The military would have its airplanes and other supplies, with no serious delays, and the shortage of aluminum for civilian uses did not impose a great hardship on the American people. Historian Wyatt Wells notes that the monopolistic complexion of the aluminum industry did not "affect mobilization in more than a marginal way" because ALCOA reacted to prewar market conditions by raising supply and lowering price. If the aluminum industry had been competitive rather than monopolistic, Wells speculates, overall production would have been only "somewhat higher."[35]

IMD also supported pioneering projects designed to increase supplies of rubber. Assistant Group Executive W. L. Finger of the Rubber Products Group looked into the feasibility of extracting 50,000 to 75,000 tons of crude rubber from the rabbit bush, a plant that grew in the American West.[36] Although Finger's rabbit bush project did not pan out, Stettinius and his Synthetic Rubber Group encouraged the development of synthetic rubbers such as Buna-S.[37] In combination with RFC's Rubber Reserve Corporation, IMD convinced President Roosevelt to authorize expenditures on government-owned, privately operated synthetic rubber plants.[38] Although the rubber situation remained precarious throughout 1940, Stettinius and his allies took the first tottering steps in the right direction. In later years, enough rubber was amassed to meet military demand with something left over.[39]

Like Stettinius, Knudsen secured the assistance of numerous businessmen whom he organized into commodity sections. Key personnel of the Production Department included George J. Mead, former vice president of United Aircraft Corporation, in charge of the Aircraft Section; Harold S. Vance, chairman of Studebaker Corporation, who headed the Machine Tools and Heavy Ordnance Section; E. F. Johnson, retired vice president of GM (Ammunition and Light Ordnance); and John D. Biggers, president of Libby-Owens-Ford Glass Company (Tanks, Trucks, and Tractors).[40] Only Rear Admiral Emory S. Land (Shipbuilding) lacked a business background, but he more than made up for it given his experience as chairman of the U.S. Maritime Commission.[41] Knudsen selected individuals who had engineering and assembly line knowledge, keys to elimination of production snafus and to mass production of weapons.

The Production Department saw to it that the manufacture of arms and munitions went as smoothly as possible. The emphasis was on controlled expansion of output and elimination of bottlenecks. Knudsen advocated judicious "use of all our manufacturing facilities—bigger plants where bigger plants are needed, conversion of plants to war work that are now engaged in peace work, and finally, construction of new plants."[42] He also identified kinks in production and explained how to get rid of them. Through him, private contractors obtained engineering know-how, equipment they lacked, and capital. He facilitated military procurement in other ways as well, especially by steering large defense contracts to established firms that could get the job done. In this way, he minimized the complications that had arisen during World War I, when "in some cases a ten-cent fellow got a million-dollar job and we didn't get the work."[43]

A classic example of the Production Department in action involved the automobile industry and tanks. Drawing on his unparalleled knowledge, Knudsen determined that the man best suited to the task of making medium-weight tanks was K. T. Keller, president of Chrysler Corporation. At Knudsen's request, Keller consented to do the job. Knudsen directed Keller to the Rock Island Arsenal, where tanks were available for study, and Keller traveled there, along with Chrysler engineers and production experts. They consulted with their military counterparts and returned with 186 pounds of blueprints. A wooden tank, complete with all the parts of the real thing, quickly materialized. The wooden tank served as a model for the medium tanks that Chrysler would later produce in volume. Detailed knowledge of a very complicated machine replaced industrial inexperience. In this instance, as in so many others, Knudsen brought the public and private sectors together, and they learned from each other.[44]

The Production Department did not own or operate defense plants; it merely dispensed recommendations. Initially, federal arsenals or private companies supplied the factories and equipment. From September 1940 on, RFC's Defense Plant Corporation (DPC) put up public funds for construction of new government-owned facilities.[45] On September 3, DPC entered into an agreement with the Packard Motor Car Company for construction of an aircraft engine plant. This was the first of some 2,300 defense plants underwritten by DPC.[46] Typically, DPC provided the money, private companies handled plant specifications and daily operation, and Production Department advice covered ideal plant location and ways to bust the logjams that sometimes arose.[47] Unlike other top production men in the country, such as Henry Ford, Knudsen willingly joined government and shared his expertise. He made many valuable suggestions to companies, trade associations, the military, DPC, and other agencies.

Stettinius, Knudsen, and Nelson knew that the success of preparedness depended on the willingness of private firms to convert from peacetime production to defense production. In order to ensure conversion, NDAC insisted that businesses engaged in defense work receive incentives ranging from antitrust cessation through rapid amortization to suspension of profit ceilings. All parts of the federal government must come to understand the importance of these incentives. A safe and profitable economic environment, alone, guaranteed that companies would take defense contracts and industrial mobilization flourish. And although Roosevelt was sometimes hesitant to act in this way, his commitment to business–government collaboration proved strong enough that he allowed business to reap these benefits while steadfastly refusing the pleas of Ickes and others for widespread conscription of management.[48] FDR followed the path of business–government cooperation rather than that of a state-run munitions complex or socialism.

Antitrust suits brought by the Justice Department against corporations involved in the defense buildup tested Roosevelt's resolve. Ardent New Dealers favored the use of the antitrust laws as a means of regulating big business, whereas corporate liberals thought antitrust suits endangered national security. From their perspective, a corporation under the threat of imminent dissolution might well channel all its energies into the struggle for survival, putting off military orders. In July 1940, the NDAC therefore asked "that industrial combinations deemed necessary for the effectiveness of the defense program" be exempt from prosecution under the Sherman Anti-Trust Act or other applicable laws.[49] Much time passed before this matter would be decided, but in the end the corporate liberals had their way.

Profit issues concerned NDAC's corporate liberals. Stettinius, Knudsen, and Nelson stressed the need for a workable amortization policy, which would do more than any other single measure to persuade corporations to accept defense business. Profit ceilings, the corporate income tax, and the question of an excess-profits tax also received scrutiny. The bottom line, as always, was vital. If defense work generated reasonable profits, then it would be simpler to locate industrial plants, wean business away from civilian production, and recruit expert manufacturers.

American business viewed a sound amortization law as indispensable to the future of industrial mobilization, and NDAC concurred. Both insisted that corporations be allowed to write off expenditures on defense-related plant over the period of "emergency." The shorter the amortization period, the better. By charging off new defense plant over 5 years, rather than 20 or 30, taxable income would be reduced. Diminution of taxable income translated into less taxes for the firm and more retained earnings. An amortization policy of this type offered producers a considerable inducement to build new defense plants.

Businesses also factored in profit ceilings, the corporate income tax, and the probability of an excess-profits tax when they considered whether or not to take defense business. The Vinson-Trammell Act of 1934 and the Merchant Marine Act of 1936 established profit ceilings on airplane manufacturers and shipbuilders of 8 and 12 percent, respectively.[50] A corporate income tax of 18 percent on large-earning corporations remained from the 1939 Revenue Act.[51] As of summer 1940, no excess-profits tax had been enacted, but one was expected soon. The business community, sensitive to all these matters, argued for removal of profit caps, retention of the 18 percent corporate income tax, and a reasonable excess-profits tax. NDAC supported each of these requests, on the grounds that preparedness required the voluntary assistance of corporate America and that firms that risked their capital in this way should be adequately compensated.

Congress responded to NDAC recommendations, passing the Second Revenue Act of October 8, 1940, which addressed these issues. Title III of the Second Revenue Act authorized the much anticipated amortization deduction, wherein approved defense facilities could be written off over a 5 year period, with subsequent tax savings to the firm. Title IV discontinued the Vinson-Trammell Act, thereby freeing airplane manufacturers and shipbuilders from burdensome profit ceilings and making it easier for them to find subcontractors. The corporate income tax rose by 4.1 percent, a relatively modest increase. A livable excess-profits tax was established, ranging from 25 percent on excess profits up to $25,000 to 50 percent for excess profits beyond $500,000. Blackwell Smith, now general counsel for the Industrial Materials Department, concluded that "the Ways and Means Committee of the House [has] been outstanding in its cooperation in pushing through the amortization bill recommended by this commission with cooperation from . . . the Treasury."[52]

By November 1940, the gains registered by NDAC's corporate liberals were obvious enough, and the tempo of industrial mobilization quickened. Stettinius's Industrial Materials Department had launched a $330 million stockpiling program.[53] Accumulations of rubber, aluminum, antimony, tungsten, copper, steel, and other raw materials increased.[54] Knudsen's Production Department facilitated conversion. The machine tool industry—one in which machines made the machines that in turn cranked out weapons—underwent a $34 million expansion.[55] Manufacturers switched to production of military items: a toy manufacturer churned out fuses; a mechanical pencil maker constructed bomb parts; a canner retooled in order to fashion parts for merchant vessels; and so on.[56] Tanks moved from the blueprint phase to actual assembly, some light tanks appearing before 1941 and medium and heavy tanks thereafter.[57] Between July and December 1940, $400 million worth of ships materialized, and they were faster than the old ones.[58] Airplane production vaulted from 2,141 in 1939 to 6,086 in 1940, nearly a threefold increase.[59] Overall defense expenditure rose from $1.24 billion in 1939 to $2.2 billion in 1940, and this was just a beginning.[60] Knudsen and Nelson cleared billions of dollars of defense contracts with deliveries scheduled for 1941 and beyond.[61] Companies such as Pratt & Whitney (machine tools), Glenn L. Martin (aircraft), Newport News Shipbuilding (aircraft carriers), United Shoe Machinery Corporation (guns and parts), Eastman Kodak (aiming circles), and Packard joined General Electric, Scovill, York, and the other pioneers.[62] Most significant of all, passage of the Second Revenue Act created an economic environment that encouraged business to invest heavily in defense-related plant and equipment.[63] Capacity for war production multiplied, and the outlines of Roosevelt's "arsenal of democracy" became visible.

Despite these accomplishments, several groups spoke out against the National Defense Advisory Commission. Whereas NDAC received the cooperation of RFC, Congress, the Treasury Department, and many other federal agencies, it clashed periodically with the War Department and Justice Department. Isolationists, for their part, were suspicious of NDAC. "All-outers," bolstered by the liberal press, accused the commission's corporate executives of "business as usual." Rather than doing too much, as the isolationists contended, all-outers alleged that NDAC did too little. Conservative businessmen continued their assault on the Roosevelt administration, and a few reactionaries discerned a New Deal conspiracy against NDAC's corporate liberals. NDAC's achievements, measured by the strength of its opposition and the doubts of its friends, appear more impressive than they would have otherwise.

War Department resistance to NDAC oversight centered in its new civilian leadership and in its old-line organization. In July 1940, seeking bipartisan support for defense policy, Roosevelt asked Republican Henry Stimson to become Secretary of War. Stimson agreed, but his acceptance did not indicate approval of the National Defense Advisory Commission. Indeed, he began to criticize NDAC, while his Ordnance and Quartermaster Departments disregarded its policies.

In conversations with Roosevelt, Stimson argued that NDAC exceeded its authority, infringed upon War Department prerogatives, and brought unnecessary delay. He "indicate[d] that an advisory group was exercising decision where no legal basis existed."[64] He told FDR that "the War Department had the responsibility for its contracts and that sharing it with the Defense Commission . . . was a serious administrative difficulty."[65] Furthermore, NDAC's presence "held up a lot of things."[66] Stimson suspected that the corporate liberals were trying to take control of military contracting and purchasing. The War Department wanted to deal directly with private companies; it did not see the need for an intermediary, let alone a competitor.

Production Commissioner Knudsen countered Stimson's objections. Knudsen let it be known once again that Roosevelt had set up NDAC to advise existing agencies, not to do the actual work. Thus, NDAC accepted the legitimacy of Army and Navy contracting and purchasing. Although NDAC did review defense contracts of $500,000 or more, the vast majority of them passed without objection.[67] Knudsen told FDR that "there had not been any delay in clearing almost $4 billion of Army contracts."[68]

The disagreement between Stimson and Knudsen was only the first of many between the War Department and the military, on the one side, and the various industrial mobilization agencies on the other. Throughout the preparedness period, then into the war itself, the civilian leaders of the War Department and the generals refused to subordinate themselves to the business mobilizers. Too often Stimson, Assistant Secretary of War Robert P. Patterson, Army Services of Supply Chief Lieutenant General Brehon

Somervell, and others ignored the mobilization agencies or attempted to bully the corporate liberals. Historians and social scientists who generalize about the formation of the military-industrial complex routinely overlook or downplay struggles between the two sides, which generated substantial friction and heat. Far from being some great, unmarked monolith, the early military-industrial complex was cut through with fracture lines.

Price Commissioner Henderson echoed Knudsen's complaints about Stimson. Henderson showed Roosevelt how the War Department intended to construct "its own version of a War Resources Board" by "paralleling the Defense Commission with experts on powder, airplanes, machine tools, etc. . . ."[69] This type of duplication undermined NDAC's mission: it made mobilization planning more difficult and prevented the most efficient use of public and private resources.

Roosevelt did not take a firm stand. He refused to side with either the NDAC or War Department, though he heard both out. An uneasy coexistence, never completely devoid of tension, prevailed. Sometimes the two agencies cooperated, sometimes not. The War Department, through its ordnance and quartermaster offices, let contracts and arranged purchases. NDAC ensured that the biggest contracts went to firms that could handle them and that various agencies did not bid against one another. The basic framework of military procurement was preserved, because by law and tradition this was the accepted mode of operation and time was of the essence.

Disagreement between the Justice Department and NDAC over the antitrust issue remained a constant. Assistant Attorney General Thurman Arnold believed in the vigorous use of federal antitrust laws against corporations in restraint of trade. He viewed lawsuits as a proper means to enforce fair competition, ensure economic freedom, and protect the consumer interest. NDAC's corporate liberals objected to Arnold's approach because they believed it jeopardized defense production. A corporation threatened by the Anti-Trust Division could postpone construction of new defense facilities, neglect conversion of existing plant, or fall behind schedule on delivery of arms. NDAC therefore took up where the War Resources Board left off, repeatedly requesting safeguards from antitrust action for corporations doing defense business.[70] Corporations required insulation from government coerciveness, as well as a profitable environment, if they were to proceed with a greater volume of defense work.

Despite NDAC protests, Arnold persisted. In August, he proposed filing an antitrust action against 22 major firms in the oil industry. He charged that the firms in question rigged prices and forced service stations to sell only their products.[71]

NDAC's corporate liberals led the fight against the "atomizing" suit. Nelson claimed that "the oil-disintegration action would cause the big oil companies to lose valuable time which they should be devoting to the

expansion of their industry."[72] After all, the military was anxiously awaiting plain, ordinary gasoline for jeeps, 100-octane gasoline for fighter
planes, toluene for explosives, and petroleum for synthetic rubber.
Stettinius pointed out that "novel prosecutions" of the Arnold type would
compel "chief executives in not only the oil industry but other large
industry to divert their attention [away from] efforts in defense against a
life and death sort of internal attack. . . ."[73] According to the corporate
liberals, national security considerations justified a temporary retreat from
antitrust.

Price Commissioner Henderson entered into delicate negotiations
with the Justice Department.[74] Henderson met with Attorney General
Jackson and Arnold. Jackson, while conceding that "the question of national
defense is more important than the settlement of the theory on which the
oil industry is to operate," proved reluctant to "let down the bars" for large
oligopolistic firms.[75] The Justice Department temporized, then initiated the
oil lawsuit.[76] The case dragged on and on in court, with no resolution. In
1942, after the United States had been thrust into the war, President
Roosevelt finally intervened, suspending antitrust prosecution against companies vital to defense production.[77] New Deal regulators such as Arnold,
Jackson, and Ickes suffered a great defeat. Safeguarded now, the oil industry—and other big industries—produced a wide array of goods indispensable to the U.S. war machine. The corporate liberals had advocated this
policy all along; they contributed greatly to its implementation.

Most isolationists, like vociferous New Dealers, viewed NDAC with
distrust. They objected to the magnitude of the defense buildup, which they
deemed excessive. They saw the corporate liberals in a poor light, not as
dedicated public servants but as self-interested partisans of big business. They
insisted that Roosevelt wanted war, not peace, and that NDAC represented
a step in that direction.

During the presidential campaign of 1940, FDR declared emphatically
that the United States "wants no war with any nation" and that "keeping
this nation and the other Republics at peace with the rest of the world" was
"uppermost" in his thinking.[78] He repeatedly asserted that American boys
"are not going to be sent into any foreign wars."[79] Roosevelt, however, did
emphasize his hatred of totalitarianism, the need for preparedness, the necessity of aiding freedom-loving peoples, and his grave responsibility "to
awaken this country to the menace for us and for all we hold dear."[80]

Isolationists, led by Senators Hiram Johnson (R–Calif.) and Gerald
P. Nye (R–ND), claimed that Roosevelt's statements were deceptive but that
they knew the truth. Johnson insisted that the president was "bending every
effort now, and by every trick and device known, to get us into" war.[81] Nye
agreed, declaring that FDR "talks sweetly of peace, but his acts for the past
two years have been . . . taking us ever closer to war."[82] Although isolationists

sometimes professed support for industrial and military preparedness, their hearts were not always in it.[83]

NDAC set its sights on a defense program of substantial size, one much larger than isolationists thought desirable. In June 1940, NDAC took as its initial objective an army of 1.2 million men. Subsequently, it accepted War Department plans for an army of at least 4 million soldiers.[84] By contrast, isolationist leaders believed a 500,000 man army sufficient.[85] Whereas NDAC believed that the army ought to be able to project force abroad if necessary, isolationists opposed sending U.S. forces overseas. They wanted a smallish, defensive force that "could be moved quickly to any spot [in the Americas] to repel invaders."[86] If the military grew too big, or became offensive-minded, so isolationist logic ran, the chances for continued peace would diminish.

The corporate liberal complexion of NDAC also bothered many isolationists, as did questions of the agency's legitimacy. General Hugh Johnson, an isolationist himself, wrote that Stettinius and Knudsen were inappropriate choices for any defense commission because of their connection to the Morgan-DuPont crowd.[87] A conflict of interest could arise between company well-being and national well-being, or at least the appearance of such a conflict, which in and of itself would be detrimental. Senator Nye and his followers, typically farmers who viewed the corporation as a natural enemy, suspected that businessmen-bureaucrats would put profits ahead of the lives of American boys if they got the chance. For them, Stettinius, Knudsen, Nelson, Budd, and the rest might well become "merchants of death," in the ghoulish tradition of the World War I munitions-makers.[88] Furthermore, Nye objected to Roosevelt's use of ad hoc emergency powers, including authorization of preparedness agencies by issuance of executive orders. The senator from North Dakota alleged that the president "has assumed powers that were never intended to be that of the Executive, has assumed them without even consulting a Congress, has seemed to want to make himself the policeman of all the world."[89] At root, isolationists were averse to any NDAC actions that might draw the country even an inch closer to European war. Since the Defense Commission adhered to Roosevelt's "aid-short-of-war" policy, isolationists found it suspect.

In stark contrast to the isolationists, all-outers such as journalist I. F. Stone and the United Automobile Workers' Walter Reuther complained that the National Defense Advisory Commission moved in too leisurely a fashion. At NDAC's 1940 pace, Stone estimated, the U.S. might be ready to tackle the Axis by 1947. He cried out for a more rapid mobilization of the steel, aluminum, automobile, and shipbuilding industries. The chemical industry also moved too slowly, perhaps because of its close ties to I. G. Farben, the giant German chemical company.[90] Stone, Reuther, and other all-outers also advocated far greater defense production than NDAC deemed wise.[91] Corporate liberals were caught in the middle: some Americans thought they were too aggressive, others not aggressive enough.

Motivated first and foremost by a sincere desire to preserve the American way of life against totalitarianism, and secondarily by an urge to help small businessmen and workers, all-outers viewed NDAC as a bumbling, stumbling body too solicitous of large corporate interests like U.S. Steel Corporation, the Aluminum Company of America, General Motors, and DuPont. From this perspective, corporate liberals such as Stettinius, Knudsen, and Biggers valued oligopolistic stability, managerial rights, and profits more than the type of massive defense expansion needed to launch an effective counterattack against Axis dictatorship. All-outers, including editorial writers for the *Nation,* the *New Republic,* and similar liberal publications, insisted that NDAC and its corporate executives were pursuing "business as usual." "Business as usual," in turn, was preventing the successful integration of small business and labor into the defense program, undercutting New Deal social reforms and needlessly imperiling precious American freedoms. This conclusion seemed most evident to them when the Reuther plan, calling for rapid conversion of automotive plant to fighter plane production, vastly expanded fighter plane output, and a say for labor on a new industrial council, met with opposition from Knudsen and the automobile and airplane industries that ultimately doomed it to defeat.[92]

Corporate liberals rebutted the all-outers point by point. According to the corporate liberals, all-outers did not appreciate either the complexities of industrial mobilization or how long it would take. Nelson reminded Stone and others like him that large-scale, sustainable defense production must rest upon the solid foundation provided by the civilian economy. Any attempt to ignore the civilian economy, or to gut it for maximum, immediate defense production, would be counterproductive, ending in a smaller output of weapons in the long run.[93] Knudsen, Stettinius, and William Batt publicized the intricacies of defense production. Machine tools "take from six weeks to two years to construct. They range from the size of a desk to that of a two-story house. . . ."[94] On occasion, companies found that the type of machine tool they needed did not exist and they were forced to build one from scratch.[95] A gun carriage for a new 155 mm howitzer demanded "a thousand separate drawings and five hundred more . . . for the recoil mechanism."[96] Welds that held the pieces of a gun mount together needed to withstand terrific firing pressure and were therefore checked for strength by using state-of-the-art X-ray equipment.[97] An average airplane engine consisted of slightly less than 8,000 separate metal parts.[98] As many as 536 subcontractors participated in the fabrication of a heavy bomber.[99] Given all this, and more, industrial mobilization for war required 15 to 24 months to reach high gear.[100] Even then, some classes of weapon (such as battleships) were so complicated that experts declared that they could not be constructed in less than four years.[101] Corporate liberals knew that global democracy would be far better served by controlled, precision expansion of U.S. economic and military capabilities than by a headlong rush. Finally, the defense emergency was no time for social engineering: the Reuther plan only invited labor–management controversy at a moment when it would be extremely hurtful. Corporate liberals therefore resisted the pleas of the more reckless all-outers, just as they tried to ignore the charges of the isolationists.

Corporate liberals called for patience, but their cries went unheeded. Stettinius repeatedly warned that mobilization would be an extended task. He asked for "full cooperation" and forbearance.[102] Deputy Industrial Materials Commissioner Batt echoed his chief, saying conversion "is a big job, a job that no [one] man and no commission could do overnight. . . ."[103] They spoke the truth: although the anxieties of the all-outers were understandable given Axis triumphs, they did not allow sufficiently for the underlying realities of industrial mobilization. Though industrial inexperience diminished with each passing day, the rate of progress was never fast enough to please the Stones of the world.

While all-outers demanded that the National Defense Advisory Commission speed it up, conservative business organizations voiced other, more familiar complaints about the New Deal. From 1938 through 1941, the Chamber of Commerce maintained its "negativistic opposition" to Roosevelt administration policies. The Chamber favored tax relief for corporations, revision of the Wagner Act, retreat from securities regulation, and an end to government involvement in the utilities industry. More than anything else, it wanted a balanced budget; it described deficit spending "as the greatest single obstacle to faith in the free-enterprise system and to recovery from the Depression."[104] The National Association of Manufacturers objected just as strenuously to the growing federal deficit. NAM blamed New Deal Keynesians for this problem and asked for vigilance against "substitution of an unknown measure of . . . government operation of the economy for private enterprise" and the eventual loss of personal liberties.[105]

A handful of business reactionaries proved even more extreme in their thinking, visualizing a New Deal conspiracy against industrialists engaged in defense work. For them, FDR was an erstwhile dictator, New Dealers were akin to fascists, the corporate liberals were pawns, and—if the American people were not vigilant—the 1930s social experiment might well end in despotism.

The conspiracy school expressed towering confidence in laissez-faire capitalism but held that it was under attack by the New Deal. According to its critique, Roosevelt administration laws, rules, and regulations undermined individualism, foisting on the nation and its citizens an insidious paternalistic state. At best, the people forfeited their work ethic because of government handouts: the spirit that energized capitalism was sapped.

At worst, the state itself might exploit the national emergency to take over the economy and then replace democracy with totalitarianism. Even if the New Dealers' plans for preparedness should somehow go awry, they were free to pin the blame on industrialists in the defense agencies.

Business publicist and author Samuel Crowther, politician and advertising man Bruce Barton, and corporate executives Wilson Foss and Edgar Monsanto Queeny were among the leading conspiracy theorists. More than any of them, Crowther hated the New Deal. On occasion, Barton matched Crowther's invective; Foss and Queeny were only slightly less outspoken.

Industrial Materials Commissioner Stettinius received a large volume of correspondence from Crowther and the others, and a smattering went to Knudsen and Nelson. Just after Stettinius's appointment to NDAC, Crowther admonished him not to "permit the palace press to oversell you. . . ."[106] Foss, chairman of the board of the New York Trap Rock Corporation, implored Stettinius to "keep your guard up and your chin in. . . ."[107] He guessed that Stettinius would be served up as "political breakfast" if the preparedness program went badly and the Roosevelt administration needed an alibi.[108] Barton, like the others, warned Stettinius to watch his step: "Don't let these New Dealers put you in the position of defending their failures. Don't pull a damn one of their chestnuts out of the fire."[109] Crowther, echoing Foss, predicted that defense preparedness "will fall short" and that FDR "will try and probably succeed in shifting the blame on business."[110] Barton saw the 1940 Democratic National Convention, where Roosevelt maneuvered for an unprecedented third presidential term, as "an attempt to start this democracy down the road to fascism."[111] President Queeny of Monsanto Chemical Company spoke for them all when he summarized the whole matter: "My fear is that the New Deal will use the good work that [Stettinius] and Knudsen are doing, in spite of the obstacles . . . placed in [their] way, to continue themselves in power, and that then there will be no need to defend ourselves against totalitarianism because we will already have it."[112]

NDAC's corporate liberals, though only too well aware of this scurrilous talk, refused to take it seriously. They did not deviate from their longstanding commitment to "intelligent collaboration," nor did they hesitate to fulfill their functions as the president desired. Averell Harriman, about to become a member of NDAC, declared: "Business should have no quarrel with politicians. The politicians do what they think their constituents want. If business is doing what the people want . . . the politicians will take care of themselves."[113] Stettinius agreed, ultimately severing his friendship with Crowther after the business publicist branded New Dealers "gutter-snipes" and Secretary of State Cordell Hull a "backstairs politician" who had gone "senile."[114] Better than anyone else, corporate liberals knew that there was no New Deal conspiracy aimed at them. The conspiracy theorists simply did not understand the dynamics of the new collaborative relationship between business and government; trapped in a past they could not escape, they had become irrelevant.

Doubts about the effectiveness of the National Defense Advisory Commission were not so easily dispelled as the more outlandish claims of the conspiracy theorists. Criticism from NDAC's enemies mounted during the winter of 1940. As the international situation worsened and anxiety at home intensified, NDAC's achievements received short shrift, and its short-comings were magnified many times. Shortages of aluminum, rubber, and specialty steels did not really handicap the military, but frustrated civilians. Given his initial optimism about raw materials, Stettinius was discredited and became a popular whipping boy. Questions about weapons arose. Why didn't we have a torpedo dive bomber, an equivalent to the German Panzer, or lots of 105 mm howitzers? When Knudsen explained that auto industry conversion, machine tool expansion, or some other adjustment would take care of the problem in due time, that did not seem good enough. The *New Republic* lamented "that Herr Hitler's industry is organized to fight the world, while America's industry is organized to fight inflation, or labor, or the administration."[115] A consensus developed that much more could be accomplished.

The corporate liberals themselves acknowledged the need for institutional change. They wanted more certain authority, either in congressional statute or by executive order. Leadership of the emergency defense apparatus had to be consolidated, and a cleaner chain of command established. Nelson, for one, considered himself only a "consulting purchasing agent."[116] He had always been dissatisfied with the seven-headed configuration of NDAC, as were Stettinius and Knudsen as well. Additional rank-and-file personnel and more money were also needed if the more ambitious of Roosevelt's military goals were to be attained. Institutional deficiencies of many kinds certainly had to be overcome in order to expand operations much beyond the relatively restrained June 1940 targets. The corporate liberals agreed with the assessment of *Nation's Business:* "Conditions are not that bad, but no one is satisfied. General feeling is that the [defense] program will dawdle until someone—Knudsen or another—is given real authority and told to use it."[117]

Roosevelt responded cautiously to the "insistent demand for a stronger defense production agency"; he was waiting for just the right moment.[118] Public opinion and the imminent presidential election were his primary considerations. By autumn 1940, public opinion had shifted toward FDR. Most Americans came to believe that "it was more important for the United States to assure a British victory over the Axis than to stay out of the European war."[119] November witnessed Roosevelt's electoral triumph over Republican Wendell Willkie. By this point, then, the president's "aid-short-of-war" policy

had won widespread acceptance and he was assured a third term. The isolationist challenge had been rebuffed as well, and preparedness was far less
controversial.

In this new, more hospitable environment, FDR felt free to act. In
December, he formed a defense policy committee whose members
included Knudsen, Hillman, Stimson, and Secretary of the Navy Frank
Knox. The defense policy committee, in turn, recommended creation of a
more powerful ad hoc preparedness agency capable of reaching higher
defense production objectives. Established on January 7, 1941, the Office of
Production Management (OPM) superseded NDAC, although the latter
continued to function until October 22, 1941.[120]

The National Defense Advisory Commission practiced non-statist
planning. A tiny agency endowed with minimal resources, which increased
the size of the state only marginally, NDAC offered President Roosevelt a
way to begin rationalizing the preparedness program without threatening
administration control or provoking too great a backlash from business.
NDAC supplied an important, albeit limited, increment of central direction
to a host of unruly, often contentious governmental structures, and brought
them into contact with the private sector. In this manner, NDAC traveled
some distance toward remedying the problem of bureaucratic incapacity
that had been so visible in 1939.

The role of NCAC's corporate liberals was significant. They insisted that
the educational orders program be expanded. The largest War Department
bulk orders received Knudsen and Nelson's assent. Through the corporate
liberals, businessmen were introduced to Army and Navy ordnance experts
and instructed in the fine art of munitions manufacture. This knowledge was
then applied to the mass production of weapons in private facilities.
Knudsen, Nelson, Stettinius, Batt, Folsom, and the others advised trade associations, corporations, and individual businessmen regarding defense plant
locations, financing of new plant and equipment, raw materials, assembly-
line techniques, elimination of bottlenecks, finished goods, transportation,
military attitudes, and so forth. Government took advantage of the corporate
liberals to obtain business expertise and information previously unavailable
to it. Through Stettinius, Knudsen, Nelson, and their associates, the government greatly augmented the federal arsenal by joining private plant and
equipment to it. Corporate liberal efforts, it follows, counteracted industrial
inexperience and weapons shortfalls just as surely as they contributed to state
building. The corporate liberals performed an enormously difficult task with
not inconsiderable skill and, for the most part, moved preparedness forward.

Rapprochement between business and government, under way since
1938–1939, accelerated because of the defense emergency, and the outlines of
a new partnership took shape. Both sides benefited from the exchange. The
Roosevelt administration secured a public–private network of organizations,

facilities, legislation, intelligence, and cooperation, which produced more rifles, planes, tanks, and ships in the short run and made mass production of arms and munitions in later years a likelihood. The glaring absence of weapons, which received so much attention in 1939, plagued America for a surprisingly short time. America's defenses grew stronger. Business, for its part, retained considerable autonomy when it came to productive processes, received splendid profits, and positioned itself well to influence national economic policy during wartime.

Perhaps this result was inevitable. In a capitalistic country with a democratic political system, mobilization of the economy for national defense required active, voluntary participation of business. What is more, the U.S. government of 1940 did not possess the capability or even the desire to undertake preparedness itself. Business sensibilities, rampant isolationism, and political calculations associated with the presidential election precluded the development of an expanded New Deal state. The government therefore relied on the willingness of dozens and dozens of industries and thousands and thousands of firms to lend their resources to the cause of national security. Given earlier strains between the New Deal and the business community, Roosevelt found himself in a disadvantageous bargaining position when he issued the call for help. To win capital over, sweeteners such as five-year amortization, suspension of Vinson-Trammel, a halt to antitrust prosecutions, and cost-plus contracts became necessary. The National Defense Advisory Commission, acting as an intermediary, helped prepare the way for each of these measures while FDR's "pet businessmen" absorbed flack from betrayed liberals, isolationists, all-outers, and business reactionaries alike.

Chapter 6

One Step Short of War
The Corporate Liberals and the Office
of Production Management

Axis advances in Europe and Asia during the last part of 1940 fueled demands for a more effective American preparedness agency. The result was the creation of the Office of Production Management (OPM), staffed by corporate liberals who moved over from the National Defense Advisory Commission (NDAC). A greater sense of urgency gripped them now, as the rush of events broadened the scope of their activities, increased overall defense production demands, and drew the United States deeper into the escalating conflict. In the spring of 1941, lend-lease replaced cash-and-carry, permitting the United States to supply arms and munitions to the British. Aid-short-of-war gave way to an unofficial naval war between the United States and Germany in the fall. Under these circumstances, corporate liberals redoubled their mobilization efforts and preparedness advanced further.

Under intense strain now, corporate liberals struggled to put the economy of a neutral nation on something approaching a wartime footing. Construction of an emergency administrative state designed to accomplish this end provided their focus. They constantly emphasized the interdependence of the public and private sectors, and the resultant need for teamwork. President Roosevelt and the military generally supported corporate liberal exertions. On the other hand, ideologically inclined New Dealers, all-outers, the liberal press, and isolationists kept up their attack on the evolving emergency state. Despite formidable opposition, corporate liberals prevailed, and U.S. industry substantially increased production of weapons and related goods. Corporate liberal guidance of the United States'"near wartime state," though imperfect, proved successful enough.

President Roosevelt created the Office of Production Management on January 7, 1941. Executive Order 8629 defined OPM's mission. Like NDAC, OPM was a temporary, emergency organization designed to work with numerous federal agencies, the military, trade associations, private firms, and individuals to "increase, accelerate, and regulate" defense production.[1] Also like NDAC, OPM dispensed advice rather than orders. Alarmed by German and Japanese gains and by British vulnerability, Roosevelt pushed U.S. rearmament forward, ordering OPM to secure more raw materials, plant, and equipment for the manufacture of arms, munitions, and related goods. He also asked for a workable priorities system, given that certain raw materials were in scarce supply and ought to be parceled out in the order of their usefulness to the defense program.[2] Altogether, Roosevelt called on OPM to do whatever it took to supply a four-million-man army, a two-ocean navy, and an air force that he hoped would grow by 50,000 airplanes each and every year.[3]

OPM's organizational structure quickly took shape. Located within the Office of Emergency Management, a "presidential holding company," OPM resembled a pyramid. The Office of Production Management Council, the top policymaking body, occupied the point. Beneath it, the Director General and Associate Director General ran day-to-day operations. The Purchases Division, Production Division, and Priorities Division formed the broad base of the pyramid.

Roosevelt selected OPM's leaders and they quickly assumed their posts. NDAC Production Commissioner William Knudsen became Director General of the Office of Production Management and Labor Commissioner Sidney Hillman Associate Director General. They sat on the OPM Council with Secretary of War Henry Stimson and Secretary of the Navy Frank Knox. Donald Nelson headed the Purchases Division, John Biggers the Production Division, and Edward Stettinius the Priorities Division. Nelson, Biggers, and Stettinius, like Knudsen, entered into OPM from NDAC; corporate liberal stewardship of the preparedness program was an unvarying theme, as was business–government cooperation. Once again, FDR disappointed supporters of a New Deal national security state.[4]

The Knudsen-Hillman pairing was highly significant. Knudsen dominated OPM, while Hillman was clearly subordinate. Indeed, Roosevelt made Hillman Associate Director General almost as an afterthought. Perhaps Hillman was a sop for labor and ardent New Dealers, as the *New Republic* believed. FDR certainly did not want to be accused of excluding certain special interests, as he had been in the days of the War Resources Board. Given that this was the case, Roosevelt still intended that Knudsen and other corporate liberals exercise control over the daily operations of OPM. While corporatism prevailed, labor's place was insignificant compared to those of government and business.[5]

Subject to the approval of Knudsen, the Purchases, Production, and Priorities Divisions performed the essential functions of OPM. Nelson's Purchases Division helped the Army and Navy technical services, and their contract officers, with buying. It pointed the Armed Services to companies that sold quartermaster goods, medical supplies, and other necessary items. It gave advice regarding consolidation of purchases and tried to spread out government buying over the course of the business cycle, encouraging the

Army and Navy to purchase more heavily during slack times and less heavily during boom periods. Biggers' Production Division bolstered the output of arms and munitions, including most prominently airplanes, tanks, and ships. Biggers, of course, worked in close conjunction with Knudsen, whose production expertise remained a great asset. Stettinius's Priorities Division assigned preference ratings to goods deemed essential to national defense, trying to ensure that the most vital items appeared before any others. Though raw materials such as aluminum, copper, and specialty steels most often demanded priority attention in 1941, priorities were also attached to end products, machinery, power, fuel, credit, transportation, and even workers.[6]

Each divisional director shaped and molded his own organization. Nelson took his old Coordinator of National Defense Purchases team into OPM almost intact.[7] The resultant Purchases Division therefore tapped the experience, knowledge, and abilities of some of the nation's best merchants. Biggers split the Production Division into three branches: Industrial Materials; Aircraft, Ordnance, and Tools; and Ships, Construction, and Supplies.[8] NDAC veterans Averell Harriman, E. F. Johnson, and W. H. Harrison led these branches. Airplane output continued to be a primary concern. Stettinius's Priorities Division housed five major branches: Mining and Metals, Chemicals, Commercial Aircraft, Tools and Equipment, and General Products.[9] Again, NDAC provided much of the personnel, an example being Blackwell Smith, former general counsel for the Industrial Materials Department. Stettinius selected his key subordinates with general expertise in mind, expecting them to apply their broad understanding to particular cases.[10]

OPM did not exist in a vacuum. Similar to NDAC, the Office of Production Management interacted with a host of public and private agencies and individuals. The Army and Navy placed many contracts with corporations after receiving OPM advice on which company could do the best job. Delivery dates within military contracts were sometimes influenced by OPM officials, looking to even out defense production so as to avoid assembly-line overloads and prevent price hikes. RFC subsidiaries operated with OPM input: Defense Plant Corporation invested public money in armament and munitions factories after due consultation; Rubber Reserve Corporation and Metals Reserve Corporation continued buying as during the NDAC period. OPM branches, staffed by former trade association officials and others with specialized knowledge of materials and production processes, answered countless questions from trade groups, corporations, and individuals about complementary goods, substitutes, proper scheduling of orders, contact persons, and much more. Trade associations, businesses, and executives also funneled ideas to OPM. Corporate liberals Knudsen, Nelson, Stettinius, and Biggers conducted more and more information back and forth between the public and private sectors. Their role as liaisons expanded dramatically.

Knudsen captured the essence of OPM and the corporate liberal contribution. Testifying before Congress in April 1941, he described OPM as "a service organization" that existed only to help the War Department, the Navy Department, and other interested parties in the mutual quest for maximum development of the United States' "productive capacity for defense."[11] He noted once again that OPM was "created to expedite, rather than to formulate or execute, the defense program."[12]

Knudsen was right. Ultimate success for preparedness depended on construction of an emergency form of administrative state. The corporate liberals did not "formulate" orders: President Roosevelt did. Corporate liberals did not really "execute" orders either: operating agencies performed this function. Rather, corporate liberals "expedited" and "facilitated" and "coordinated." They held the evolving national security apparatus together, seeking to improve it as conditions permitted.

The relationship between the military establishment and corporate liberals illustrates well the complex exchange under way. After Stimson's original misunderstanding with NDAC, he and other military leaders generally saw eye to eye with corporate liberals. Both groups believed that the United States must construct an economic environment conducive to increased production of defense materiel. Both groups insisted on the necessity of business turning a profit in the process. Both groups objected to reform efforts that might get in the way of preparedness. Most important of all, the military and corporate liberals supported business–government cooperation "based on extensive corporate discretion" as a means of mobilizing, rather than construction of an enhanced New Deal state or some other alternative.[13] If they did not always agree on specific issues, corporate liberals and military men worked within the same broad parameters during most of the preparedness period.

Throughout the latter part of 1940, and beyond, military spokesmen urged Roosevelt and Congress to pass laws favorable to greater defense production. The War Department, Army, and Navy added their voices to those of NDAC's corporate liberals. The military, like the corporate liberals, advocated such measures as five-year amortization, removal of burdensome profit ceilings, beneficial tax legislation, and suspension of antitrust.[14] Whereas Secretary of the Interior Ickes opposed five-year amortization, declaring that he wanted no more "war millionaires" who made their money off public largesse, Stimson and Knox offered countervailing arguments.[15] They considered rapid amortization one key to adequate military supply during an international crisis. When Assistant Attorney General Arnold clung to his antitrust vision, the military pressed for cessation in the name of national defense.[16] The military–industrial alliance ultimately beat back ardent

New Dealers, helping win passage of the Second Revenue Act of 1940 and suspension of antitrust. Rapid amortization of defense plant, lucrative profits for business, and considerable managerial autonomy were assured.[17] The juridical and economic climate that emerged was favorable to big business.

The profit issue went the way of the business community. As early as autumn 1939, General Charles Tillman Harris Jr. had assured leading businessmen that corporations that chose to enter into defense contracts would be insured against losses. At that point, Harris did not guarantee large profits but his words all but said it.[18] In 1940, Stimson displayed similar sentiments. He wrote that the United States was a capitalistic country preparing for the possibility of war. Given these circumstances, "you have got to let business make money out of the process or business won't work."[19] Little wonder that the Army and Navy began to award cost-plus-a-fixed-fee contracts under terms of the National Defense Expediting Act of July 1940.[20] Oligopolistic corporations, in particular, generated big profits.

Military leaders perceived New Dealers and labor representatives as potential obstructionists. Soldiers and sailors needed arms and munitions that only corporate America could supply. Anyone that upset business, or otherwise interfered with the flow of weapons, imperiled national security.

The preparedness emergency, the military argued, was not the right time to quibble over business practices or to institute liberal reforms. Stimson believed that New Dealers and labor leaders hindered mobilization because their actions alienated the business community, possibly resulting in a lower output of weapons.[21] Under Secretary of War Robert P. Patterson, himself a Wall Streeter, told Congress that "preparation for defense is the worst possible vehicle for relieving economic and social conditions."[22] He thought lucrative defense contracts only right and proper, because they guaranteed arms shipments. Intrusive questions about profit margins and contract distribution, however, were detrimental. Contracts, according to Patterson, should go to reliable companies that could produce weapons quickly, whether or not they observed existing labor or social legislation.[23] Preparedness came first; reforms that got in the way must be postponed for the duration of hostilities.

Dramatic new state-building departures, of course, were even less welcome. The military wished to follow the World War I and inter-war precedents. It believed that industrial mobilization depended on creation of an agency similar to the War Industries Board or the Industrial Mobilization Plan's War Resources Administration. Whatever the exact name or names used, mobilization agencies should be staffed with the patriotic business leaders of the nation, who would collaborate with Army and Navy brass.[24] Patterson certainly thought that the combination of military institutions and corporate expertise in and of itself was equal to the mobilization task.[25] Other parties, as Stimson viewed the matter, were only likely to cause trouble.

An expanded New Deal state, with objectives other than simple provision of weapons, jeopardized U.S. defense preparations.

OPM fit the military's conception of the proper way to organize the mobilization effort. It was a temporary emergency body equipped with appropriate mechanisms to bring into contact corporate executives, business firms, and military officers. Although Stimson would have preferred a mobilization network entirely his own, and direct contact between the War Department, military services, and the nation's firms, he made do with the civilian mobilization agencies Roosevelt put into place.[26] More accurately, perhaps, Stimson cooperated with OPM and the other agencies when it suited him and overlooked them when convenient.

OPM officials got along well enough with their War Department counterparts, but their views were not identical. Stimson, after all, had attempted to carve out an independent mobilization network during NDAC days. In October 1940, Knudsen himself had alerted FDR to Stimson's efforts to parallel NDAC's commodity groups and experts.[27] During April–May 1941, Nelson threatened to resign from OPM unless the military awarded a greater volume of defense contracts. He thought that the War Department and the services were proceeding too slowly when it came to the matter of letting contracts to individual companies.[28]

Stimson, for his part, took advantage of the great power of the War Department to fend off the majority of the challenges he faced. NDAC and OPM simply lacked the strength to make the War Department toe their line. More fundamental still, their design required them to assist operating agencies rather than run them. Knudsen ultimately became an "ally and advocate" of the War Department.[29] Nelson gave in, too, fearing that confrontation with the military would mean delay at a moment when armament and munitions production must go forward. Later, when Nelson acquired the power to rein in the military and take charge of contracting and purchasing, he opted to leave it in Army and Navy hands. If corporate liberals let military contracts, he believed, charges of favoritism and conflict of interest would most assuredly mount.[30] Nelson also agreed with Roosevelt that "the final determination of the character of Army and Navy material has to be made by the people who know best about it."[31] OPM's corporate liberals occasionally resented Stimson's high-handedness; friction occurred periodically between civilian mobilization agencies and the military establishment; but both groups were united by their desire to fend off New Deal innovations and win over individual firms and businessmen to the preparedness program.

Corporate liberal exertions contributed to a marked growth of state capacity. As we have seen, corporate liberals forged linkages between public and private organizations that allowed for the completion of numerous defense-related projects that could not have been undertaken otherwise.

Corporate liberals also lobbied government and business for additional resources. Under their ministrations, OPM itself grew, and so did its ability to guide the activities of institutions larger and more powerful than itself. In January 1941, NDAC got along with a yearly budget of $1 million and 1,000 employees.[32] By December 1941, only 11 months later, the Office of Production Management spent over $2.5 million per quarter and deployed 7,600 workers.[33] Increases in OPM's funding and personnel, along with consequent expansion of its outreach activities, pointed to the presence of a modified American state, one better equipped to harness the industrial strength of the nation in event of war and thus better able to safeguard national security.

Manufacture of defense articles became more efficient as the state brought its growing strength, and newfound expertise, into play. S. R. Fuller Jr., president of the American Bemberg Corporation, accepted a position as Industrial Materials chief within the OPM Production Division. Fuller suggested that Bessemer steel could be used instead of open-hearth steel under the right conditions, and it was done.[34] Hans W. Huber of the J. M. Huber Corporation wrote a letter to OPM outlining ways in which chrome ore, lead, and zinc might be conserved. Huber listed peacetime production processes that could be altered without significant harm, yielding savings of essential metals which should then be channeled into the defense program and the production of defense goods. He did not see any reason to use chromium and lead in paint and wallpaper, or zinc dust in the paper industry, when the military needed these substances.[35]

Technical knowledge possessed by OPM's corporate liberals, and their associates outside government, was applied to industrial mobilization, with telling effect. OPM branches touched trade associations, corporations, and businessmen to the benefit of national defense, and vice versa. Output of arms, munitions, and related goods jumped as a result. By May 1941, Knudsen reported that production of machine tools had doubled from a year before, and there were gains in many other areas as well.[36] The United States produced three times as many aircraft as 12 months earlier. Production of tanks increased by sixfold. The country saw production of Garand rifles rise by 360 percent; powder was up by 1,000 percent, small-arms ammo by 1,200 percent. Biggers told the House Military Affairs Committee that the manufacture of many categories of small arms, including submachine guns, was "running ahead of schedule."[37] Nelson and his purchases group bought the U.S. Army "3 million sheets, 9 million pairs of shoes, 11 million khaki shirts, 18 million pairs of pants, 33 million pieces of cotton underwear, and 63 million pairs of socks."[38] Altogether, a $40 billion–plus defense program was under way, made possible by a state-building process that emphasized business–government cooperation, achieved for the most part through corporate liberal diplomacy.[39] Corporatism of this type promised to yield even greater gains in the future; the potential for business–government cooperation to mobilize the U.S. economy was immense.

Events, however, seemed to conspire against OPM's corporate liberals. Throughout 1941, international developments brought only unrelenting gloom. Demand for materials and weapons constantly increased. Stress of this type revealed that the Office of Production Management suffered from serious internal defects that needed to be fixed. Interagency conflict appeared, complicating matters further. Zealous New Dealers, all-outers, and the liberal press slammed OPM for overall munitions objectives they considered too low, while downplaying the fact that the United States was officially at peace. These groups insisted that businessmen were using the preparedness agencies to their own selfish advantage, at the expense of social reform. Isolationists counterbalanced all-outers, leery of OPM's potential to involve America in war. They condemned Roosevelt's use of emergency presidential powers and extraordinary defense agencies. Knudsen, Nelson, Stettinius, Biggers, and the other businessmen-bureaucrats felt besieged but fought on.[40]

The news from Europe and Asia was bad. Germany dominated Western and Central Europe. Britain was still recovering from its poor start. In April 1941, Hitler overran Yugoslavia and Greece, completing his conquest of the Balkans. The Japanese, moving closer to their dream of a "greater East Asian co-prosperity sphere," incorporated more Chinese territory into their expanding empire. The threat to Southeast Asia increased. Totalitarianism moved forward.

Like Roosevelt, corporate liberals watched these developments with dismay. They wanted to thwart Axis plans without resort to an American declaration of war. Knudsen loved his native Denmark, which had fallen into Nazi hands a year before, and wished to see it independent once again. An "instinctively democratic man," he was repelled by totalitarian dictatorship. Up to 1940, Nelson had not devoted much attention to the European and Asian wars, but in hindsight he was "appalled" by them. Stettinius, Biggers, and Batt felt much the same. Restoration of peace promised a renewal of stability and profitability in world commerce, with subsequent gains for General Motors, General Electric, U.S. Steel, Standard Oil, and other firms with overseas branches and operations. Knudsen, Swope, Stettinius, and those corporate liberals affiliated with multinational corporations recognized the economic benefits that the termination of hostilities must confer. Simple human decency, too, persuaded each of them that British and Chinese victory over the Germans and Japanese, without forfeiture of American lives, was the preferred outcome, and they sided wholeheartedly with Roosevelt in pursuit of this goal.[41]

Allied setbacks put additional pressure on the corporate liberals. The American public expected more of them, and their job became bigger and harder. The clamor for raw materials, arms, munitions, and related products grew louder. The Army and Navy requisitioned weapons and other items essential to their operations in an increasingly hazardous world, then upped their demands further. OPM found it necessary to make numerous adjustments in order to reach higher targets. Passage of the Lend-Lease Act on March 11, 1941, over vehement isolationist objections, added another claimant. England issued plea after plea for a variety of defense articles, increasing OPM's production burden still further. The press for basic materials and military goods proved unrelenting.[42]

By this stage, OPM's corporate liberals had been asked to protect the United States' civilian economy, meet the needs of the military services, and provision Britain. The addition of lend-lease increased the load significantly. Corporate liberals watched as Congress enacted into law the initial lend-lease appropriation of $7 billion on March 24.[43] More appropriations followed. Somehow, corporate liberals would have to find a way to get the British mountains of military equipment and related goods. The defense articles that began to pass from the United States to Great Britain included tanks, aircraft, ships, railroad locomotives, train rails, projectiles, aviation fuel, boots, other types of clothing, and foodstuffs.[44] Corporate liberals such as Stettinius and Averell Harriman helped arrange for the production and distribution of these items, sometimes overcoming substantial shipping problems. American aid amounted to a substantial percentage of overall British requirements. By November–December 1941, lend-lease shipments were going not only to Great Britain but to the Soviet Union as well.[45]

OPM's organizational scheme, though workable at the beginning, hampered it more and more as the size of its task swelled to near wartime proportions. Most observers noted the lack of one-man leadership or the need for additional statutory authority, but other, equally serious problems developed.[46] OPM's functional organization resulted in an unwise proliferation of commodity groups, and a satisfactory priorities system was desperately needed.

OPM divisions were arranged according to the function they facilitated: production, purchases, or priorities. As the weeks and months passed, each division set up its own commodity groups. Ultimately, three commodity groups operated for all significant commodities: steel, aluminum, magnesium, ships, airplanes, and so forth. Businessmen who came to Washington seeking contacts and contracts quickly became frustrated when they found themselves shuffled from commodity group to commodity group within the OPM labyrinth. Manufacturers cried out for a central point of contact; their bewilderment and anger owed as much to preexisting weaknesses of the American state as it did to the inefficiencies of OPM's design.[47]

As had been the case with NDAC, OPM struggled to devise an adequate priorities system. This task proved enormously challenging. Priorities

Director Stettinius occupied the "hot seat." From January to August 1941, he dealt with the military, civilian agencies, and corporations on a regular basis. As always, he worked extremely hard and unstintingly invested his considerable energies. Some small gains were registered, but in the end Stettinius failed to do the job.

The Priorities Division (PD) faced numerous difficulties. Stettinius's overoptimism about the availability of raw materials, coupled with a reluctance to coerce business, mitigated against establishment of rationing or even quick imposition of mandatory priorities. Roosevelt's tardiness in passing on priorities power further delayed the implementation of strong priority controls. The administrative machinery Stettinius installed soon fell behind, unable to process priorities applications fast enough. Although OPM was supposedly the top priorities agency, control of one kind or another was vested in many other bodies, including most prominently the Army and Navy. Together, these impediments produced the priorities mess.

Reliance on voluntary priorities generated poor results. Companies sometimes complied but on many occasions ignored directives. Machine tool corporations were prime offenders. Steel manufacturers also turned down orders placed by freight car builders and farm machinery makers, which carried voluntary priority ratings, so that they could supply the auto industry, their traditional customer.[48] Up to late August, with a few notable exceptions, private firms retained their prerogative to decline defense orders, thus effectively evading the skeletal priorities system. In this way, unnecessary civilian production continued even after OPM endorsed curtailment.

As it became clear that voluntary priorities were not the answer, and that aluminum, copper, and specialty steels were indeed in short supply, Stettinius took corrective measures. On January 31, 1941, he asked that the largest machine tool corporations "deliver their products only to customers who could present a preference rating."[49] When that request proved insufficient, he took more decisive action. On February 24, the entire machine tool industry found itself under mandatory priorities: the first industry so affected.[50] On the same day, aluminum was placed under a similar restraint; magnesium and other key metals followed.[51] Yet most industries and materials still escaped mandatory priorities. More telling, Stettinius and his PD subordinates showed insufficient recognition that even mandatory priorities orders must be accompanied by thoroughgoing rationing if the most important defense needs were to be satisfied above all else.

Stettinius might have acted more vigorously had he been more certain of his authority. His indecisiveness stemmed from several factors. OPM's role was essentially to give advice, not commands. Stettinius believed in the voluntary association of business and government; he shied away from the use of force in their relationship. Moreover, he was waiting for FDR to give him additional power. On May 31, 1941, Congress had granted Roosevelt sweeping authority under Public Law 89 "to extend . . . priorities and allocate material," but the president paused before passing this authority on.[52] Stettinius noted that the absence of an "Executive Order from the President to delegate powers under the new priority act" was seriously hindering him.[53] He wanted a clear mandate permitting the Priorities Division to prioritize indirect defense, maritime, and British requirements. Barring this, he felt constrained, and hesitated before issuing necessary directives.

A backlog of priorities applications plagued Stettinius. Through June 30, 1941, the Priorities Division managed to keep pace with the priorities applications (PD-1s) it received. A total of 11,000 had come in, and the appropriate forms (PD-2s), complete with the assigned preference ratings, went out.[54] Unfortunately, a rapid increase in priorities applications during July and early August caused a severe overload. From July 1 to August 15 alone, 28,000 PD-1s arrived at the Priorities Division.[55] Given the space and personnel Stettinius had at his disposal, he could not keep up. Eventually, 18,500 applications piled up: roughly 4,500 required attention from the Priorities Division itself, while the rest awaited approval from the various commodity sections.[56] This breakdown prevented some businesses from getting raw materials quickly, and therefore delayed defense production. Stettinius beseeched Knudsen, Hillman, and Roosevelt for additional room and workers but did not get them.[57] A more efficient deployment of available resources was the only way out, but an answer eluded Stettinius.

Sharing the priorities responsibility with so many other agencies complicated matters. In theory, OPM was the top agency. In practice, the priorities function was badly divided. The Interstate Commerce Commission handled railroad priorities, the Maritime Commission shipping priorities, the Federal Power Commission power priorities, and so on.[58] Worse by far, OPM's Priorities Division permitted the military to exercise some control over the Priorities Critical List (PCL).

The PCL was a constantly growing roster of items essential to warfare, including arms, munitions, and raw materials, for which Army and Navy supply officers unilaterally determined priorities.[59] Items on this list as of March 1941 included guns, rifles, grenades, mortars, torpedoes, aircraft, aluminum, magnesium, rubber, and tungsten.[60] Altogether, some 200 items were included.[61] All of them were of vital importance, and each might be prioritized by three separate agencies.

The result of such folly should be self-evident. OPM, Army, and Navy officials all performed the same basic function, with scant reference to each other. So many A-1-a ratings were minted for items on the Priorities Critical List that companies holding A-1-b and A-1-c ratings found them severely devalued. Ratings below that (from A-1-d down) were worth even less; holders often learned that they could not obtain desired materials or equipment. Encroachment on OPM priorities jurisdiction by the Army, Navy, and several civilian agencies became a very serious subject indeed.[62]

On August 27, 1941, Stettinius made one last bid to resolve the priorities crisis. After much soul-searching—which critics labeled unconscionable delay—he compelled U.S. manufacturers to take defense orders and comply with all preference certificates.[63] Companies no longer had any choice. This step facilitated expansion of numerous wartime industries, including transportation, steel, and agriculture. Additional defense production gains were registered, and industrial mobilization lurched forward. Stettinius's inability to deal so effectively with the paperwork nightmare or military competition led to rumors that his job was in jeopardy. Unimaginative leadership on his part, combined with a fragmented priorities power, led him to this strait.

Stettinius's difficulties, of course, did not result entirely from his own defects. The nature of the preparedness state hampered him as well. Although the use of ad hoc emergency powers and temporary, emergency agencies benefited Roosevelt enormously, allowing him to concentrate power in his own hands, bypass Congress, and exert some degree of control over the pace of mobilization, Stettinius and the other corporate liberals found themselves in a tight spot. Their advice was non-binding; the directives they eventually issued dependent on ill-defined executive orders or vague congressional statutes. Little wonder that the military and other agencies often did their own thing. Business–government cooperation yielded considerable messiness, yet other state-building approaches might not have fared any better and would have lacked even the political advantages the president reaped.

Roosevelt had created another headache for OPM on April 11, 1941, with establishment of the Office of Price Administration and Civilian Supply (OPACS). OPACS' roots stretched back to the National Defense Advisory Commission. With the departure of the purchases, production, and priorities functions for OPM, NDAC's price stabilization and consumer protection departments were deserted. Unwilling to let them die, Commissioners Leon Henderson and Harriet Elliot argued that a new organization should be fashioned. The result was OPACS, with Henderson as administrator.[64]

FDR designed OPACS with two concerns in mind. He wanted to restrain prices because he was leery of the high inflation that the United States had experienced during World War I.[65] He also wished to maintain the "essential" civilian economy, which required basic materials and priorities, just as the defense program did. Although military needs increasingly came first, the civilian economy demanded attention if it was to be healthy.

Leon Henderson was one of a group of New Deal economists who had in mind social engineering in the midst of the turmoil created by preparedness. Henderson envisioned the creation of a civilian economy characterized by high wages and low prices. In this type of economy, consumers could buy the massive amount of goods cranked out by producers, so over-production would no longer be a threat. If OPACS prevailed, producer prices and profits would not be excessive. Along these lines, Henderson can be seen as a consumer advocate and OPACS as an agency intent on fashioning a state-building coalition between parts of the federal government, labor, and consumers. This type of planning, wherein the state sought "to play a direct role in overseeing the wage, price, and production policies of private enter-prise," ran contrary to the interests of the mainstream business community. Even corporate liberals winced at such a prospect, advocating instead a far less intrusive government regulatory presence for the time being and a post-emergency return toward the free market.[66]

Henderson strenuously pursued his objectives, clashing with OPM in the process. OPACS and OPM disagreed on the pace of the defense buildup and on the distribution of scarce raw materials. OPACS advocated maximum defense production consistent with national income and legiti-mate needs of the civilian economy. It pushed hard for materials to go into the core economy, while insisting that non-essential civilian production be curtailed and defense production boosted. For its part, OPM thought OPACS' estimate of maximum defense production too high. It resisted rapid curtailment of civilian industry on the grounds that no acceptable definition of "non-essential" existed. A product that appeared to be "non-essential" might become indispensable under certain circumstances but would be unavailable if production was entirely halted. Better to continue production at a reduced volume.[67] As for materials, OPM asserted the basic principle that military needs must come first and noted the regrettable fact that this sometimes left very little for civilians. Army, Navy, Maritime Commission, and Lend-Lease supply officers competed against one another for the scarcest materials, with the result that OPACS got very little or none. Naturally, Henderson, his subordinates, and elements of their labor-consumer constituency resented this situation.[68]

Friction between OPM and OPACS continued throughout the life-time of the latter, symbolic of the organizational infighting that character-ized preparedness. Roosevelt frequently pitted one agency against another, as in this case. In this way, he received a wide array of opinions, was free to pick the course he liked best, and consolidated authority in his own hands. Nor did organizational-institutional disarray preclude positive develop-ments. OPACS' emphasis on higher defense production put pressure on OPM to move forward, counteracting the inherent cautiousness of Knudsen and Stettinius. Curtailment of civilian industry accelerated, as in the case of automobiles. Knudsen and Henderson arranged a compromise here, releas-ing a joint order commanding that passenger car production be slashed 26 percent by November 30, 1941, and 50 percent by July 1942.[69] Similar reductions transpired in other consumer durables industries. Yet there were many complaints about "divided authority," and conflicts always took time to resolve.[70] Only so much inter-agency squabbling could be tolerated before it turned counterproductive, and at that point reform became necessary.

All-outers, like OPACS' Henderson, constantly questioned the scope of OPM's military supply program. They believed that the powerful U.S. economy was capable of underwriting a defense program well in excess of the contemplated $40 billion. For them, the return of economic vitality, reflected in an expanding national income, justified greater expenditures on weapons and related goods. Though OPM statistician Stacy May announced in March 1941 that a total defense program of $48.7 billion was underway and "will place an unprecedented load on American industry for the calendar years 1941 and 1942," all-outers such as Robert Nathan and I. F. Stone insisted that even more was possible.[71] Nathan, perhaps the foremost expert in the country on national income, argued for a figure in excess of $60 billion.[72] Stone, a leading journalist, called for up to $100 billion.[73] They believed that idle plant should be employed and new plant constructed, which would make such large production figures feasible.

The *Nation,* the *New Republic,* and other liberal publications shared the views of the all-outers and ardent New Dealers. The *Nation* assumed "that we must increase supplies of planes, tanks, warships, and guns rapidly. . . ."[74] Public production of weapons and separation of armaments from profits, though intriguing ideas that had some merit, were not practical because of the delays and animosities they would bring. Because private enterprise must therefore do the job, and did not respond adequately to patriotism, "we must expect to pay through the nose."[75] Even at that, the *New Republic* noted, the National Defense Advisory Commission had "failed to call for expansion of capacity" and OPM was going along the same lines.[76] Both agencies, instead, "served as . . . inside pressure group[s] for the interests that were delaying the defense program."[77] Giant monopolies and Wall Street financial manipulators, in league with corporate executives like Knudsen, had "been largely successful in driving the New Deal out of the defense program," and OPM "represents an attempt by business to seize control of defense."[78] If Roosevelt and the people did not recognize these truths, or refused to act, then big business would amass vast profits; the New Deal would be shut down; and groups such as labor, consumers, and the disadvantaged would lose out.

Festering organizational-institutional inefficiencies, coupled with nonstop criticism from businessmen, corporations, trade associations, all-outers, and the press, led to three separate reorganizations of the defense program during the last half of 1941. Each reorganization addressed specific problems that had become highly visible in the preceding months. A more rational defense program emerged out of this ferment.

The June reorganization focused heavily on OPM's overlapping commodity groups. Two out of every three commodity groups were wiped away, leaving just one commodity group for each commodity. Surviving commodity groups were housed within either the Production, Purchases, or Priorities Divisions, depending on the chief problem presented by the particular good or material.[79] The Production Division was assigned materials such as aluminum, magnesium, chemicals, and steel, as well as the machine tools, construction, ordnance, automotive, and shipbuilding sections. Commodity sections placed within the Purchases Division ranged from Subsistence to Drugs, Firefighting Equipment, Fuels, and Refrigeration. Food, clothing, drugs, and hoses were among the more prominent goods represented. Rubber, copper, manganese, zinc, and tin fell under the Priorities Division.[80] Consultation between OPM and trade organizations yielded corresponding "war service committees," which were officially labeled "industry advisory committees."[81] The Aluminum Section met with the Aluminum Advisory Committee, and so forth. OPM's new, more efficient shape resembled the IMP model, and the old War Industries Board, more closely than ever.

Additional reforms stand out in the June reorganization. Priorities Division priority committees, which had been arranged along commodity lines, were abolished. After June 24, remaining commodity groups reported directly to the Priorities Division, which retained final responsibility for determining priorities and issuing certificates.[82] Knudsen also forbade the employment of paid trade association officials by the Office of Production Management.[83] Stone, New Dealers like Ickes, and others had accused these men of favoring their peacetime employers and industries over the public interest; this became less likely now.

The changes of June 1941 remedied obvious institutional defects. Needless duplication of commodity sections ceased, and businessmen discovered a central point of contact. Their pursuit of expertise, information, and defense contracts became less complicated. The commodity group–industry advisory committee nexus fostered additional public–private exchange. With the elimination of priority committees, more unnecessary bureaucracy disappeared. The prohibition on paid trade association executives deflected conflict-of-interest charges. Unfortunately, the priorities backlog demanded more attention, threatening to get worse before it got better; the OPM–OPACS feud showed little sign of abating; and all-outers were still upset about OPM's defense production goals.

Even as the first reorganization effort petered out, clamor for a second began. Tensions between OPM and OPACS, which attracted public notice, forced Roosevelt to become involved. He referred the dispute to White House adviser Samuel Rosenman. Rosenman met with Knudsen and Henderson, securing general agreement that there should be a single, preeminent agency in charge of all supply and priority matters. Though

Rosenman thought OPM should be that agency, Roosevelt created the Supply Priorities and Allocation Board (SPAB) instead.[84]

Executive Order 8875, issued on August 28, 1941, established SPAB as the chief policymaking body for the national defense program, with control over all materials, commodities, and priorities, whether intended for military or civilian use.[85] In this capacity, SPAB formulated top policy directives, estimated overall defense requirements, and saw to distribution of basic materials among competing claimants. Having been demoted, OPM became SPAB's chief operating agency.[86] SPAB issued orders; OPM, the military, and other agencies carried them out. As a part of this general shake-up, OPACS was dismembered. The Office of Price Administration became a separate entity, vitally concerned with price control, rent control, and rationing.[87] Henderson kept his position as head of OPA, where he continued his losing struggle for "a high-wage, low-price economy capable of sustaining mass consumption."[88] Civilian Supply, ironically enough, found itself a new division within its old adversary, OPM.[89] Thus, centralization of defense requirements proceeded, while internal governmental debates over the magnitude of defense production and competing state-building models temporarily grew less heated.

Leadership of the defense agencies shifted along with the agencies themselves. Though Knudsen stayed on as OPM Director General, his standing diminished with SPAB's appearance. His production expertise and connections were no less valuable than they had been 15 months before, and would be retained throughout World War II, but he had become a political liability.[90] An easy target for all-outers, who alleged that Knudsen was in bed with auto makers and other large corporate interests to forestall conversion, he gradually lost favor with Roosevelt and ended up in the War Department. Unable to escape the priorities quagmire, Stettinius was transferred from OPM to leadership of the Office of Lend-Lease Administration (OLLA), where he facilitated the flow of American weapons and related items to Britain and Russia.[91] Meanwhile, Donald Nelson's star rose. Nelson became Executive Director of SPAB, replaced Stettinius as OPM Priorities Director, and took Knudsen's spot as the dominant businessman-bureaucrat of the Roosevelt administration preparedness program. Business–government cooperation remained a constant, with Nelson as the United States' new Bernard Baruch.[92]

Donald Marr Nelson was born in Hannibal, Missouri, in 1888. In 1911, he took his Bachelor of Science degree in chemical engineering from the University of Missouri. After a brief flirtation with teaching, he secured "temporary" employment with the merchandising giant Sears, Roebuck and Company. He remained with Sears thereafter, from April 1, 1912, up to World War II. During these decades, Nelson advanced from the chemical laboratory, becoming manager of the men's and boys' clothing department, merchandising assistant, general merchandise manager, vice president in charge of merchandising, and finally executive vice president and chairman of the executive committee. His subordinates described him as a good boss and a reasonable man. Though a perfectionist, who pursued information "like a dentist after an ailing tooth," he preferred the use of patience, tact, and diplomacy rather than brute force to get results.[93]

Because Nelson believed that government and business should work together, iron out differences, and sustain a true understanding of each other, he agreed to take a leave of absence from Sears, Roebuck and Company during 1934 to serve with the National Recovery Administration. He became an assistant to then–NRA Administrator Clay Williams, joining forces with Stettinius, Harriman, and other businessmen-bureaucrats. Four years later, in 1938, Nelson returned to Washington as chairman of the wage committee for the textile industry. At this point, the Fair Labor Standards Act had just been enacted, and he grappled with "the problem of raising wages above the 25 cent minimum."[94] Nelson's commitment to corporatist undertakings, and his liberal proclivities, increasingly attracted Roosevelt's attention.

European developments now played a decisive part in shaping Nelson's career. Up to mid-1939, he had been only "vaguely disturbed" by the predatory actions of totalitarian states.[95] War brought him back to government once more, this time for a prolonged stay. The Roosevelt administration seized on his retail experience and expertise, asking him to sign up with the Treasury Department as a procurement officer. In that capacity, he influenced government purchases of defense-related commodities. From there, Nelson became Coordinator of National Defense Purchases for NDAC and head of the Purchases Division, OPM.[96]

Nelson occupied a commanding position after August 1941. As SPAB's leader and an important OPM official, he united policy formulation and execution in his single person. Using power with uncommon restraint, he sought to minimize discord and maximize efficiency. Nelson calculated the overall size of the defense program, balanced the claims of the Armed Services and civilian industry for scarce resources, moved toward more extensive rationing of materials, and exhibited sufficient mastery over administrative detail to bring a measure of order out of untidiness. Though some contemporaries and historians judged him permissive in terms of exercising power, particularly in relation to dealings with the military during War Production Board days, his diplomatic temperament was a boon in the preparedness period.[97]

After considerable study, Nelson's Supply Priorities and Allocation Board arrived at a figure of $40 to $45 billion for total munitions production and construction during calendar year 1942.[98] Of this, $27 billion worth had already been scheduled. Roughly $6 billion more would go to ground Army munitions, $3.5 billion for aircraft, and the remainder to all other purposes.[99] Authorities expected that these expenditures would equip a four-million-man-plus army and provide for up to 45,000 tanks and 60,000 planes.[100] Since expected gross national product for 1942 was $90 billion, up to 50 percent of total U.S. output was slotted for defense.[101] A preparedness program of this size hardly amounted to "business as usual."

Nelson was strongly committed to a program of this magnitude. Indeed, he thought $50 billion obtainable with some massaging. Called to testify before the U.S. Senate Special Committee Investigating the National Defense Program, Nelson told his listeners that defense contracts ought to be larger and delivery dates should be moved forward. He insisted that this would force companies to use three or four shifts per day and to place heavier reliance on those subcontractors who possessed idle machine tools. Prior to Pearl Harbor, he advocated greater production of arms and munitions than the military itself. He took this advanced position, and stood his ground, despite strong opposition.[102]

Isolationists, proclaiming that the United States was still at peace, charged that excessive defense expenditures made it more likely that the nation would get caught up in war. Lend-lease, in particular, infuriated them because U.S. naval ships accompanying British merchant vessels might well be attacked by German submarines, making U.S. involvement in the war more likely. Senator Henrik Shipstead warned the Senate that lend-lease approval meant that the U.S. "will pay the bill with our money, our resources and the precious blood of American boys."[103] Senator Burton Wheeler described lend-lease as "the New Deal's triple 'A' foreign policy— it will plough under every fourth American boy."[104] Senator Gerald Nye, a long-time enemy of the corporate liberals, disliked OPM because it was another method Roosevelt had found to "govern through administrative proclamation," thereby bypassing Congress and normal constitutional processes.[105]

Certain industries and businessmen still had reservations about the type of program Nelson envisioned. Many automobile industry executives preferred civilian production and profits to conversion; some resented the steps that government had compelled them to take. The *Wall Street Journal* accepted the need for emergency defense appropriations but advocated a corresponding reduction of $2 billion per annum in non-defense expenditures such as public works and farm aid. Reductions of this type made an "inflation of disastrous proportions" less likely.[106] The *Financial and Commercial Chronicle* also wished to cut non-defense budget items, including farm relief, unemployment, and housing. Other businessmen thought overproduction a good possibility. Complaints about OPM "red tape" never completely vanished, and joblessness showed up in civilian industries (such as construction and refrigerators), which were denied high priority or received no priority at all.[107]

Nelson was undeterred by the criticism of isolationists and conservative or reactionary businessmen. He regretted priorities unemployment but justified it by noting that preparedness was "burdensome, but we cannot afford impairing bold action because of our reluctance to bear burdens."[108] He also disagreed with all-outer claims that many more billions of dollars should be devoted to military supply. Given American national income, he insisted, the defense program was about the right size. Economists active in preparedness, including May and ultimately Nathan, backed him up.[109]

Preservation of the essential civilian economy took the other 50 percent of GNP. Nelson made certain that core civilian industries received enough raw materials to keep functioning. He never deviated from the assumption that modern war depended on the foundation provided by numerous peacetime industries. To deprive them of necessary sustenance would be shortsighted and ultimately disastrous. For these reasons, he sent a stream of basic inputs to civilian producers while simultaneously supplying military manufacturers. Even after Pearl Harbor, when the military flip-flopped, demanding preposterously large amounts of ordnance when before it had not asked for enough, Nelson held firm.[110]

Materials allocation and the priorities system benefited from Nelson's attention. He perceived that priorities in and of themselves were not sufficient, and explained it this way: "A manufacturer can only make things out of physical materials. A priority rating doesn't entitle him to materials—it only fixes his place in the line. If he has an A-10 rating for a certain steel (or any other commodity), and all of it is taken by the A-4's, his ticket is obviously no good. To guarantee him his rightful share, you've got to ration—that is, divide what there is and say this much is for you and you and you and you."[111] Nelson's point was that priorities must be combined with rationing if scarce materials were to be used in the most effective manner possible.

This insight guided Nelson's actions, but first he put the bureaucracy of the OPM Priorities Division back on track. To help him out with paperwork, Nelson brought in three experts on forms and procedures from Sears, Roebuck and Company, his old employer.[112] They combined two forms, the application for priority rating (PD-1) and the notice of priority rating (PD-2), into one.[113] Other small but significant adjustments were implemented as well, resulting in a startling increase in efficiency: the maximum number of priorities applications processed in a day rose from 500 to 12,000![114] By the time the Sears men departed, the priorities backlog had disappeared, and all correspondence entering the Priorities Division left within 48 hours.[115] OPM Materials Division Director Bill Batt, who watched this transformation, expressed his admiration: "Those boys from Sears sure treat paper rough."[116]

Freed from the paperwork impasse, Nelson extended rationing. By October 1941, 35 materials, including aluminum, steel, and copper, were on a partial allocation basis, and many others followed.[117] More thoroughgoing rationing was just ahead. Nelson's emphasis on comprehensive rationing and balanced distribution foreshadowed Ferdinand Eberstadt's Controlled Materials Plan of 1942–1943, which resolved the chronic materials crunch.

In December 1941, the Office of Production Management underwent its third and final reorganization. A study finished on December 10 urged establishment of a single Commodities Division to "take over the activity, responsibility, and personnel of the industrial branches (presently) under the Purchases Division, Civilian Supply Division, and Materials Division."[118] Although Knudsen chose not to set up the Commodities Division, he achieved much the same effect by ordering commodity branches within the Civilian Supply and Materials Division to report directly to himself and Hillman, bypassing divisional directors. OPM therefore stepped away from the old functional pattern, which had hindered it from the beginning, toward centralized control of all industry branches. A system more like that employed by Baruch's War Industries Board emerged. This process culminated with the advent of the War Production Board's Bureau of Industry Branches in 1942.[119]

Three major reorganizations left their mark on the preparedness program. OPM as a whole became less unwieldy. For industry and trade organizations, it was now easier to find a government contact point, expediting their search for defense business. In the factories, machine tools were put into place, assembly-line techniques refined, and output stepped up. Nelson had made a decent start on rationing, though more work in that area was needed because of the shortage of key raw materials. The SPAB-OPM team, while clearly an institutional stopgap, more closely resembled WIB or WRA than NDAC, and it was functioning fairly well by the end of 1941.

Statistics support this contention. In 1940, total sales of turning, boring, grinding, milling, planing, and other machines amounted to $450 million.[120] In 1941, buoyed by Stettinius's priorities order, that figure approached $800 million.[121] In 1940, the Charlestown, Indiana, smokeless powder plant did not even exist. By July 1941, this plant was producing 300,000 pounds of smokeless powder every day, and it doubled that amount by year's end. Indeed, the Charlestown smokeless powder plant became the largest of its kind anywhere in the world by 1942. Slowed only slightly by the paucity of aluminum, fabricated materials like steel forgings, and skilled labor, aircraft output soared from just over 6,000 planes in 1940 to 18,000 in 1941.[122] Mass production and continuous-flow techniques in the airplane industry improved as well.[123] Even tank production registered impressive gains, jumping from virtually nothing in the summer of 1940 to almost 1,000 per month by the end of 1941.[124] Lend-lease, it should also be noted, contributed 11.5 percent of Britain's military equipment for 1941 and 29.1 percent of its food.[125] In aggregate terms, munitions output rose from $2.047 billion in the last six months of 1940 to $8.4 billion during 1941.[126] Additional contracts, amounting to billions of dollars, had already been placed for 1942–1943. Under SPAB-OPM, industrial mobilization far exceeded its 1940 pace, a mass production trajectory was assured, and relatively little time was wasted. Given the isolationist challenge and the official U.S. policy of neutrality, Roosevelt had pushed ahead as far as he dared.

The Japanese attack on Pearl Harbor ushered in a new reality. Some 2,400 servicemen were killed, the Pacific Fleet was crippled, and the United States was at war.[127] The American people wanted retribution. Isolationist strength instantly drained away to almost nothing. All-outers were freer to pursue the demise of fascism. Business and government shared in the general feeling of unity that swept the nation. Finally, the debate over the effectiveness or ineffectiveness of OPM meant little now: everyone knew that a new supreme defense agency would soon be forthcoming.

Business–government relations received a final boost from U.S. entry into World War II. The 1938–1939 Roosevelt administration business "appeasement" campaign, which offered corporate America good words and tax help, had signaled government's initial desire to conciliate business. General improvement in the national economy from 1939 on calmed both parties. Evidence that government and business had embarked on a cooperative course could be found in corporate liberal inclusion within the War Resources Board, the National Defense Advisory Commission, and the Office of Production Management. Corporate liberals, once in place, brought the state and firms throughout the national economy into closer contact with each other. Incentives such as five-year amortization and cost-plus contracts helped win over a larger and larger segment of the business community to government. A partnership was in the making.

As early as May 1941, six months before Pearl Harbor, *Fortune* reported on the increasing convergence between corporate executives and government leaders. More than 90 percent of businessmen polled endorsed a rearmament program at least as energetic as the one underway.[128] The vast majority saw "danger or disaster resulting from a Hitler victory. . . ."[129] When the Japanese smashed Pearl Harbor, only victory mattered.[130] Even *Nation's Business,* formerly a bitter foe of the Roosevelt government, urged cooperation. It repudiated whatever "finagling" businessmen engaged in during preparedness, convinced now that all industrialists and manufacturers "found their hearts in their jobs. . . ."[131] Direct U.S. engagement in World War II cemented the business–government partnership, a result that corporate liberals welcomed but wished had come under happier circumstances.

SPAB-OPM, of course, became expendable. Preparedness was one thing; war was another. The scale of military and industrial operations expanded dramatically after Pearl Harbor, and labored progress was simply not good enough anymore. Moreover, political conditions now permitted Roosevelt vast leeway to do what he deemed appropriate to defeat the Axis.

Nelson explained that the SPAB-OPM team was not "big enough or strong enough—or, perhaps, smart enough—to build for the global war which was upon us."[132] In January 1942, Roosevelt scrapped both agencies and established the War Production Board.[133]

The demise of the Office of Production Management should not obscure its central contribution. OPM, like the National Defense Advisory Commission before it, orchestrated industrial mobilization, seeing that the civilian government, military, and business worked together in the realm of economic defense. In the eleven months before Pearl Harbor, OPM was the chief coordinating and planning entity of the U.S. government; its presence permitted the state to make more effective use of public and private resources, thereby vastly expanding war-making capacity. OPM engaged in a special type of state building, defined by the worsening international crisis and by "emergency state" and "broker state" impulses. As a result of its efforts, American territory, American citizens, and American ideology were better protected from Axis barbarity than they would have been otherwise.

Stettinius, Knudsen, Nelson, and the other corporate liberals must not be forgotten either. They reintroduced the government and business after years of separation and hostility, then forged an alliance that allowed the U.S. to become Roosevelt's "arsenal of democracy." The U.S. military obtained the weapons it needed. U.S. companies, aided by the acumen of businessmen-bureaucrats, passed from the tooling-up stage to mass production of weapons with surprisingly little delay. When the United States declared war against Japan, on December 8, 1941, OPM had already laid the foundation for a gigantic output of arms and munitions. With formidable American help, the Allies immediately began to outproduce the Axis. A long step toward victory was assured, though military reversals in the Pacific and Russia temporarily hid this truth.

Epilogue

Corporate liberal thought changed dramatically from 1920 to 1941. During the New Era, corporate liberals espoused welfare capitalism. Private approaches to economic questions still predominated. A few corporate liberals, like Henry Dennison, did welcome Hooverian associationalism, but the contacts between business and government were infrequent and brief compared to the later period. The Great Depression forced corporate liberals to adjust course; increasingly, they forsook welfare capitalism and informal public–private linkages in favor of sustained periods of service within the federal government. Intelligent collaboration between big business and big government, for the purpose of economic renewal, became their new credo. European war provided an even better opportunity for the corporate liberals to advance their cooperative agenda, as they came to dominate the U.S. preparedness campaign. Edward Stettinius, William Knudsen, and Donald Nelson labored intensely to construct a national security apparatus up to the challenges posed by a world gone mad. The organizational edifice they built, though imperfect, facilitated industrial mobilization, pushing American industry to mass production of weapons by the time of the Japanese attack on Pearl Harbor. This development boosted the U.S. war effort considerably while helping to ensure big-business domination of public policy during the war years and beyond.

Corporate liberals depicted welfare capitalism as a way to counteract the few negative side effects of capitalism. Thus, company cafeterias served low-cost, nutritious meals that stretched a decent salary further. Group insurance paid sick or disabled workers; when a worker died, loved ones received life insurance payments. Unemployment insurance offered protection against layoffs, and so on. Most important, workers who received non-wage benefits were less likely to disrupt production by striking. Thus, welfare capitalism ultimately yielded stability and the best guarantee of sustainable prosperity possible in an uncertain world.

From this perspective, maintenance of economic prosperity was primarily a responsibility of private enterprise. Accordingly, corporate liberals concentrated their attention on their own firms. Throughout the 1920s, Dennison, Stettinius, Gerard Swope, Marion Folsom, and Averell Harriman focused on company-specific solutions to general economic maladies. Individual company policies were contrived to minimize swings of the business cycle, maximize employment, and ensure worker satisfaction. The workers themselves characterized welfare capitalism as paternalistic, and would have preferred wage increases anyway, but the American Federation of Labor was too weak to alter the existing state of affairs.

Corporate liberals, with the exception of Dennison and a few others like him, were not yet greatly interested in public service. Government might play a supporting role in the economy, supplying information and advice to industry or sponsoring an occasional conference, but should stop there. Associationalism of the type Hoover put forward from the Commerce Department was acceptable, but not coercion. Privatism, as they saw it, must prevail.

The performance of welfare capitalism depended heavily on the number of firms that embraced it. To exert a decisive macroeconomic effect, most industries and most firms needed to pick it up. Unfortunately, this never happened.

Dennison preached the virtues of welfare capitalism up to the early 1930s, in hopes of converting the skeptical. He thought "good management" essential to continued economic well-being.[1] Moderate and conservative businessman, however, did not want to pay for innovative, non-wage benefits for their employees. Dennison concluded that if 5 percent of the companies in a trade refused to implement welfare capitalistic programs, the system would not work, "and we could never manage even to get 5% interested, much less 95%."[2] Clearly, the vast majority of companies did not take welfare capitalism seriously, trade unionists and many among the rank-and-file deemed it condescending, and the Great Depression made a mockery of it.

The economic collapse of the 1930s devastated welfare capitalism. Small and medium-size companies with non-wage programs simply could not maintain them. Claims exhausted unemployment insurance funds, as at Dennison Manufacturing Company. Other programs fell victim to cost cutting. Welfare capitalism survived only in the largest firms. Worst of all, the welfare-capitalist vision of never-ending prosperity and progress was destroyed.

Associationalism did not work either. President Herbert Hoover watched glumly as one industry after another laid off workers, ignoring the admonitions of trade association groupings to maintain employment and wage rates. Joblessness mounted, family incomes fell, investment bottomed out, and associational structures and mechanisms could not halt this erosion. Hooverian associationalism simply was not powerful enough to hold off the contractionary forces that had been unleashed and was discredited.

Reassessment became a necessity. It was a painful process for the corporate liberals, who had to admit the failure of private and semiprivate prescriptions for the perpetuation of American economic vitality. Swope devoted considerable thought to a system of cartelization featuring industrial self-regulation with minimal federal supervision. Folsom edged toward involvement with government, first establishing limited contacts with the Rochester city government and then with New York State. The inadequacy of the Rochester unemployment plan of 1931, coupled with the increasing severity of the Depression, compelled him to give up associationalism and endorse more extensive ties with the federal establishment. Stettinius and Harriman eventually accepted government posts in Washington, DC. Dennison preferred to "work our way out in evolutionary fashion [rather] than to have revolutionary results tried out on us."[3] He believed a return to the old system of unfettered private enterprise, minus welfare capitalism, would result in "a worse tailspin than '32 ever thought of being. . . ."[4] Corporate liberals therefore joined the Roosevelt government as an alternative to irrelevance or disaster, thereby separating themselves even more from mainstream businessmen. Their transition from privatism through associationalism to a rather more intense public–private partnership complete, the era of "intelligent collaboration" had begun, and it would be prolonged.

Corporate liberalism, at root, accepted government supervision and regulation of the macroeconomy. Conservative and moderate businessmen could not stomach such a revolting prospect, but the corporate liberals saw no other viable option under prevailing economic and political conditions. "Pragmatic realists," they gave in to the inevitable, hoping to turn it to their advantage over time. Over the course of the next dozen years, only a handful of enlightened businessmen would remain committed to this philosophy.

Corporate liberals accepted positions in a variety of New Deal agencies. They started with the National Recovery Administration and the Business Advisory Council. At one time or another, Swope, Dennison, Folsom, Harriman, and others filled these bodies.[5] Corporate liberals eventually took up posts in social security agencies, the Department of Commerce proper, the Treasury Department, and other organs of government. Although NRA made little mark, and BAC was often only of marginal utility, the businessmen-bureaucrats shaped social security to their liking. They understood the Social Security Act at least as much in terms of business stabilization as for the benefits conferred upon unemployed workers and retirees.

Intelligent collaboration between Roosevelt and Stettinius, Harriman, and Swope was very much in evidence, even as business–government antipathy reached its height from 1935 to 1938. Not surprisingly, Harriman, John W. Hanes, Robert Wood, and other corporate liberals enthusiastically participated in the Roosevelt administration business recovery and appeasement drive of 1938–1939. This campaign led to the abolition of the undistributed-profits tax and granted business social security tax relief, thereby tempering business–government hostility and hinting at better days to come.

FDR acted differently, too. He moved away from the type of harsh criticism he had leveled at particular businessmen in 1936. His antibusiness rhetoric softened and gradually disappeared. By 1938–1939, when he launched the business appeasement campaign, the Roosevelt administration offered the business world both good words and real concessions. It also found more and more places in government for liberal and moderate businessmen. Business, not labor, came to the forefront in the corporatist arrangements of the late 1930s.

Germany's thrust into Poland in September 1939 provoked British and French declarations of war, further enlarging the corporate liberal role in the U.S. government. Roosevelt wanted to assist the democracies, but confronted formidable opposition to U.S. involvement. Isolationists, including a strong isolationist bloc in Congress, stood in his way. FDR moved cautiously to circumvent them. In November he gained repeal of the Neutrality Act; "cash and carry" followed. The Roosevelt administration, with valuable corporate liberal assistance, supplied Britain and France with arms and munitions in their fight against the Third Reich.

Roosevelt had found an unlikely ally in the business community. Corporate liberals like Stettinius and Harriman, sure that Hitler must be vanquished, backed administration foreign policy from the start. Knudsen, Budd, Nelson, Batt, Folsom, and others enlisted slightly later. As time passed, conservative businessmen joined the rearmament effort. Corporate liberal diplomacy had something to do with it; profits and patriotism proved a greater incentive. FDR curried the favor of business by offering quick amortization, other tax breaks, and lucrative contracts. He welcomed whatever business support he could get in his ongoing struggle to outmaneuver non-interventionists and confront Axis power.

FDR and the corporate liberals not only agreed on the danger posed by Nazi Germany and on incentives for business, they were united by their common desire to move carefully on industrial mobilization. The corporate liberal inclination to play it safe, on economic and ideological grounds, meshed nicely with Roosevelt's political sensibilities when confronted by isolationism. Corporate liberals, recalling World War I and the Great Depression, wished to avoid the evils of overproduction and inflation. Lingering mistrust between the mainstream business community and the New Deal administration also recommended caution. Roosevelt did not wish to hurry defense preparedness, either, what with isolationists such as Wheeler, Nye, and Johnson lurking. Careful, controlled expansion of defense plant and output was expedient for both FDR and the corporate liberals.

The president also knew that the federal government was not well suited to perform the preparedness function. The state needed business plant, equipment, and expertise in order to keep Britain armed and to mobilize the U.S. economy properly. Industrial mobilization required the addition of corporate resources to federal stock so as to bolster state capacity. Even before that, the overall pattern of state building had to be determined.

Crisis abroad generated organizational ferment and controversy at home. New Dealers Ickes, Perkins, Wallace, Corcoran, and Arnold, among others, argued that industrial mobilization should be carried out by existing government agencies. Corporate liberals and military men insisted on creation of temporary emergency bodies to do the work. Roosevelt chose the latter course, ultimately rejecting what social scientist Brian Waddell has called the New Deal civilian-state.[6] Instead, FDR relied on one defense preparedness agency after another. Back in August 1939, Stettinius had been appointed chairman of the War Resources Board, with Wood and Gifford as members. In May 1940, the National Defense Advisory Commission reappeared. Knudsen, Harriman, Folsom, Batt, Biggers, and Nelson joined Stettinius. In January 1941, the Office of Production Management materialized. Roosevelt created these bodies in order to upgrade U.S. national security. He put corporate liberals in the top spots because they were already friendly toward him and could be counted on to placate those elements within the business community that remained disgruntled because of earlier New Deal economic and social policies. With the corporate liberals as expert advisers and mediators, industrial mobilization proceeded.

The War Resources Board finished its work late in 1939. Stettinius, Wood, and Gifford heartily endorsed the military blueprint for industrial mobilization. They accepted the predominant features of the various industrial mobilization plans authored during the 1930s, including establishment of a War Resources Administration under emergency conditions, accompanied subsequently by a commodity committee–war service committee interlock. Although FDR pigeonholed the final War Resources Board report, he did not reject the basic premise that business–government cooperation should underlie any industrial mobilization effort.

Rather than place reliance entirely on a state-run munitions complex, a market-driven system, or even an augmented New Deal civilian state, Roosevelt opted for a public–private model reminiscent of both the World War I War Industries Board and the National Recovery Administration. A state-run munitions complex of sorts existed in the United States, but it was too tiny to be of any great use by itself. More important, dramatic expansion of government arsenals conjured up visions of an overgreat state, which might well become oppressive. Nationalization of defense industries also ran counter to the hallowed tradition of free enterprise; socialism was not the answer. A market-driven system to meet defense needs did not seem feasible either, as it was likely to be inadequate. Business was still more attuned to economic recovery in 1939–1940 than to the requirements of the military. The automobile industry, for example, preferred to produce cars rather than tanks. Construction of a New Deal state capable of upholding national security proved impractical (even if it was doable), as a result of the unswerving opposition of the business community, the military, and conservative forces both inside and outside of Congress. The opposition was too strong for Roosevelt to overcome easily, and the risk of losing private production facilities was too great. To the grave disappointment and sorrow of New Dealers, FDR abandoned the fight for overt New Deal control over the rapidly evolving national security apparatus. A public–private approach, featuring moderate federal regulation of industrial mobilization for the possibility of war, seemed best precisely because it minimized statist coercion while promoting gradual but vital growth of U.S. defense production. Roosevelt depended heavily on corporate liberal diplomacy and on voluntary compliance of private enterprise to fuse the small federal arsenal with private defense plant.

Public–private cooperation, of course, implies some degree of government regulation of industry. The degree of regulation might be small or great; indeed, there exists a fairly wide range of possible outcomes. Given that this was the case for the period from 1939 to 1941, Roosevelt might have brought greater pressure to bear against large, oligopolistic companies as a way to accelerate defense production. He might also have pushed harder to reduce corporate profits from defense contracts, to spread out military work to smaller firms located in areas of lingering unemployment, and to help labor. FDR made a conscious decision not to move forward more vigorously on these matters because business–government harmony and victory over the totalitarian powers was more important in the short run than saving some money or fostering social reform.

At a time of worldwide crisis and uncertainty at home, Roosevelt played it safe. The state wanted greater and greater defense production from industry, especially from established firms, but feared the consequences of employing coercion and largely refrained from it. With so much at stake, cutting it close on business profit margins made little sense. Spreading out defense contracts among small companies, which might or might not be up to the production task, seemed too risky, and the oligopolistic complexion of the U.S. economy—already seventy years or so in the making—was beyond effective challenge. Roosevelt made no strenuous effort either to put labor councils on a coequal footing with management councils. Defense preparedness and the eventual demise of the Axis, Roosevelt thought, demanded caution until victory was assured.

The National Defense Advisory Commission pushed industrial mobilization from the planning stage to actual implementation. NDAC helped amass raw materials; saw to it that more plant and equipment were made available for defense production; directed educational orders to willing firms; and ratified large arms contracts that extended far into the future. Even more significant, Knudsen, Stettinius, and Nelson championed five-year amortization and other economic incentives for business that would spur defense output. Their efforts, before the Administration and Congress, resulted in passage of the Second Revenue Act of November 1940. This legislation created a legal and economic order conducive to tremendous expansion of defense industries, especially machine tools, tanks, airplanes, and ships.

The Office of Production Management and the Supply Priorities and Allocation Board followed NDAC. They continued stockpiling efforts; oversaw an increasingly large number of defense factories; saw to it that bulk orders went to industry; balanced civilian, military, and lend-lease demands; and set the magnitude of the evolving defense program. The demise of the 1940 Reuther plan for rapid conversion of idle automobile plant to production of military aircraft illustrates both the measured pace of mobilization and business control over the process. Labor had been effectively marginalized; not even the corporate liberals advocated putting labor on par with business in the boardroom or the war room. Nevertheless, the SPAB-OPM combination moved the United States from the tooling-up stage to the beginnings of genuine mass production.

Even at this stage, problems remained. An adequate rationing system for scarce raw materials did not yet exist, though Nelson was getting close to a solution. Additional curtailment of non-essential civilian industry was needed. More factory space was a must after the attack on Pearl Harbor. Most important, Roosevelt had not yet decided on the total amount of defense production that would be required should war come. For that reason, the corporate liberals still lacked a final arms and munitions target.

The groundwork, however, had been laid. By December 7, 1941, the structure of the American national security state was more rational and its ability to mobilize the economy greater. Bureaucratic incapacity was not the problem it had been. Industrial inexperience was disappearing. The United States possessed an abundance of weapons that it had lacked in 1939. A military-bureaucratic regime guided by a surprisingly small number of corporate liberals had been constructed in less than two and a half years, insuring that the powerful U.S. economy could be brought to bear against the Axis with crushing force.[7]

By this juncture, the United States was actively engaged in the fight. Roosevelt responded by replacing the SPAB-OPM duo with the War Production Board (WPB) during January 1942. The WPB exercised "general responsibility" over the economy.[8] FDR named Nelson WPB chairman, transferring him from SPAB to the new office.

Nelson's authority was much greater than it had been. He received congressional authorization to speed curtailment and set priorities.[9] His stature was such that military contracting and purchasing were within his reach.[10] Indeed, almost no area of economic activity was outside his purview.

Nelson used his power with restraint, but effectively enough. Raw materials edicts helped accumulate additional rubber, tin, scrap iron, and other vital inputs.[11] In February 1942, Nelson ordered the automobile industry not to build any more civilian passenger cars "for the duration" of the war.[12] This move forced Detroit to construct more planes and military vehicles such as jeeps and half-tracks. The WPB banned production of more than 400 other civilian products, including home appliances, lawn mowers, home oil burners, bird cages, and cocktail shakers.[13] Late in 1942, under Nelson's direction, the WPB's Ferdinand Eberstadt developed the Controlled Materials Plan. It gave shares of aluminum, steel, and copper to major claimants such as the Army, Navy, and Maritime Commission. They got only so much and no more, distributing it to prime contractors as they saw fit. Prime contractors then distributed available materials to subcontractors. This method ended the raw materials free-for-all and introduced order into the equation.[14]

Unfortunately, Nelson clashed with the War Department and the military brass. Perhaps he was too permissive here. Though he might have taken control of wartime contracting and purchasing, he decided against it. Rather than cause unnecessary delay, he left the Army and Navy in charge. Assistant Secretary of War Robert P. Patterson and General Brehon Somervell, head of Army Services of Supply, pegged Nelson as a weakling who was too solicitous of the civilian economy and not willing enough to make sacrifices for the sake of military advantage.[15] For his part, Nelson viewed Patterson and Somervell as economic neophytes who did not understand that the U.S. economy was incapable of infinite production.

These views were at the heart of the feasibility dispute of 1942–1943. The War Department demanded a military supply program of $115 billion for 1943.[16] Nelson, Batt, and other corporate liberals knew this was out of the question. Such an astronomic production figure threatened the economy with total breakdown, while it would plunge the standard of living of the American people to a level 40 percent below that of 1932.[17] Even more to the point, a catastrophic economic collapse of the type implied here would imperil the entire war effort—the flow of American weapons to the U.S. military and the Allies could stop, with terrifying results. Nelson therefore stood his ground; built an alliance with New Dealers such as Henderson, Harry Hopkins, and Henry Wallace; and succeeded in arranging a sane compromise with Patterson and Somervell. The total military supply program for 1943 was pared down by $35 billion, to $80 billion overall.[18] The U.S. economy thus provided both guns and butter, but only so much of each, and the mix helped achieve final victory over the Axis.

Increasing friction between the War Production Board and the military did disturb Roosevelt. In October 1942, he established the Office of War Mobilization (OWM), under former South Carolina Senator James F. Byrnes, to arbitrate between the WPB and the Armed Services. Byrnes became a "super-umpire," who made the tough calls before feuds reached the point where they brought either adverse publicity or real damage to the industrial mobilization effort.[19] Despite doing valuable work, Nelson had been demoted, although he wielded considerable influence until he finally left the WPB.[20]

Events after his demotion showed that Nelson and the corporate liberals under him could still make a major contribution to the war effort. In the summer of 1943, another dispute broke out between the War Department and the emergency wartime agencies. The WPB and the War Manpower Commission (WMC) insisted that the U.S. Army discharge a certain number of soldiers with mining experience for immediate employment in the copper mines out West, but Patterson refused to go along. Nelson and WMC's Paul McNutt noted that a shortage of copper, brought on by the draft and the resulting lack of experienced labor, prevented the manufacture of .30 caliber ammunition for semiautomatic weapons and machine guns. In their estimation, the urgent need for this ammunition more than justified the release of a comparatively small number of soldiers. Patterson, however, stood squarely and resolutely in the way. Somehow or other, he could not see that the production of eight billion rounds of .30 caliber ammunition outweighed the release of fewer than 5,000 troops from an army of many millions. The whole matter had to be referred to Jimmy Byrnes. Byrnes sided with Nelson and McNutt over Patterson, and the soldier-miners were reallocated from the Army to the copper mines. Production of the requisite .30 caliber ammunition was achieved; U.S. troops received their "bullets" and were much better off for it.[21]

The feasibility dispute and the .30 caliber ammunition controversy once again illustrate the stubborn, unbending nature of much of Nelson's opposition during the war and the fact that the military-industrial alliance lacked homogeneity. Secretary of War Henry Stimson, Undersecretary Patterson, and Lieutenant General Somervell were autocrats, who preferred to plow straight through obstacles when possible. They often interpreted Nelson's conciliatory manner as a sign of weakness, even when that did not necessarily follow. Their narrow focus on Army manpower and supply—indeed, it amounted to myopia—necessarily brought them into occasional conflict with Nelson, whose responsibilities and vision were much broader and projected further into the future.

Recent historical scholarship has not been flattering to the corporate liberals or to the mobilization agencies they ran. Stettinius, Knudsen, and Nelson emerge as men with good intentions who tried their best but were neither smart enough nor tough enough to convert the economy to a wartime footing in an effective manner. The military, supposedly ran roughshod over them, nullifying their desire to assist small business and labor.[22] NDAC and OPM have been depicted as puny, ineffectual bodies. The WPB, for its part, averted outright disaster but was never fully in control and just barely muddled through. Nelson fares poorly in comparison to World

War I industrial czar Bernard Baruch, and WPB comes out in second place behind the War Industries Board.

This interpretation is too harsh. The World War II mobilization experience was of much greater magnitude than mobilization for World War I, making Nelson's job harder than Baruch's. Moreover, U.S. soldiers of the Great War routinely fought the Hun with French and British guns, ammunition, artillery pieces, and tanks. A thoroughgoing mobilization of U.S. industry was never completed during World War I. In World War II, of course, U.S. troops carried their own arms, and American-made weapons also showed up in British, Russian, and Chinese hands. The U.S. economy was more completely mobilized for total war than ever before or since. Nelson and his assistants finished the job, whereas Baruch never had to.

We should not suppose, either, that the "arsenal of democracy" resulted simply from the efforts of the weak American state or from the individual exertions of thousands of American firms scattered across a vast continent. In 1939, the federal government lacked the bureaucratic capacity to wage a modern war or even the connections necessary to plug into private plant and equipment. Capitalists objected to the Roosevelt administration's New Deal policies and stood apart from the state. Throughout 1940, CEOs preferred taking advantage of a reviving civilian economy to procurement of defense-related orders.

Only the corporate liberals could bridge the divide between the state and business. The corporate liberals helped bind together the two entities and establish a public–private bureaucracy capable of carrying out all vital wartime functions. In the process, they overcame a daunting number of impediments: old animosities between the New Deal and business; uncertainty regarding conversion to defense production; FDR's messy administrative proclivities (i.e., creation of too many defense-related agencies during the preparedness period), a practice the corporate liberals surely would not have tolerated at their own firms; and the absence of a suitable aggregate production goal for so long. Given the many constraints they faced, the performance of the corporate liberals and their agencies looks considerably better than the standard interpretation would allow.[23]

Rather than proceeding in a sluggish manner, the United States' corporate liberals prepared for war relatively quickly. In the two-year-plus interval from August 1939 to December 1941, they made up for more than twenty years of military and industrial neglect. When the Japanese struck Pearl Harbor, the infrastructure and mechanisms for mass production of weapons were already in place. A frenetic, haphazard, but ultimately effective period of industrial mobilization lay behind the United States; only regulation and fine-tuning of the military-industrial complex, and more mass production, lay ahead.

Statistics tell the story, as do the words of world leaders. From 1941 to mid-1945, U.S. factories churned out 3.3 million rifles, 41 billion rounds of ammunition, 2.6 million machine guns, 100,000 tanks, 79,125 landing craft, 300,000 airplanes, and so many other articles of war that space does not permit their recounting.[24] Preparedness ensured truly massive production of weapons only one year after Pearl Harbor, by which time "the nation was producing more than all its enemies combined."[25] During 1944, the last full year of World War II, roughly "60 percent of all the combat munitions of the Allies . . . were produced in the United States."[26] Lend-lease to Great Britain alone "saved [that country] from something like disaster." Roosevelt, as we saw in the introduction, praised U.S. businessmen for their mighty contribution. Soviet premier Joseph Stalin agreed, concluding that the war could not have been won without the "nation of machines."[27]

U.S. industrial mobilization might have been accomplished without the corporate liberals. Nevertheless, the task would have been far harder and would have entailed a radical departure from tradition. More friction between the New Deal and business, not less, would have been the result, with longer production delays. Sweeping changes in the organization of our economy and political system, though less likely, might have occurred.

Nelson himself once said that the U.S. state could become a manufacturer and make its own weapons. The question in his mind was whether that approach would be better or worse than public–private cooperation, and what effect this course might ultimately have on the American way of life. He concluded that government manufacturing would be the "more laborious way" of carrying out mobilization. Greater inefficiency and delay must surely result. Even worse, a 100 percent state-run munitions operation threatened to transform American capitalism into "fascist industry," and that, in turn, imperiled "democracy in government." With the European war on, Nelson, other corporate liberals, and politicians such as President Roosevelt and Senator Harry S Truman thought it preferable to fashion a truly effective alliance between the state and private enterprise.[28] When this feat was accomplished by the end of 1941, the United States was able to join its awesome industrial might with the manpower of other Allied nations. In this way, World War II was not only won but shortened, Western civilization survived Hitler's barbarity, and countless lives were saved. The corporate liberals deserve a sizable part of the credit for this outcome; they most assuredly took their reward.

The business–government partnership, which had been sealed under wartime pressure, grew stronger after 1945. Retention of the military-industrial complex brought large corporations big profits while undergirding and sustaining postwar economic prosperity. Tax cuts favored corporate America up through the early 1960s. Until the advent of President Lyndon Johnson's Great Society in the mid-1960s, social spending was restrained and was managed in a way compatible with corporate liberal sensibilities. Organized labor, handicapped by the narrowly focused brand of corporatism that emerged out of World War II, could not escape its subordinate position. In 1945–1946, labor leaders pushed for full employment while corporate liberals advocated "maximum" employment. The Employment Act of 1946 contained the watered-down version. The Office of Price Administration, which once represented the hopes of New Deal economists for establishment of a high-wage, low-price economy beneficial to workers and consumers, died out later in 1946. The OPA went down because it could not force meat producers to send their product to market—meanwhile, consumers could not get beef, and black market prices soared. Once the Truman administration phased out the OPA, the meat producer boycott ended.[29] A more obvious loss for labor and trade unionism occurred in 1947 with passage of the ultraconservative Taft-Hartley Act. Whether corporate liberals or more reactionary business forces prevailed, labor lost out, and the general pro-business trend in politics and public policy became more and more obvious.

For better or worse, the corporate liberals ensured that things would happen this way. Once the alternatives of a state-run or a market-driven mobilization were rejected, public–private planning went forward. This type of hybrid planning continued after the war as well. Highly decentralized in nature, featuring a retreat from New Deal liberalism, a minimal role for labor and consumers, a cozier relationship with Washington politicians, and an openly solicitous military establishment, this approach gave big business the supportive environment it needed to achieve most of its specific goals.

Corporate liberals celebrated this outcome. Central planning threatened business autonomy and managerial prerogatives. Only wartime conditions justified the WPB, the OWM, the OPM, and the other bodies. With victory in hand, they were no longer needed, and were liquidated so as to protect corporate capitalism and its beneficiaries, the American people, from unwarranted government power and the excesses it could bring.

Corporate liberals preferred decentralized planning, relying on quasi-public and quasi-private bodies to reach their economic objectives. The Business Advisory Council and the Committee for Economic Development (CED) were peopled by corporate liberals, who pursued goals such as a high national income, maximum production and employment, economic growth, and anti-communism. Folsom, a CED founder, made it clear that business planning of this sort, featuring loose cooperation between industrialists, trade associations, and federal authorities, should take the place of central planning. Batt, while still vice chairman of the War Production Board, had noted that the American people did not like "controls that are maintained merely for the power of controlling." He asked that wartime price controls and other measures be eliminated, and they were removed.[30] Biggers considered friendly interaction between business and government essential, and antagonism counterproductive, but warned that in many parts of the world "the state is supreme and absolute, imposing its rule upon its subjects without their consent."[31] He did not want that here. Walter D. Fuller, another prominent CED member, asked for full elaboration of the BAC-CED concept, noting that "postwar planning either is going to be done by us, or it will be done for us."[32] Although wartime agencies such as WPB and OWM disappeared quickly after the war's end, other less visible but significant linkages between business and government remained.

Folsom, Batt, Biggers, Fuller, and the other corporate liberals need not have worried about the overgreat state. Elected officials and civil servants cooperated with the Committee for Economic Development, the Business Council, the Ad Council, and other business groups. Government chose to regulate the capitalist economy but not necessarily capitalist institutions. Compensatory fiscal and monetary policy allowed the federal government to manipulate economic aggregates without encroaching unduly on the autonomy of corporations and trade associations. Within this framework, business retained substantial independence, while labor continued at a disadvantage. The corporate liberal vision for the future, featuring de facto business planning and a pro-business public policy, carried the day and is still in vogue. Given the innate conservatism of present-day American politics, this pattern of affairs is not likely to change anytime soon.

Notes

Introduction

1. Left-wing scholars were the first to use the term "corporate liberalism." See Martin J. Sklar, "Woodrow Wilson and the Political Economy of Modern United States Liberalism," *Studies on the Left* 1 (1960): 17–47; James Weinstein, *The Corporate Ideal in the Liberal State, 1900–1918* (Boston: Beacon Press, 1968); and Ronald Radosh and Murray N. Rothbard, eds., *A New History of Leviathan: Essays on the Rise of the American Corporate State* (New York: E. P. Dutton, 1972). William Appleman Williams's introduction to *A New History of Leviathan* (pp. 1–6) is particularly revealing. Three more worthwhile studies are G. William Domhoff, *The Power Elite and the State* (New York: Aldine de Gruyter, 1990), esp. pp. 33–39; Brian Waddell, *The War Against the New Deal* (DeKalb: Northern Illinois University Press, 2001); and Howell John Harris, *The Right to Manage* (Madison: University of Wisconsin Press, 1982). See, in particular, Waddell, pp. 15–16, and Harris, p. 136. Organizational historians and others have also examined corporate liberalism. See Ellis W. Hawley, "The Discovery and Study of a 'Corporate Liberalism,'" *Business History Review* 52 (Autumn 1978): 311; Kim McQuaid, "Corporate Liberalism in the American Business Community, 1920–1940," *Business History Review* 52 (Autumn 1978): 342–43; and Gerald Berk, "Corporate Liberalism Reconsidered: A Review Essay," *Journal of Policy History* 3, no. 1 (1991): 71. Jacob S. Hacker and Paul Pierson, "Business Power and Social Policy: Employers and the Formation of the American Welfare State," *Politics and Society* 30 (June 2002): 277–325, is also worth consulting.

2. Robert M. Collins's *The Business Response to Keynes, 1929–1964* (New York: Columbia University Press, 1981) first alerted me to the flexibility of the corporate liberals. See, for example, p. ix.

3. A significant literature on welfare capitalism exists. See David Brody, "The Rise and Decline of Welfare Capitalism," in John Braeman, Robert H. Bremner, and David Brody, eds., *Change and Continuity in Twentieth Century America: The 1920s* (Columbus: Ohio State University Press, 1968), pp. 147–78; Stuart D. Brandes, *American Welfare Capitalism, 1880–1940* (Chicago: University of Chicago Press, 1976), pp. 5–6; Edward Berkowitz and Kim McQuaid, *Creating the Welfare State: The Political Economy of Twentieth-Century Reform* (New York: Praeger, 1980), pp. 1–24; and Stuart Bruchey, *Enterprise: The Dynamic Economy of a Free People* (Cambridge, MA: Harvard University Press,

1990), p. 417. A chapter on employers' welfare capitalist strategies in a single city can be found in Lizabeth Cohen,' *Making a New Deal: Industrial Workers in Chicago, 1919–1939* (Cambridge: Cambridge University Press, 1990). A fine historiographical essay, though quite critical of welfare capitalism and the employers' part in it, is H. M. Gitelman, "Welfare Capitalism Reconsidered," *Labor History* 33 (1992): 5–31. The best of the most recent works on welfare capitalism are Andrea Tone, *The Business of Benevolence: Industrial Paternalism in Progressive America* (Ithaca, NY: Cornell University Press, 1997), and Sanford M. Jacoby, *Modern Manors: Welfare Capitalism Since the New Deal* (Princeton, NJ: Princeton University Press, 1997).

4. See, for example, Guy Alchon, *The Invisible Hand of Planning: Capitalism, Social Science, and the State in the 1920s* (Princeton, NJ: Princeton University Press, 1985), p. 5. Also helpful is Kim McQuaid, *Big Business and Presidential Power: From FDR to Reagan* (New York: William Morrow, 1982), p. 23.

5. Ellis Hawley's *The Great War and the Search for a Modern Order: A History of the American People and Their Institutions, 1917–1933* (New York: St. Martin's Press, 1979) contains a discussion of "anti-Hooverian alternatives." See pp. 199–202.

6. Ibid.

7. Many authors make this point. See, for example, Irving Bernstein, *The Lean Years* (Boston: Houghton Mifflin, 1960), p. 187, and Brandes, *American Welfare Capitalism,* preface through p. 7.

8. Kim McQuaid, "Henry S. Dennison and the 'Science' of Industrial Reform, 1900–1950," *American Journal of Economics and Sociology* 36 (January 1977): 88–89; Brody, "The Rise and Decline of Welfare Capitalism," pp. 171–78.

9. David M. Kennedy, *Freedom from Fear: The American People in Depression and War, 1929–1945* (New York: Oxford University Press, 1999), p. 180; Hawley, *The Great War and the Search for a Modern Order,* pp. 184–86; Alchon, *The Invisible Hand of Planning,* p. 152.

10. I borrow the phrase "intelligent collaboration" from McQuaid, "Corporate Liberalism in the American Business Community, 1920–1940," p. 342.

11. Theda Skocpol, "Bringing the State Back In: Strategies of Analysis in Current Research," in Peter Evans, Dietrich Rueschemeyer, and Theda Skocpol, eds., *Bringing the State Back In* (Cambridge: Cambridge University Press, 1985), p. 12; Theda Skocpol, "A Society without a 'State'? Political Organization, Social Conflict, and Welfare Provision in the United States," *Journal of Public Policy* 7 (October–December 1987): 349–71; Stephen Skowronek, *Building a New American State: The Expansion of National Administrative Capacities, 1877–1920* (Cambridge: Cambridge University Press, 1982), esp. pp. 3–16, 207–8, 287–90; and Alan Brinkley, "The New Deal and the Idea of the State," in Steve Fraser and Gary Gerstle, eds., *The Rise and Fall of the New Deal Order, 1930–1980* (Princeton, NJ: Princeton University Press, 1989), p. 102. Other significant works on the state, and state building, include Ellis W. Hawley, "The New Deal State and the Anti-Bureaucratic Tradition," in Robert Eden, ed., *The New Deal and Its Legacy: Critique and Reappraisal* (Westport, CT: Greenwood Press, 1989); Roger Benjamin and Stephen L. Elkin, eds., *The Democratic State* (Lawrence: University

Press of Kansas, 1985); and Barry D. Karl, *The Uneasy State* (Chicago: University of Chicago Press, 1983). Finally, Robert Wiebe's seminal work (*The Search for Order, 1877–1920,* New York, 1967) should not be omitted, as it has influenced much of this scholarship in one way or another.

12. Hawley, "The New Deal State and the Anti-Bureaucratic Tradition," pp. 77–92. See esp. pp. 80–81.

13. Unflattering assessments of the corporate liberals and their agencies can be found in many books. See, for example, I. F. Stone, *Business As Usual* (New York: Modern Age, 1941); Bruce Catton, *The War Lords of Washington* (New York: Harcourt, Brace, 1948); and Eliot Janeway, *The Struggle for Survival* (New Haven: Yale University Press, 1951). More recent accounts that also view the corporate liberals negatively include Robert C. Perez and Edward F. Willett, *The Will to Win: A Biography of Ferdinand Eberstadt* (New York: Greenwood Press, 1989), esp. p. 3; and Keith E. Eiler, *Mobilizing America* (Ithaca, NY: Cornell University Press, 1997), esp. pp. 80–96.

14. *New York Times,* January 4, 1936, p. 8; June 28, 1936, p. 25. See also George Wolfskill, *The Revolt of the Conservatives: A History of the American Liberty League, 1934–1940* (Boston: Houghton Mifflin, 1962) pp. 121, 146–49.

15. *New York Times,* January 4, 1936, p. 8.

16. *Nation's Business,* August 1936, p. 7.

17. Franklin D. Roosevelt to Averell Harriman, January 19, 1940, BAPC File Folder (1940–1943), Box 9, Official File (Department of Commerce), Franklin D. Roosevelt Papers, Franklin D. Roosevelt Library, Hyde Park, New York.

18. Donald M. Nelson, *Arsenal of Democracy: The Story of American War Production* (New York: Harcourt, Brace, 1946), p. 431.

19. Ibid.

Chapter One

1. Andrea Tone, *The Business of Benevolence: Industrial Paternalism in Progressive America* (Ithaca, NY: Cornell University Press, 1997), p. 14.

2. *National Cyclopaedia of American Biography,* Vol. 45, 1962, p. 14; David Loth, *Swope of G.E.* (New York: Simon and Schuster, 1958), p. 112.

3. Loth, *Swope of G.E.,* p. 66.

4. *National Cyclopaedia of American Biography,* Vol. 45, pp. 14–15.

5. *American National Biography,* Vol. 7, 1999, pp. 248–51; *Business Leader Profiles for Students,* 1999, pp. 233–35; Blake McKelvey, "A Semi-Centennial Review of Family Service of Rochester, Inc.," *Rochester History,* Vol. 23, no. 2 (April 1961): 5; *National Cyclopaedia of American Biography,* Current Vol. 1 (1953–1959), 1960, p. 170; Edward Berkowitz and Kim McQuaid, "Businessman and Bureaucrat: The Evolution of the American Social Welfare System, 1900–1940," *Journal of Economic History* 38 (March 1978): 128.

6. M. B. Folsom, "Wage Dividend Plan and Industrial Relations Program of Eastman Kodak Company," November 21, 1938, *Speeches,* Vol. 2 (Tab 27), pp. 8–9, Marion B. Folsom Papers, University of Rochester Library, Rochester, New York.

7. Eastman Kodak Unemployment Benefit Plan Proposal, p. 1, January 13, 1927, File Folder 2, Box 39, Folsom Papers; *Saturday Evening Post,* December 3, 1955, p. 134; Berkowitz and McQuaid, "Businessman and Bureaucrat," p. 128.

8. "Responsibility of the Individual Community toward the Unemployment Problem," February 27, 1931, *Speeches,* Volume I (Tab 12), Folsom Papers, p. 16.

9. Larry I. Bland, *W. Averell Harriman: Businessman and Diplomat, 1891–1945* (Ann Arbor, MI: University Microfilms, 1972), p. 20.

10. *Time,* August 4, 1986, p. 28; Bland, *W. Averell Harriman,* p. 22; Maury Klein, *Union Pacific: The Rebirth, 1894–1969* (Garden City, New York: Doubleday, 1987), p. 378. For greater detail, see Rudy Abramson, *Spanning the Century: The Life of W. Averell Harriman, 1891–1986* (New York: William Morrow, 1992), pp. 64–90. Abramson is a good source on Harriman's whole life.

11. Report of the Twenty-First Meeting of the Union Pacific Retired Employees Association, speech by G. O. Brophy, June 4, 1936, Union Pacific, Retired Employees Association 1935–1941 File Folder, Box 669, W. Averell Harriman Papers, Library of Congress, Washington, DC, p. 12.

12. Ibid.

13. Ibid.

14. Edward R. Stettinius Jr.'s University of Virginia Commencement Address, June 15, 1937, Bound Vol. 21, Edward R. Stettinius Jr. Papers, University of Virginia Library, Charlottesville, Virginia.

15. Henry S. Dennison, *Ethics and Modern Business* (Boston: Houghton Mifflin, 1932), p. 5.

16. *National Cyclopaedia of American Biography,* Vol. 40, 1955, pp. 52–53; Kim McQuaid, "Henry S. Dennison and the 'Science' of Industrial Reform, 1900–1950," *American Journal of Economics and Sociology* 36 (January 1977): 80.

17. McQuaid, "Henry S. Dennison and the 'Science' of Industrial Reform," p. 80.

18. *System, the Magazine of Business,* June 1926, p. 796.

19. Ibid.

20. *National Cyclopaedia,* Vol. 40, p. 53.

21. Guy Alchon, *The Invisible Hand of Planning: Capitalism, Social Science, and the State in the 1920s* (Princeton, NJ: Princeton University Press, 1985), pp. 77–78.

22. Ibid., pp. 71–76; Ellis W. Hawley, *The Great War and the Search for a Modern Order: A History of the American People and Their Institutions, 1917–1933* (New York: St. Martin's Press, 1979), pp. 59–61, 100–104.

23. Hawley, *The Great War and the Search for a Modern Order,* pp. 101–3.

24. See, for example, Alchon, *The Invisible Hand of Planning,* p. 3; Barry D. Karl, *The Uneasy State: The United States from 1915 to 1945* (Chicago: University of Chicago Press, 1983), pp. 74–75.

25. Dennison, *Ethics and Modern Business,* pp. 57–59.

26. Ibid., pp. 56–57.

27. Hawley, *The Great War and the Search for a Modern Order,* p. 96; Karl, *The Uneasy State,* p. 72.

28. Karl, *The Uneasy State,* pp. 72–73; James Warren Prothro, *The Dollar Decade: Business Ideas in the 1920's* (New York: Greenwood Press, 1954),

pp. 141–47; Henry S. Dennison, "Unemployment Relief—A Burden or an Investment?," *System* (June 1926).

29. Hawley, *The Great War and the Search for a Modern Order,* p. 96.

30. Daniel Nelson, *Unemployment Insurance: The American Experience, 1915–1935* (Madison: University of Wisconsin Press, 1969), pp. 45–46.

31. Berkowitz and McQuaid, "Businessman and Bureaucrat," p. 128.

32. "The Social Security Act," January 9, 1936, *Speeches,* Vol. 2 (Tab 1), Folsom Papers, p. 1.

33. Stettinius Jr.'s University of Virginia Commencement Address, June 15, 1937, Stettinius Jr. Papers.

34. Karl, *The Uneasy State,* p. 73; Hawley, *The Great War and the Search for a Modern Order,* pp. 103–4; Alchon, *The Invisible Hand of Planning,* pp. 169–70.

35. Gloria Vollmers, "Industrial Home Work of the Dennison Manufacturing Company of Framingham, Massachusetts, 1912–1935," *Business History Review* 71 (Autumn 1997): 465.

36. "Measures for the Prevention of Unemployment," Dennison Manufacturing Company, May 20, 1931, Unemployment File Folder, Case 1, Henry S. Dennison Papers, Harvard University (Baker) Library, Cambridge, Massachusetts, p. 4.

37. Vollmers, "Industrial Home Work of the Dennison Manufacturing Company of Framingham, Massachusetts, 1912–1935," pp. 447, 465; McQuaid, "Henry S. Dennison and the 'Science' of Industrial Reform," p. 89.

38. H. S. Dennison to Ida M. Tarbell, March 14, 1935, 1933–1934–1935 File Folder, Case 1, Dennison Papers, p. 1.

39. "The Social Security Act," January 9, 1936, Folsom Papers, p. 3; Richard E. Holl, "Marion B. Folsom and the Rochester Plan of 1931," *Rochester History* 51 (Winter 1999): 8–9.

40. Holl, "Marion B. Folsom and the Rochester Plan of 1931," pp. 13–15.

41. Holl, "Marion B. Folsom and the Rochester Plan of 1931," p. 13; "Wage Dividend Plan and Industrial Relations Program of Eastman Kodak Company," pp. 1–5, November 21, 1938, Folsom Papers.

42. Union Pacific Railroad Company Pension Plan, May 5, 1937, Union Pacific, Pension Plan 1937 File Folder, Box 668, Harriman Papers, p. 1.

43. *National Cyclopaedia of American Biography,* Vol. 45, p. 15.

44. Andrea Tone makes the point that "the Depression pushed private employee benefits in some firms into a state of dormancy but not oblivion. The welfare state that followed supplemented rather than supplanted welfare capitalism." Tone is right; the story of welfare capitalism does not end abruptly with the Great Depression. See Tone, *The Business of Benevolence,* pp. 247–48; Sanford M. Jacoby, *Modern Manors: Welfare Capitalism Since the New Deal* (Princeton, NJ: Princeton University Press, 1997), p. 5.

45. Marion B. Folsom Speech to Y.M.C.A., September 25, 1934, *Speeches,* Vol. 1 (Tab 41), Folsom Papers.

46. Hawley, *The Great War and the Search for a Modern Order,* pp. 184–85; Alchon, *The Invisible Hand of Planning,* p. 152.

47. Ibid.

Chapter Two

1. David Loth, *Swope of G.E.* (New York: Simon and Schuster, 1958), p. 203; Philip W. Warken, *A History of the National Resources Planning Board, 1933–1943* (New York: Garland Publishing, 1979), pp. 23–25; Kim McQuaid, "Corporate Liberalism in the American Business Community, 1920–1940," *Business History Review* 52 (Autumn 1978): 353–54.

2. Warken, *A History of the National Resources Planning Board, 1933–1943,* p. 26; Kim McQuaid, *Big Business and Presidential Power: From FDR to Reagan* (New York: William Morrow, 1982), p. 23; Robert M. Collins, *The Business Response to Keynes, 1929–1964* (New York: Columbia University Press, 1981), pp. 35–36.

3. Loth, *Swope of G.E.,* p. 198.

4. Ibid.

5. *Saturday Evening Post,* December 3, 1955, p. 136.

6. McQuaid, *Big Business and Presidential Power,* p. 25; Robert F. Himmelberg, *The Origins of the National Recovery Administration: Business, Government, and the Trade Association Issue, 1921–1933* (New York: Fordham University Press, 1976), p. 157. In addition, see Colin Gordon, *New Deals: Business, Labor, and Politics in America, 1920–1935* (Cambridge: Cambridge University Press, 1994), p. 168. Gordon notes that "Hoover advisers dismissed it (the Swope plan) as 'the most gigantic proposal of monopoly ever made in history.'"

7. Loth, *Swope of G.E.,* pp. 198–200; Himmelberg, *The Origins of the National Recovery Administration,* pp. 170–73; and David Brody, "The Rise and Decline of Welfare Capitalism," in John Braeman, Robert H. Bremner, and David Brody, eds., *Change and Continuity in Twentieth-Century America: The 1920s* (Columbus: Ohio State University Press, 1968), pp. 166–68.

8. Loth, *Swope of G.E.,* p. 220; McQuaid, *Big Business and Presidential Power,* pp. 20–21. In addition, see David E. Hamilton, *From New Day to New Deal: American Farm Policy from Hoover to Roosevelt, 1928–1933* (Chapel Hill: University of North Carolina Press, 1991), pp. 180–83, in order to compare the Swope agricultural plan to M. L. Wilson's even more elaborate three-part farm plan.

9. Henry Dennison to Roderic Olzendam, April 20, 1943, Case 1, Dennison Papers, p. 1.

10. Ellis W. Hawley, "A Partnership Formed, Dissolved, and in Renegotiation: Business and Government in the Franklin D. Roosevelt Era," in Joseph R. Frese, S. J. Judd, and Jacob Judd, eds., *Business and Government* (New York: Sleepy Hollow Press, 1985), p. 204.

11. James Warren Prothro, *The Dollar Decade: Business Ideas in the 1920's* (New York: Greenwood Press, 1954), p. 219.

12. Ibid., pp. 215–16.

13. Collins, *The Business Response to Keynes, 1929–1964,* p. 28.

14. Ellis W. Hawley, "The New Deal State and the Anti-Bureaucratic Tradition," in Robert Eden ed., *The New Deal and Its Legacy: Critique and Reappraisal* (Westport, CT: Greenwood Press, 1989), pp. 80–81. Hawley argues that the "New Deal did not turn out to be a straightforward push to create a new

administrative state." Instead, the interaction of competing state-building formulations (labeled respectively the "business commonwealth," the "populist commonwealth," the "emergency form of the administrative state," and the "interest group commonwealth") helped determine the structure of the government and, at least to a certain extent, what it could and could not do. I find Hawley's argument sophisticated as well as persuasive and therefore draw heavily from it.

15. See, for instance, David M. Kennedy, *Freedom from Fear: The American People in Depression and War, 1929–1945* (New York: Oxford University Press, 1999), p. 292. Kennedy mentions Swope by name, and writes that some other employers—though a minority—"welcomed and even encouraged the unionization of their employees."

16. Gloria Vollmers, "Industrial Home Work of the Dennison Manufacturing Company of Framingham, Massachusetts, 1912–1935," *Business History Review* 71 (Autumn 1997): 466.

17. "Brief History of Industrial Advisory Board," Section C-2, NIRA and NRA Notebook, Box 24, Stettinius, Jr. Papers, p. 2.

18. William E. Leuchtenburg, *Franklin D. Roosevelt and the New Deal, 1932–1940* (New York: Harper & Row, 1963), p. 65.

19. Ibid, p. 66.

20. See, for example, Bernard Bellush, *The Failure of the NRA* (New York: W. W. Norton, 1975), pp. 32–33; Ellis W. Hawley, *The New Deal and the Problem of Monopoly: A Study in Economic Ambivalence* (Princeton, NJ: Princeton University Press, 1966), p. 65.

21. McQuaid, "Corporate Liberalism in the American Business Community, 1920–1940," p. 356.

22. Bellush, *Failure of the NRA*, pp. 38–40; Larry I. Bland, *W. Averell Harriman: Businessman and Diplomat 1891–1945* (Ann Arbor, MI: University Microfilms, 1972), pp. 94, 97; Hawley, *The New Deal and the Problem of Monopoly*, pp. 77–98; Donald R. Brand, *Corporatism and the Rule of Law: A Study of the National Recovery Administration* (Ithaca, NY: Cornell University Press, 1988), pp. 290–91; Louis Galambos, *Competition and Cooperation: The Emergence of a National Trade Association* (Baltimore, MD: Johns Hopkins University Press, 1966), pp. 283, 287.

23. Kim McQuaid, "The Business Advisory Council of the Department of Commerce, 1933–1961," in *Research in Economic History* 1 (1976): 172; Brand, *Corporatism and the Rule of Law*, pp. 138–39; Edward Berkowitz and Kim McQuaid, *Creating the Welfare State: The Political Economy of Twentieth-Century Reform*, 2nd ed. (New York: Praeger, 1988), pp. 95–102.

24. Henry P. Kendall to Daniel C. Roper, January 31, 1935, Business Advisory Council (1935) File Folder, Box 71, Stettinius, Jr. Papers, p. 1.

25. Ibid., p. 2.

26. Kim McQuaid, "The Business Advisory Council of the Department of Commerce, 1933–1961," p. 177.

27. Ibid. See, as well, Daniel Nelson, *Unemployment Insurance: The American Experience, 1915–1935* (Madison: University of Wisconsin Press, 1969), pp. 211–22.

28. Typescript of Gerard Swope's speech, "What the Government Can Do to Assist in Stabilizing Employment," April 10, 1938, Herbert H. Lehman Papers, Lehman Suite, Columbia University, New York, New York, p. 1.

29. "The Social Security Act," August 14, 1935, *Speeches,* Vol. 1 (Tab 48), Folsom Papers, pp. 2–3; "The Social Security Act," January 9, 1936, *Speeches,* Vol. 2 (Tab 1), Folsom Papers, p. 14; "Business and Social Security," October 20, 1936, *Speeches,* Vol. 2 (Tab 8), Folsom Papers, pp. 17, 20, 27.

30. See, for example, "What the Government Can Do to Assist in Stabilizing Employment," Lehman Papers, pp. 3–5; "Business and Social Security," Folsom Papers, p. 21.

31. "What the Government Can Do to Assist in Stabilizing Employment," Lehman Papers, pp. 2–4; Address of Gerard Swope before the War Industries Board, November 11, 1935, Lehman Papers, p. 2.

32. Nelson, *Unemployment Insurance,* p. 142; Andrea Tone, *The Business of Benevolence: Industrial Paternalism in Progressive America* (Ithaca, NY: Cornell University Press, 1997), p. 248.

33. McQuaid, "The Business Advisory Council of the Department of Commerce," pp. 177–78.

34. Ibid., p. 174.

35. "Developments at Business Advisory Council Meeting Last Week," July 15, 1935, Business Advisory Council (1935) File Folder, Box 71, Stettinius Jr. Papers.

36. McQuaid, "The Business Advisory Council of the Department of Commerce," p. 181.

37. "Developments at Business Advisory Council Meeting Last Week," July 15, 1935, Stettinius Jr. Papers.

38. *Newsweek,* May 16, 1938, p. 36; McQuaid, *Big Business and Presidential Power,* pp. 47–48; Thomas Ferguson, "From Normalcy to New Deal: Industrial Structure, Party Competition, and American Public Policy in the Great Depression," *International Organization* 38, no. 1 (Winter 1984): 88; and Loth, *Swope of G.E.,* pp. 229, 256.

39. Walter LaFeber, Richard Polenberg, and Nancy Woloch, *The American Century: A History of the United States Since the 1890s,* 4th ed. (New York: McGraw-Hill, 1992), p. 218.

40. Edward Berkowitz and Kim McQuaid, *Creating the Welfare State: The Political Economy of Twentieth Century Reform* (New York: Praeger, 1980), p. 90.

41. Collins, *The Business Response to Keynes,* p. 42.

42. *New York Times,* June 28, 1936, p. 25. For similar comments from FDR, see George Wolfskill, *The Revolt of the Conservatives: A History of the American Liberty League, 1934–1940* (Boston: Houghton Mifflin, 1962), p. 121.

43. *Business Week,* July 13, 1935, p. 8.

44. On the realignment of big business during the 1920s and 1930s, see Ferguson, "From Normalcy to New Deal," pp. 41–94. Pages 85–94 are most relevant to my study. See, as well, Michael J. Hogan, *Informal Entente: The Private Structure of Cooperation in Anglo-American Economic Diplomacy, 1918–1928* (Columbia: University of Missouri Press, 1977), pp. 1–12, 181–83. Hogan applies the organizational synthesis to foreign affairs with telling effect; he suggests that

Teagle and others like him sought economic stability and prosperity at home and abroad through government-sanctioned private arrangements.

45. *Current Biography,* 1941, "Donald Nelson," p. 609.

46. Ibid.

47. *Washington Post,* February 25, 1939, p. 7.

48. *New York Times,* February 25, 1939, p. 1.

49. Ibid.; *Vital Speeches,* Vol. 5, October 15–October 1, 1938–1939, "The Administration's Program for Recovery," p. 337.

50. *Washington Post,* December 25, 1938, p. 2; February 25, 1939, p. 5.

51. Ibid., February 25, 1939, p. 5.

52. Ibid.

53. Ibid., April 13, 1939, p. 4.

54. Ibid., April 18, 1939, p. 1.

55. Ibid., April 13, 1939, p. 4.

56. Ibid., January 29, 1939, p. 2.

57. *Dun's Review,* May 1939, pp. 8–9.

58. *Fortune,* June 1939, p. 104.

59. *Dun's Review,* May 1939, p. 10.

60. Hawley, *The New Deal and the Problem of Monopoly,* p. 412.

61. *Dun's Review,* May 1939, p. 9; Hawley, *The New Deal and the Problem of Monopoly,* p. 185; William J. Barber, "Government as a Laboratory for Economic Learning in the Years of the Democratic Roosevelt," in Mary O. Furner and Barry Supple, eds., *The State and Economic Knowledge: The American and British Experiences* (Cambridge: Woodrow Wilson International Center for Scholars and Cambridge University Press, 1990), pp. 116–20.

62. *Washington Post,* March 11, 1939, p. 1.

63. Ibid., April 18, 1939, p.1.

64. McQuaid, "The Business Advisory Council of the Department of Commerce," p. 182. See, as well, George McJimsey's *Harry Hopkins* (Cambridge, MA: Harvard University Press, 1987).

65. *New York Times,* March 9, 1939, p. 1; *Washington Post,* March 9, 1939, p. 1; March 11, p. 1.

66. *Digest of Public General Bills,* 76th Congress, 1st Session, Final Issue, H.R. 6851, p. 338; Mark H. Leff, *The Limits of Symbolic Reform: The New Deal and Taxation, 1933–1939* (Cambridge: Cambridge University Press, 1984), p. 274; *Washington Post,* June 13, 1939, p. 4.

67. *Washington Post,* March 28, 1939, p. 2.

68. *Digest of Public General Bills,* 76th Congress, 1st Session, Final Issue, 1939, H.R. 6635, p. 329; *Washington Post,* June 11, 1939, pp. 1, 14.

69. See, for example, "Business and Social Security," October 20, 1936, Folsom Papers, pp. 17–18.

70. *Digest of Public General Bills,* 76th Congress, 1st Session, Final Issue, 1939, H.R. 6635, p. 329.

71. Leff, *The Limits of Symbolic Reform,* pp. 281–82.

72. Roosevelt to Harriman, January 19, 1940, BAPC File Folder (1940–1943), Box 9, Official File (Department of Commerce), Roosevelt Papers.

73. *Washington Post,* February 25, 1939, p. 7.

74. Address by George Mead before the Congress of American Industry in conjunction with Annual Meeting, NAM, December 10, 1936, Business Advisory and Planning Council Folder (1936–May 1937), Box 9, Official File, Roosevelt Papers, pp. 3–4.

75. See, for example, *Nation's Business,* June 1939, p. 64; July 1939, p. 31.

76. Leff, *The Limits of Symbolic Reform,* p. 282.

Chapter Three

1. *Fortune,* September 1940, p. 132.

2. See, for example, John Keegan, *The Second World War* (New York: Penguin Books, 1990), p. 537.

3. Dwight D. Eisenhower, *Crusade in Europe* (Garden City, NY: Doubleday, 1948), p. 2.

4. Ibid; Ronald H. Spector, *Eagle Against the Sun: The American War with Japan* (New York: Free Press, 1985), p. 10.

5. Eisenhower, *Crusade in Europe,* p. 2.

6. Donald M. Nelson, *Arsenal of Democracy: The Story of American War Production* (New York: Harcourt, Brace, 1946), p. 41. Consult *The Nation* as well (May 25, 1940, p. 644; June 8, 1940, p. 710.)

7. Yet by 1942–1943, the U.S. Army possessed too many of these weapons. See R. Elberton Smith, *The Army and Economic Mobilization* (Washington, DC: Office of the Chief of Military History, Department of the Army, 1959), p. 159.

8. *Fortune,* September 1940, p. 59.

9. Christopher R. Gabel, *The U.S. Army GHQ Maneuvers of 1941* (Washington, DC: Center of Military History, U.S. Army, 1991), p. 36.

10. Eliot Janeway, *The Struggle for Survival: A Chronicle of Economic Mobilization in World War II* (New Haven, CT: Yale University Press, 1951), p. 25.

11. *Fortune,* September 1940, p. 59; Janeway, *The Struggle for Survival,* p. 25.

12. Walter Millis, *Arms and Men: A Study in American Military History* (New York: G. P. Putnam's Sons, 1956), p. 270.

13. Memorandum from H. K. Rutherford to War Resources Board (WRB) members, August 17, 1939, War Resources Board Subject File, Robert E. Wood Papers, Herbert Hoover Presidential Library, West Branch, Iowa, p. 3.

14. David M. Kennedy, *Freedom from Fear: The American People in Depression and War, 1929–1945* (New York: Oxford University Press, 1999), p. 429.

15. Spector, *Eagle Against the Sun,* p. 17.

16. Gabel, *The U.S. Army GHQ Maneuvers of 1941,* p. 13.

17. Ibid., pp. 13–14.

18. Russell F. Weigley, *History of the United States Army* (Bloomington: Indiana University Press, 1984), pp. 419–20.

19. *Fortune,* November 1939, p. 66.

20. Ibid.

21. Ibid., p. 114.

22. Ibid., p. 28.

23. Ibid., p. 110.

24. Memo from Rutherford to WRB members, August 17, 1939, Wood Papers, p. 6.

25. I. F. Stone, *Business As Usual: The First Year of Defense* (New York: Modern Age Books, 1941), p. 20.

26. Ibid.

27. Ibid., p. 22.

28. *Fortune,* September 1940, p. 124; Spector, *Eagle Against the Sun,* p. 19.

29. Gabel, *The U.S. Army GHQ Maneuvers of 1941,* p. 12.

30. *Fortune,* November 1939, p. 108.

31. *Newsweek,* August 28, 1939, p. 11; Weigley, *History of the United States Army,* pp. 395–420; Burnham Finney, *Arsenal of Democracy: How Industry Builds Our Defense* (New York: Whittlesey House, 1941), pp. 8–9; Smith, *The Army and Economic Mobilization,* pp. 100–101.

32. Theda Skocpol, "A Society Without a 'State'? Political Organization, Social Conflict, and Welfare Provision in the United States," *Journal of Public Policy* 7, Part 4 (October–December 1987): 359. For more specific information along these lines, consult Samuel P. Huntington, *Political Order in Changing Societies;* Bernard Bailyn, *The Ideological Origins of the American Revolution;* and Gordon S. Wood, *The Creation of the American Republic.*

33. Stephen Skowronek, *Building a New American State: The Expansion of National Administrative Capacities, 1877–1920* (Cambridge: Cambridge University Press, 1982), p. 24.

34. Margaret Weir and Theda Skocpol, "State Structures and Social Keynesianism," *International Journal of Comparative Sociology* 24, nos. 1–2 (January–April 1983): 21.

35. The tension between autonomous individualism and planned efficiency is a major theme in Barry Karl's fine book *The Uneasy State* (Chicago: University of Chicago Press, 1983). See esp. Karl's introduction and conclusion.

36. John E. Wiltz, *In Search of Peace: The Senate Munitions Inquiry, 1934–1936* (Baton Rouge: Louisiana State University Press, 1963), p. 228; Robert H. Ferrell, *Peace in Their Time: The Origins of the Kellogg-Briand Pact* (New Haven, CT: Yale University Press, 1952), p. 27.

37. Wayne S. Cole, *Roosevelt and the Isolationists, 1932–1945* (Lincoln: University of Nebraska Press, 1983), p. 266.

38. Smith, *The Army and Economic Mobilization,* p. 121.

39. See, for example, Ferrell, *Peace in Their Time,* p. 13; Arnold A. Offner, *American Appeasement: United States Foreign Policy and Germany, 1933–1938* (Cambridge, MA: Harvard University Press, 1969), p. 280. The idea that mere distance safeguarded the United States can be found in numerous other sources as well, including Samuel Flagg Bemis's piece, "The Shifting Strategy of American Defense and Diplomacy," in Dwight E. Lee and George E. McReynolds, eds., *Essays in History and International Relations in Honor of George Hubbard Blakeslee* (Worcester, MA: Clark University, 1949), pp. 1–14. Bemis described the period between World War I and World War II as the "Fool's Paradise of American history."

40. Alan S. Milward, *War, Economy and Society, 1939–1945* (Berkeley: University of California Press, 1977), p. 25.

41. Smith, *The Army and Economic Mobilization,* pp. 498, 708; Finney, *Arsenal of Democracy,* p. 8. Also see U.S. Senate Special Committee Investigating the National Defense Program, Hearings, 77th Congress, 1st session, 1941, Part 1, 12.

42. Finney, *Arsenal of Democracy,* p. 9. The same basic information can also be found in statements made by Secretary of War Henry Stimson and Under Secretary of War Robert Patterson before the U.S. Senate Special Committee Investigating the National Defense Program (Hearings, 77th Congress, 1st session, 1941, Part 1, 12, 22).

43. Memo from Rutherford to WRB members, August 17, 1939, Wood Papers, p. 3.

44. Tentative draft of the final section of the War Resources Board report (H. S. Moulton to Robert E. Wood), October 1, 1939, WRB Subject File, Wood Papers, p. 3.

45. Finney, *Arsenal of Democracy,* p. 9.

46. Tentative draft of the final section of the WRB report (Moulton to Wood), October 1, 1939, Wood Papers, p. 3.

47. Financier Baruch and corporate executive Walter S. Gifford, among other civilians, pressed for an emergency-preparedness agency. See, for example, Paul A. C. Koistinen, *The Military-Industrial Complex: A Historical Perspective* (New York: Praeger, 1980), p. 59, and Smith, *The Army and Economic Mobilization,* p. 100. The Baruch quote comes from Jordan A. Schwarz, *The Speculator: Bernard M. Baruch in Washington, 1917–1965* (Chapel Hill: University of North Carolina Press, 1981), p. 429.

48. U.S. Senate Special Committee Investigating the National Defense Program, Hearings, 77th Cong., 1st sess., 1941, Part 1, 12–13; Smith, *The Army and Economic Mobilization,* p. 38.

49. Finney, *Arsenal of Democracy,* p. 7.

50. Smith, *The Army and Economic Mobilization,* pp. 123–26.

51. Millis, *Arms and Men,* p. 270; Nelson, *Arsenal of Democracy,* pp. 33–34.

52. Nelson, *Arsenal of Democracy,* pp. 31–35; Milward, *War, Economy and Society,* pp. 189–90.

53. Brian Waddell, "Economic Mobilization for World War II and the Transformation of the U.S. State," *Politics and Society* 22, no. 2 (June 1994): 165–71; Alan Brinkley, "The New Deal and the Idea of the State," in Steve Fraser and Gary Gerstle, eds., *The Rise and Fall of the New Deal Order, 1930–1980* (Princeton, NJ: Princeton University Press, 1989), esp. pp. 87–88.

54. Waddell, "Economic Mobilization for World War II and the Transformation of the U.S. State," pp. 167–70, 185.

55. Ellis W. Hawley, "The New Deal State and the Anti-Bureaucratic Tradition," in Robert Eden, ed., *The New Deal and Its Legacy: Critique and Reappraisal* (Westport, CT: Greenwood Press, 1989), pp. 77–90.

56. Koistinen, *The Military-Industrial Complex,* pp. 57–58.

57. Brinkley, "The New Deal and the Idea of the State," p. 102; Karl, *The Uneasy State,* pp. 166–67.

58. Alan Brinkley argues that the New Deal state, by itself, lacked the bureaucratic capacity needed to conduct industrial mobilization. For this reason, the state "would turn to the private sector for its administrative talent." See Brinkley, "The New Deal and the Idea of the State," p. 102.

59. See, for example, Nelson Lichtenstein, *Labor's War at Home: The CIO in World War II* (Cambridge: Cambridge University Press, 1982), p. 39.

60. Brinkley, "The New Deal and the Idea of the State," p. 102.

61. Hawley, "The New Deal State and the Anti-Bureaucratic Tradition," pp. 80–81.

62. Waddell, "Economic Mobilization for World War II and the Transformation of the U.S. State," pp. 166–67; Koistinen, *The Military-Industrial Complex,* pp. 59–61.

63. Hugh Heclo, *Modern Social Politics in Britain and Sweden* (New Haven, CT: Yale University Press, 1974), pp. 305–6. Also see Theda Skocpol and Kenneth Finegold, "State Capacity and Economic Intervention in the Early New Deal," *Political Science Quarterly* 97 (Summer 1982): 255–78.

64. Alan Brinkley, "Prosperity, Depression, and War, 1920–1945," in Eric Foner, ed., *The New American History* (Philadelphia: Temple University Press, 1990), p. 131.

65. Nelson, *Arsenal of Democracy,* pp. 25–36; Waddell, "Economic Mobilization for World War II and the Transformation of the U.S. State," esp. pp. 165–167, 185.

66. See, for example, Walter Johnson's entry in the *Dictionary of American Biography (Supplement Four, 1946–1950),* 1974, p. 777.

67. Samuel Crowther to Edward R. Stettinius Jr., August 5, 1940, Samuel Crowther File Folder (May–December 1940), Box 119, Edward R. Stettinius Jr. Papers, University of Virginia Library, Charlottesville, Virginia.

68. *Dictionary of American Biography (Supplement Four, 1946–1950),* 1974, p. 777; Crowther to Stettinius (dated only 1943), Samuel Crowther File Folder 2, Box 119, Stettinius Jr. Papers.

69. *Dictionary of American Biography (Supplement Four, 1946–1950),* 1974, p. 457.

70. Ibid.

71. Bruce Catton, *The War Lords of Washington* (New York: Harcourt, Brace, 1948), p. 69.

72. Nelson, *Arsenal of Democracy,* p. xii.

73. Ibid., p. 415.

74. Gabriel Kolko, "American Business and Germany, 1930–1941," *Western Political Quarterly* 15, no. 4 (December 1962): 724–25; *Dictionary of American Biography (Supplement Four, 1946–1950),* 1974, p. 458.

75. Nelson, *Arsenal of Democracy,* p. 65.

76. Christy Borth, *Masters of Mass Production* (Indianapolis, IN: Bobbs-Merrill, 1945), p. 59.

77. General Motors, for example, constructed and operated the massive $35 million Adam Opel plant in Germany. See *The New Yorker,* March 8, 1941, p. 32. Also consult Mira Wilkins's *The Maturing of Multinational Enterprise* (Cambridge, MA: Harvard University Press, 1974). Wilkins provides an excellent description of the overseas activities of some large U.S. corporations.

78. Nelson, *Arsenal of Democracy*, p. 41.

79. Ibid., p. 28.

80. Weigley, *History of the United States Army*, p. 419.

81. Nelson, *Arsenal of Democracy*, p. 54.

82. Ibid., p. 49.

83. Edward R. Stettinius Jr., *Lend-Lease: Weapon for Victory* (New York: Macmillan, 1944), pp. 12–13.

84. Gabel, *The U.S. Army GHQ Maneuvers of 1941*, p. 39.

85. Nelson, *Arsenal for Democracy*, p. 41.

86. Gabel, *The U.S. Army GHQ Maneuvers of 1941*, pp. 27, 39; Keegan, *The Second World War*, p. 59; Nelson, *Arsenal of Democracy*, p. 49; Doris Kearns Goodwin, *No Ordinary Time: Franklin & Eleanor Roosevelt: The Home Front in World War II* (New York: Simon & Schuster, 1994) p. 52.

87. Nelson, *Arsenal of Democracy*, p. 35.

88. Ibid., p. 31.

89. Ibid., pp. 33–34.

90. Ibid., p. 34.

91. Stettinius, *Lend-Lease*, p. 45.

92. Nelson, *Arsenal of Democracy*, p. 35.

93. Rutherford to Wood, November 3, 1939, WRB Subject File, Wood Papers.

94. Finney, *Arsenal of Democracy*, p. 6.

95. Waddell, "Economic Mobilization for World War II and the Transformation of the U.S. State," p. 166; Lichtenstein, *Labor's War at Home*, pp. 38–42. In addition, see David Vogel, "Why Businessmen Distrust Their State: The Political Consciousness of American Corporate Executives," *British Journal of Political Science* 8 (1978): 45–78. Vogel discusses the apprehensions of big business-men toward the expansion of state authority.

96. See, for example, Waddell, "Economic Mobilization for World War II and the Transformation of the U.S. State," p. 174.

97. Ibid., pp. 183–85; Brinkley, "The New Deal and the Idea of the State," pp. 100–109.

98. Smith, *The Army and Economic Mobilization*, p. 100.

99. Cole, *Roosevelt and the Isolationists*, pp. 436–37.

Chapter Four

1. Under Roosevelt and Secretary of War Harry W. Woodring, the U.S. Army's command structure "finally accepted army dependence on the civilian economy in order to fulfill the military mission." See Paul A. C. Koistinen, *The Military-Industrial Complex: A Historical Perspective* (New York: Praeger, 1980), p. 52.

2. I borrow the term *antibureaucratic* from Ellis W. Hawley. See Hawley, "The New Deal State and the Anti-Bureaucratic Tradition," in Robert Eden, ed., *The New Deal and Its Legacy: Critique and Reappraisal* (Westport, CT: Greenwood Press, 1989), pp. 77–92. Also see Brian Waddell, "Economic Mobilization for

World War II and the Transformation of the U.S. State," *Politics and Society* 22, no. 2 (June 1994): 165–94.

3. I encountered the phrase "economic potential for war," and the concept it implies, in Alan S. Milward, *War, Economy and Society, 1939–1945* (Berkeley: University of California Press, 1977), pp. 19–23.

4. R. Elberton Smith, *The Army and Economic Mobilization* (Washington, DC: Office of the Chief of Military History, Department of the Army, 1959), p. 39.

5. James W. Fesler et al., *Industrial Mobilization for War: History of the War Production Board and Predecessor Agencies, 1940–1945* (Washington, DC: U.S. Government Printing Office, 1947), p. 7.

6. *The National Cyclopaedia of American Biography*, 1953, p. 62; Thomas M. Campbell and George C. Herring, eds., *The Diaries of Edward R. Stettinius, Jr., 1943–1946* (New York: New Viewpoints, 1975), pp. xiii–xiv.

7. Campbell and Herring, *The Diaries of Edward R. Stettinius, Jr.,* p. xiv.

8. *The National Cyclopaedia of American Biography*, 1953, p. 62.

9. Ibid; New Group Insurance Plan, General Motors, 1928, Box 7, Edward R. Stettinius Jr. Papers, University of Virginia Library, Charlottesville, Virginia, p. 1.

10. Campbell and Herring, *The Diaries of Edward R. Stettinius, Jr.,* pp. xvi–xvii.

11. *The National Cyclopaedia of American Biography*, Current Volume G (1943–1946), 1946, p. 75; Biographical Brief of Edward R. Stettinius Jr., 1938, Box 49, Stettinius Jr. Papers, p. 2.

12. Koistinen, *The Military-Industrial Complex,* p. 59.

13. Fesler et al., *Industrial Mobilization for War,* pp. 7–8.

14. *Current Biography,* 1941, p. 933.

15. *Fortune,* May 1938, p. 106.

16. *Current Biography,* 1941, p. 934.

17. Ibid.

18. Wayne S. Cole, *Roosevelt and the Isolationists, 1932–1945* (Lincoln: University of Nebraska Press, 1983), p. 380.

19. Memorandum from Robert E. Wood to Franklin D. Roosevelt, October 14, 1936, Box 156, W. Averell Harriman Papers, Library of Congress, Washington, DC, pp. 1–3.

20. Ibid., p. 1.

21. Ibid., p. 2.

22. Cole, *Roosevelt and the Isolationists,* p. 380.

23. *Fortune,* May 1938, p. 104.

24. Memorandum from Wood to Roosevelt, October 14, 1936, Harriman Papers, p. 2.

25. Cole, *Roosevelt and the Isolationists,* pp. 436–37.

26. Suggested News Reel Remarks of Mr. Stettinius, August 17, 1939, Bound Vol. 31, Stettinius Jr. Papers.

27. Ibid.

28. *Washington Post,* August 10, 1939, p. 1.

29. Waddell, "Economic Mobilization for World War II and the Transformation of the U.S. State," p. 175.

30. Bernard M. Baruch to Edward R. Stettinius Jr., August 30, 1939, Bound Volume 31, Stettinius Jr. Papers.

31. Koistinen, *The Military-Industrial Complex,* pp. 51–52; "Industrial Mobilization Plan" (Revision of 1939), U.S. Government Printing Office, Washington, DC, 1939, pp. 7, 12. Copies of the 1939 Industrial Mobilization Plan can be found in the National Archives, the Franklin D. Roosevelt Library, the Stettinius Papers, and elsewhere. See, for example, National Archives (NA), Record Group (RG) 107, File Number 334/117.3, Planning Branch (PB), Assistant Secretary of War (ASW), Office of the Secretary of War (OSW).

32. Koistinen, *The Military-Industrial Complex,* pp. 52, 59.

33. "Industrial Mobilization Plan" (Revision of 1939), p. 7.

34. John Hancock's draft of War Resources Board report (to Robert E. Wood), October 2, 1939, War Resources Board Subject File, Robert E. Wood Papers, Hoover Presidential Library, West Branch, Iowa, p. 11.

35. "Industrial Mobilization Plan" (Revision of 1939), p. 12.

36. See, for one example, Waddell, "Economic Mobilization for World War II and the Transformation of the U.S. State," p. 180.

37. Hancock's draft of WRB report (to Wood), October 2, 1939, Wood Papers, pp. 6–7.

38. Assignments and Studies Given Each Member of the Board, September 20, 1939, WRB–Pending File Folder, Box 75, Stettinius Jr. Papers, p. 1.

39. Minutes of the Meetings of the War Resources Board, August 29, 30, and 31, 1939, War Resources Board (Miscellaneous: SCD, Etc.) File Folder, Box 74, Stettinius Jr. Papers, p. 3.

40. Stettinius met with both Gibson Carey and Howard Coonley, presidents of the Chamber of Commerce of the United States and National Association of Manufacturers, respectively. They assured him of the cooperation of their organizations. See Box 74, Stettinius Jr. Papers.

41. Assignments and Studies Given Each Member of the Board, September 20, 1939, Stettinius Jr. Papers, p. 2.

42. Ibid.; Minutes of the Meetings of the War Resources Board, August 29, 30, and 31, 1939, War Resources Board (Miscellaneous: SCD, Etc.) File Folder, Box 74, Stettinius Jr. Papers, p. 3.

43. Assignments and Studies Given Each Member of the Board, September 20, 1939, p. 1; Minutes of the Meetings of the War Resources Board, August 29, 30, and 31, 1939, Stettinius Jr. Papers, p. 3.

44. Organization Chart Showing Possible Organization of Power and Fuel and Transport Sections of Service Industries Division, WRB (Undated) File Folder, Box 75, Stettinius Jr. Papers.

45. Ibid.

46. Alan Brinkley, "The New Deal and the Idea of the State," in Steve Fraser and Gary Gerstle, eds., *The Rise and Fall of the New Deal Order, 1930–1980* (Princeton, NJ: Princeton University Press, 1989), pp. 87–89; Jordan A. Schwarz, *The Speculator: Bernard M. Baruch in Washington, 1917–1965* (Chapel Hill: University of North Carolina Press, 1981), pp. 356–63.

47. Albert A. Blum, "Birth and Death of the M-Day Plan" in Harold Stein, ed., *American Civil-Military Decisions: A Book of Case Studies* (Tuscaloosa: University of Alabama Press, 1963), p. 77.

48. Harold L. Ickes, *The Secret Diary of Harold L. Ickes: Volume III, The Lowering Clouds, 1939–1941* (New York: Simon and Schuster, 1954), p. 181.

49. George Martin, *Madam Secretary: Frances Perkins* (Boston: Houghton Mifflin, 1976), p. 444.

50. Ibid.

51. Blum, "Birth and Death of the M-Day Plan," p. 77.

52. John W. Jeffries uses the term "'new' New Deal" and points out who the new New Dealers were in his article "The 'New' New Deal: FDR and American Liberalism, 1937–1945." See *Political Science Quarterly* 105 (Fall 1990), esp. pp. 403–4.

53. Ibid.; Brinkley, "The New Deal and the Idea of the State," pp. 87–88.

54. Blum, "Birth and Death of the M-Day Plan," p. 77.

55. Brinkley, "The New Deal and the Idea of the State," pp. 90–91.

56. Jeffries, "The 'New' New Deal," pp. 397–404.

57. Schwarz, *The Speculator,* pp. 401–8.

58. Appearing on a radio program, Ickes blasted the WRB. Numerous newspaper articles also captured the essence of this debate, including several in the *Wall Street Journal.* See Blum, "Birth and Death of the M-Day Plan," p. 77, and Schwarz, *The Speculator,* p. 362.

59. Blum, "Birth and Death of the M-Day Plan," p. 77.

60. *Portland (Maine) Evening Express,* "Brains for Defense," May 23, 1940, Miscellaneous Newspaper Clippings, Box 75, Stettinius Jr. Papers.

61. Blum, "Birth and Death of the M-Day Plan," p. 77.

62. Ibid.

63. Schwarz, *The Speculator,* p. 361.

64. Ibid.

65. Since Baruch wanted to keep inflation down, he pursued this strategy. See Schwarz, *The Speculator,* pp. 402–8.

66. Blum, "Birth and Death of the M-Day Plan," p. 78.

67. Mae R. Fitz Maurice to Edward R. Stettinius Jr., October 17, 1939, War Resources Board (General Correspondence) File Folder, Box 74, Stettinius Jr. Papers, p. 1.

68. Harold L. Ickes, *The Secret Diary of Harold L. Ickes: Volume II, The Inside Struggle, 1936–1939* (New York: Simon and Schuster, 1954), p. 710; Koistinen, *The Military-Industrial Complex,* p. 60.

69. Minutes of the Meetings of the War Resources Board, August 29, 30, and 31, 1939, Stettinius Jr. Papers, p. 2.

70. See, for example, Fesler et al., *Industrial Mobilization for War,* p. 9.

71. Tentative Program of War Resources Board with Respect to Industrial Preparedness Plans, WRB–Pending File Folder, Box 75, Stettinius Jr. Papers.

72. Koistinen, *The Military-Industrial Complex,* p. 61 (n.).

73. Smith, *The Army and Economic Mobilization,* p. 62.

74. Ibid., p. 63.

75. Ibid.

76. *Iron Age,* June 22, 1939, p. 58.

77. *American Machinist,* Vol. 83, 1939, p. 10.

78. See, for example, *Iron Age,* June 15, 1939, pp. 58, 61.

79. *American Machinist,* May 31, 1939, p. 405.

80. Ibid., pp. 411–16.

81. Tentative draft of the final section of the War Resources Board report (H. S. Moulton to Robert E. Wood), October 1, 1939, WRB Subject File, Wood Papers, p. 3.

82. Smith, *The Army and Economic Mobilization,* p. 64.

83. Ibid., p. 62.

84. *New York Times,* August 10, 1939, p. 2.

85. Ibid.

86. News clipping from the *Youngstown, Ohio Vindicator,* "U.S. Industry Ready for War Emergency," September 3, 1939, Bound Volume 32, Stettinius Jr. Papers.

87. See, for example, the *American Machinist,* May 31, 1939, p. 367.

88. Fesler et al., *Industrial Mobilization for War,* p. 68; Donald M. Nelson, *Arsenal of Democracy: The Story of American War Production* (New York: Harcourt, Brace, 1946), pp. 37–41.

89. H. K. Rutherford, "Mobilizing Industry for War," *Harvard Business Review* 18, no. 1 (Autumn 1939): 8.

90. Ibid.

91. Assignments and Studies Given Each Member of the Board, September 20, 1939, Stettinius Jr. Papers, p. 1; John Morton Blum, *V was for Victory: Politics and American Culture during World War II* (New York: Harcourt Brace Jovanovich, 1976), pp. 132–35.

92. Brinkley, "The New Deal and the Idea of the State," pp. 89–91; Blum, *V was for Victory,* pp. 132–35.

93. Entry from Leon Henderson Diary, October 11, 1939, Box 36, Leon Henderson Papers, Franklin D. Roosevelt Library, Hyde Park, New York.

94. Ibid.

95. Ibid.

96. News clipping from the *New York Times,* "Maps First Steps on War Resources," August 18, 1939, Bound Vol. 32, Stettinius Jr. Papers.

97. Ickes was afraid that the preparedness program would result in a "new crop of war millionaires" and that New Deal advances would be undercut. See Ickes, *The Secret Diary of Harold L. Ickes: Volume III, The Lowering Clouds,* pp. 295–96.

98. Entry from Henderson Diary, October 11, 1939, Henderson Papers.

99. Smith, *The Army and Economic Mobilization,* pp. 413–14; Schwarz, *The Speculator,* p. 401; Waddell, "Economic Mobilization for World War II and the Transformation of the U.S. State," pp. 178–79.

100. *Washington Post,* September 27, 1939, p. 2.

101. *New York Times,* September 28, 1939, p. 10.

102. Many epithets of this type were hurled at WRB members. See, for example, Koistinen, *The Military-Industrial Complex,* p. 60; Ickes, *The Secret Diary of Harold L. Ickes,* Vol. 2, p. 710; Richard Polenberg, *War and Society: The United*

States, 1941–1945 (Philadelphia: J. B. Lippincott, 1972), p. 7.; *New York World Telegram,* August 22, 1939, p. 15.

103. Polenberg, *War and Society,* p. 6.

104. *Washington Post,* September 27, 1939, p. 2.

105. "Report of the War Resources Board," October 13, 1939, PB, ASW, OSW, RG 107, NA, p. 10.

106. Ibid., chart facing p. 10.

107. Hancock's draft of War Resources Board report (to Wood), October 2, 1939, WRB Subject File, Wood Papers, p. 8.

108. "Report of the War Resources Board," October 13, 1939, PB, ASW, OSW, RG 107, NA, chart facing p. 10.

109. Hancock's draft of War Resources Board report (to Wood), October 2, 1939, Wood Papers, p. 9.

110. Fesler et al., *Industrial Mobilization for War,* p. 11; "Report of the War Resources Board," October 13, 1939, PB, ASW, OSW, RG 107, NA, chart facing p. 10.

111. Hancock to Stettinius, November 22, 1939, War Resources Board (Col. H. K. Rutherford) File, Box 76, Stettinius Jr. Papers.

112. Stettinius to Walter S. Gifford, November 28, 1939, War Resources Board (Rutherford) File, Box 76, Stettinius Jr. Papers.

113. See, for example, Nelson, *Arsenal of Democracy,* pp. 88–90; Koistinen, *The Military-Industrial Complex,* p. 70.

114. Harold G. Moulton to Edward R. Stettinius Jr., December 5, 1939, War Resources Board (General Correspondence) File Folder, Box 74, Stettinius Jr. Papers.

115. See Thomas Ferguson, "From Normalcy to New Deal: Industrial Structure, Party Competition, and American Public Policy in the Great Depression," *International Organization* 38, no. 1 (Winter 1984): 41–94. Michael J. Hogan's *Informal Entente* deals with an earlier time, but sensitized me to the foreign trade deals that have resulted from the collaboration of multinational businessmen, the U.S. government (particularly the State Department), and foreign nations. Alan S. Milward's *War, Society and Economy, 1939–1945* emphasizes German autarky.

116. Wood wanted to enter military service after Pearl Harbor but "was denied that privilege." He did serve in a civilian capacity during World War II, but only in relatively minor posts. See Cole, *Roosevelt and the Isolationists,* p. 508.

117. Schwarz, *The Speculator,* p. 362.

Chapter Five

1. James W. Fesler et al., *Industrial Mobilization for War: History of the War Production Board and Predecessor Agencies, 1940–1945* (Washington, DC: U.S. Government Printing Office, 1947), p. 22.

2. Ibid., pp. 18–19.

3. Ibid.

4. Joseph P. Harris, "The Emergency National Defense Organization," *Public Administration Review,* Vol. I, no. 1 (Autumn 1940): 5.

5. R. Elberton Smith, *The Army and Economic Mobilization* (Washington, DC: Office of the Chief of Military History, Department of the Army, 1959), pp. 129–31; Fesler et al., *Industrial Mobilization for War,* pp. 42–43.

6. Brian Waddell, "Economic Mobilization for World War II and the Transformation of the U.S. State," *Politics and Society* 22, no. 2 (June 1994): 165–71; Ellis W. Hawley, "The New Deal State and the Anti-Bureaucratic Tradition," in Robert Eden, ed., *The New Deal and Its Legacy: Critique and Reappraisal* (Westport, CT: Greenwood Press, 1989), esp. pp. 80–81.

7. See, for example, John Keegan, *The Second World War* (New York: Penguin Books, 1990), pp. 538–39.

8. Roosevelt was determined to do whatever it took, which certainly included manipulation of the U.S. economy, to give "material aid" to "peace-loving and liberty-loving peoples wantonly attacked by ruthless aggressors." See Wayne S. Cole, *Roosevelt and the Isolationists, 1932–1945* (Lincoln: University of Nebraska Press, 1983), p. 394.

9. Nelson Lichtenstein, *Labor's War at Home: The C.I.O. in World War II* (Cambridge: Cambridge University Press, 1982), p. 39.

10. Alan Brinkley, "The New Deal and the Idea of the State," in Steve Fraser and Gary Gerstle, eds., *The Rise and Fall of the New Deal Order, 1930–1980* (Princeton, NJ: Princeton University Press, 1989), p. 102; Brian Waddell, *The War Against the New Deal: World War II and American Democracy* (DeKalb: Northern Illinois University Press, 2001), p. 6.

11. See, for example, Kim McQuaid, *Big Business and Presidential Power: From FDR to Reagan* (New York: William Morrow, 1982), p. 73.

12. Fesler et al., *Industrial Mobilization for War,* p. 20.

13. *Current Biography,* 1940, p. 464; *Saturday Evening Post,* April 17, 1937, p. 7.

14. Ibid.

15. Ibid; *Saturday Evening Post,* April 17, 1937, p. 114.

16. *Current Biography,* 1940, p. 464; *Saturday Evening Post,* April 17, 1937, pp. 114, 116.

17. Ibid; Doris Kearns Goodwin, *No Ordinary Time: Franklin & Eleanor Roosevelt: The Home Front in World War II* (New York: Simon & Schuster, 1994), p. 55.

18. *Time,* May 6, 1940, p. 77.

19. Ibid.

20. *Newsweek,* May 16, 1938, p. 36.

21. *Time,* January 18, 1937, p. 18.

22. McQuaid, *Big Business and Presidential Power,* p. 73; Fesler et al., *Industrial Mobilization for War,* p. 19.

23. "The Defense Advisory Commission," August 8–10, 1940, NDAC– Publications File Folder, Box 11, War Production Board (WPB) Policy Documentation File, Record Group (RG) 179, Modern Military Branch (MMB), National Archives (NA), College Park, Maryland.

24. Steven Fraser, *Labor Will Rule: Sidney Hillman and the Rise of American Labor* (New York: Free Press, 1991), p. 452.

25. "The Defense Advisory Commission," August 8–10, 1940, NA.

26. Louis Galambos, *The Public Image of Big Business in America, 1880–1940* (Baltimore, MD: Johns Hopkins University Press, 1975), p. 159.

27. Fesler et al., *Industrial Mobilization for War*, p. 22.

28. Ibid.; "History of the Division of Administrative Services, War Production Board and Predecessor Agencies, May 1940–June 1945," Box 75, WPB Policy Documentation File, RG 179, MMB, NA, p. 5.

29. "History of the Division of Administrative Services, War Production Board and Predecessor Agencies, May 1940–June 1945," NA, p. 7.

30. Ibid.; Fesler et al., *Industrial Mobilization for War*, p. 30.

31. IMD (Industrial Materials Department) Meeting, June 24, 1940, IMD, NDAC–Meetings File Folder, Box 17, WPB Policy Documentation File, RG 179, MMB, NA, p. 41.

32. Fesler et al., *Industrial Mobilization for War*, p. 30.

33. IMD Meeting, June 3, 1940, IMD, NDAC–Meetings File Folder, Box 17, WPB Policy Documentation File, RG 179, MMB, NA, p. 1.

34. "High Spots Illustrative of Activities," July 24, 1940, Box 81, Edward R. Stettinius Jr. Papers, University of Virginia Library, Charlottesville, Virginia, pp. 2–3; W. J. Barrett to J. E. Cavanagh, July 1, 1940, C File Folder, Box 78, Stettinius Jr. Papers, p. 2.

35. Folsom letter to W. Averell Harriman, February 14, 1941, Materials Division, OPM–Personnel File Folder, Box 50, WPB Policy Documentation File, RG 179, MMB, NA; "Summary of Work Done on Aluminum by the Minerals & Metals Division of the National Defense Advisory Commission," June 1940–January 1941, File Folder 2, Box 109, Marion B. Folsom Papers, University of Rochester, Rochester, New York, pp. 1–8; Wyatt Wells, *Antitrust and the Formation of the Postwar World* (New York: Columbia University Press, 2002), p. 63.

36. IMD Meeting, October 30, 1940, IMD, NDAC–Meetings File Folder, Box 17, WPB Policy Documentation File, RG 179, MMB, NA, p. 175.

37. See, for example, Donald M. Nelson, *Arsenal of Democracy: The Story of American War Production* (New York: Harcourt, Brace, 1946), p. 94.

38. Jesse H. Jones, with Edward Angly, *Fifty Billion Dollars* (New York: Macmillan, 1951), pp. 404–6.

39. The Stacom Company developed and tested a machine to extract crude rubber from the rabbit bush. This experiment, though interesting, was insignificant compared to the growth of the synthetic rubber industry. By the end of World War II, synthetic rubber not only satisfied U.S. military needs but also provided 87 percent of total U.S. rubber consumption. See IMD Meeting, October 30, 1940, p. 175, NA; Bascom Timmons, *Jesse H. Jones: The Man and the Statesman* (New York: Holt, 1956), p. 311; Richard Polenberg, *War and Society: The United States, 1941–1945* (Philadelphia: J. B. Lippincott, 1972), p. 18.

40. Fesler et al., *Industrial Mobilization for War*, p. 31.

41. Ibid.

42. "The Defense Advisory Commission," August 8–10, 1940, NA.

43. Fesler et al., *Industrial Mobilization for War*, p. 31.

44. *Fortune,* December 1940, pp. 181–82.

45. Smith, *The Army and Economic Mobilization*, pp. 484–86.

46. Ibid., p. 485; Timmons, *Jesse H. Jones,* p. 294.

47. Fesler et al., *Industrial Mobilization for War,* p. 161; Smith, *The Army and Economic Mobilization,* pp. 485–86.

48. See, for example, Harold L. Ickes, *The Secret Diary of Harold L. Ickes: Volume III, The Lowering Clouds, 1939–1941* (New York: Simon and Schuster, 1954), p. 296.

49. John Morton Blum, *V was for Victory: Politics and American Culture during World War II* (New York: Harcourt Brace Jovanovich, 1976), p. 134.

50. Smith, *The Army and Economic Mobilization,* pp. 221, 351.

51. *Digest of Public General Bills,* 76th Congress, 1st session, Final Issue, H.R. 6851, p. 338.

52. *United States Statutes at Large,* Vol. 54 (1939–1941), Part I, pp. 974–1003; U.S. Senate Special Committee Investigating the National Defense Program, Hearings, 77th Congress, 1st session, 1941, Part 1, 101; IMD Meeting, August 7, 1940, IMD, NDAC–Meetings File Folder, Box 17, WPB Policy Documentation File, RG 179, MMB, NA, p. 101.

53. Nelson, *Arsenal of Democracy,* p. 291.

54. Fesler et al., *Industrial Mobilization for War,* pp. 75, 170.

55. Ibid., p. 80.

56. *Washington Post,* August 10, 1939, p. 1; Gerald D. Nash, *The Great Depression and World War II: Organizing America, 1933–1945* (New York: St. Martin's Press, 1979), p. 136.

57. I. F. Stone, *Business as Usual: The First Year of Defense* (New York: Modern Age Books, 1941), p. 10; *Fortune,* December 1940, pp. 181–82; Smith, *The Army and Economic Mobilization,* p. 9.

58. Smith, *The Army and Economic Mobilization,* p. 7.

59. Norman Polmar and Thomas B. Allen, *World War II: America at War, 1941–1945* (New York: Random House, 1991), p. 881.

60. Stuart Bruchey, *Enterprise: The Dynamic Economy of a Free People* (Cambridge, MA: Harvard University Press, 1990), p. 475.

61. Fesler et al., *Industrial Mobilization for War,* p. 24; entry from Henderson Diary, October 16, 1940, Box 36, Leon Henderson Papers, Franklin D. Roosevelt Library, Hyde Park, New York; *American Machinist,* October 30, 1940, pp. 879–88.

62. *American Machinist,* October 30, 1940, pp. 879–88.

63. Smith, *The Army and Economic Mobilization,* p. 475.

64. Entry from Henderson Diary, October 16, 1940, Henderson Papers.

65. Ibid.

66. Ibid.

67. Fesler et al., *Industrial Mobilization for War,* p. 24; Nelson, *Arsenal of Democracy,* pp. 102–3.

68. Entry from Henderson Diary, October 16, 1940, Henderson Papers.

69. Memorandum from Leon Henderson to Franklin D. Roosevelt, October 14, 1940, Box 2, Council of National Defense, Official File, Franklin D. Roosevelt Papers, Roosevelt Library, p. 1.

70. See, for example, Blum, *V was for Victory,* p. 134.

71. Polenberg, *War and Society,* p. 77.

72. Nelson, *Arsenal of Democracy,* p. 98.

73. IMD Meeting, August 21, 1940, p. 115 (excerpt of a letter from Stettinius to Henderson), IMD, NDAC–Meetings File Folder, Box 17, WPB Policy Documentation File, RG 179, MMB, NA.

74. Nelson, *Arsenal of Democracy,* p. 98.

75. Polenberg, *War and Society,* p. 77.

76. Ibid.

77. Ibid., p. 78.

78. Cole, *Roosevelt and the Isolationists,* p. 399.

79. Ibid., p. 400.

80. Ibid., p. 397.

81. Ibid., p. 389.

82. Ibid., p. 403.

83. This insight was derived from many sources. See, especially, Wayne S. Cole, *America First: The Battle Against Intervention, 1940–1941* (Madison: University of Wisconsin Press, 1953), pp. 15–16, 93–103.

84. Smith, *The Army and Economic Mobilization,* pp. 129–30.

85. Cole, *America First,* p. 99.

86. Ibid.

87. For an example of Johnson's thinking on this score, see the *New York World Telegram,* August 22, 1939, p. 15.

88. The belief that businessmen put profits ahead of the safety of U.S. soldiers goes back at least as far as the Nye Committee of 1934–1936. See, for example, Manfred Jonas, *Isolationism in America, 1935–1941* (Ithaca, NY: Cornell University Press, 1966), pp. 144–50.

89. Cole, *Roosevelt and the Isolationists,* p. 403.

90. Stone, *Business As Usual,* pp. 12, 24–25, 45; Gabriel Kolko, "American Business and Germany, 1930–1941," *Western Political Quarterly* 15, no. 4 (December 1962): 713–28.

91. Stone, *Business as Usual,* pp. 13–18; Lichtenstein, *Labor's War at Home,* pp. 38–43.

92. A succinct statement of the "business as usual" viewpoint can be found in I. F. Stone, *The War Years, 1939–1945* (Boston: Little, Brown, 1988), pp. 119–22. In addition, see *Nation,* June 8, 1940, pp. 708–9; *The New Republic,* December 23, 1940, pp. 854–55; Lichtenstein, *Labor's War at Home,* pp. 41–42, 83–89; and Barton J. Bernstein, "The Automobile Industry and the Coming of the Second World War," *Southwestern Social Science Quarterly* 47 (June 1966): 22–25.

93. Such were the ironies of preparedness that Nelson himself was considered an "all-outer," whereas other corporate liberals (notably Knudsen and Stettinius) were not. See Stone, *Business as Usual,* p. 17, for a favorable view of Nelson. Richard Polenberg notes that Nelson was "a pre–Pearl Harbor advocate of an increased defense program." This characterization also fits with the depiction of Nelson as an all-outer in 1940–1941. See Polenberg, *War and Society,* p. 222.

94. *Washington Post,* January 7, 1941, p. 4.

95. Bendix Aircraft, for example, constructed a "special cylinder boring lathe." See *American Machinist,* October 30, 1940, p. 878.

96. "Building for Defense: The Problem" (undated), NDAC–Publications File Folder, Box 11, WPB Policy Documentation File, RG 179, MMB, NA.

97. See, for example, *American Machinist,* May 31, 1939, p. 407.

98. *Washington Post,* January 7, 1941, p. 4.

99. *Factory,* October 1940, p. 50.

100. Ibid., p. 49.

101. *New York Times,* January 19, 1940, p. 4.

102. *Washington Post,* August 10, 1940, p. 6.

103. Address by W. L. Batt to *Herald-Tribune* Forum, October 22, 1940, Industrial Materials File Folder, Box 6, National Defense Advisory Commission (Council of National Defense), Roosevelt Library, p. 7.

104. Robert M. Collins, *The Business Response to Keynes, 1929–1964* (New York: Columbia University Press, 1981), p. 45; *Nation's Business,* January 1939, p. 11.

105. Collins, *The Business Response to Keynes,* p. 87.

106. Samuel Crowther to Edward R. Stettinius Jr., May 31, 1940, Samuel Crowther File Folder (May–December 1940), Box 119, Stettinius Jr. Papers.

107. Wilson Foss to Stettinius, August 15, 1940, Hans F. Faber–Wilson Foss File Folder, Box 120, Stettinius Jr. Papers.

108. Ibid.

109. Bruce Barton to Stettinius, July 15, 1940, B. Barton–Brown File Folder, Box 119, Stettinius Jr. Papers.

110. Crowther to Stettinius, January 9, 1941, Crowther File Folder 2, Box 119, Stettinius Jr. Papers, pp. 1–2.

111. Barton to Stettinius, July 15, 1940, B. Barton–Brown File Folder, Box 119, Stettinius Jr. Papers.

112. Edgar Monsanto Queeny to Stettinius, August 12, 1940, Advisory Commission to the Council of National Defense—Criticism and Suggestions for Improvement File Folder, Box 4, WPB Policy Documentation File, RG 179, MMB, NA, p. 1.

113. *Washington Post,* January 7, 1940, Section III, p. B7.

114. Crowther to Stettinius, February 25, 1941, Crowther File Folder 2, Box 119, Stettinius Jr. Papers; Crowther to Stettinius, 1943 (no month and day noted).

115. *The New Republic,* December 23, 1940, p. 854.

116. Fesler et al., *Industrial Mobilization for War,* p. 35.

117. *Nation's Business,* February 1941, p. 36.

118. Fesler et al., *Industrial Mobilization for War,* p. xv.

119. Cole, *Roosevelt and the Isolationists,* p. 11.

120. Fesler et al., *Industrial Mobilization for War,* pp. 93–95. See also Advisory Commission to the Council of National Defense Minutes, October 22, 1941, Box 7, WPB Policy Documentation File, RG 179, MMB, NA, pp. 708–9.

Chapter Six

1. James W. Fesler et al., *Industrial Mobilization for War: History of the War Production Board and Predecessor Agencies, 1940–1945* (Washington, DC: U.S. Government Printing Office, 1947), p. 95.

2. *Washington Post,* January 8, 1941, p. 2.

3. R. Elberton Smith, *The Army and Economic Mobilization* (Washington, DC: Office of the Chief of Military History, Department of the Army, 1959), pp. 129–33.

4. Bruce Catton, *The War Lords of Washington* (New York: Harcourt, Brace, 1948), p. 52; Smith, *The Army and Economic Mobilization,* p. 104; Fesler et al., *Industrial Mobilization for War,* p. 96.

5. See, for example, Richard Polenberg, *War and Society: The United States, 1941–1945* (Philadelphia: J. B. Lippincott, 1972), p. 7; *The New Republic,* February 17, 1941, p. 231; Steven Fraser, *Labor Will Rule: Sidney Hillman and the Rise of American Labor* (New York: Free Press, 1991), pp. 460–61.

6. Fesler et al., *Industrial Mobilization for War,* p. 60; *Nation's Business,* July 1941, pp. 29–30.

7. Fesler et al., *Industrial Mobilization for War,* p. 97.

8. Ibid.

9. Ibid.

10. Stettinius normally put "experienced executives" in charge of the branches, "whose personal business connections did not involve them with the materials (or products) which their divisions were studying." He did this to avoid conflict-of-interest charges. On the other hand, personnel who assisted branch chiefs came from industries that produced the items under consideration; these men supplied "expert knowledge." See Initial Report to the President (June 1–December 1, 1940), December 19, 1940, NDAC-IMD File Folder, Box 89, Edward R. Stettinius Jr. Papers, University of Virginia Library, Charlottesville, Virginia, p. 3.

11. Draft Statement of Mr. William S. Knudsen for Truman Investigation, April 1941, Office of Production Management–History File Folder, Box 19, War Production Board (WPB) Policy Documentation File, Record Group (RG) 179, Modern Military Branch (MMB), National Archives (NA), Washington, DC, p. 2.

12. Ibid.

13. Brian Waddell, "Economic Mobilization for World War II and the Transformation of the U.S. State," *Politics and Society* 22, no. 2 (June 1994): 170–71.

14. Paul A. C. Koistinen, *The Military-Industrial Complex: A Historical Perspective* (New York: Praeger, 1980), p. 71.

15. Harold L. Ickes, *The Secret Diary of Harold L. Ickes: Volume III, The Lowering Clouds, 1939–1941* (New York: Simon and Schuster, 1954), pp. 295–96.

16. John Morton Blum, *V was for Victory: Politics and American Culture During World War II* (New York: Harcourt Brace Jovanovich, 1976), pp. 131–40.

17. Smith, *The Army and Economic Mobilization,* p. 221.

18. Entry from Henderson Diary, October 11, 1939, Box 36, Leon Henderson Papers, Franklin D. Roosevelt Library, Hyde Park, New York.

19. Polenberg, *War and Society,* p. 12.

20. Smith, *The Army and Economic Mobilization,* p. 220.

21. Koistinen, *The Military-Industrial Complex,* p. 71.

22. Waddell, "Economic Mobilization for World War II and the Transformation of the U.S. State," p. 171.

23. Ibid., p. 187 (n. 29).

24. See, for example, "Industrial Mobilization Plan" (Revision of 1939), U.S. Government Printing Office, Washington, DC, 1939, p. 7.

25. Waddell, "Economic Mobilization for World War II and the Transformation of the U.S. State," p. 171.

26. Entry from Henderson Diary, October 16, 1940, Henderson Papers.

27. Ibid.

28. I. F. Stone, *Business As Usual: The First Year of Defense* (New York: Modern Age Books, 1941), p. 17.

29. Eliot Janeway, *The Struggle for Survival: A Chronicle of Economic Mobilization in World War II* (New Haven, CT: Yale University Press, 1951), pp. 272–73.

30. Polenberg, *War and Society,* p. 217.

31. Ibid.

32. Fesler et al., *Industrial Mobilization for War,* p. 108; "History of the Division of Administrative Services, War Production Board and Predecessor Agencies, May 1940–June 1945," Box 75, WPB Policy Documentation File, RG 179, MMB, NA, p. 5; Office of Production Management–Budget–Estimates and Justification–1942 Log, Box 22, WPB Policy Documentation File, p. 2.

33. Ibid.

34. S. R. Fuller to John Biggers, June 11, 1941, 016.206C File Folder, Box 37, WPB Policy Documentation File, RG 179, MMB, NA, p. 2.

35. H. W. Huber to H. S. Rogers, May 22, 1941, Priorities Division, OPM–Personnel, May–December 1941 File Folder, Box 36, WPB Policy Documentation File, RG 179, MMB, NA, pp. 1–2.

36. Stone, *Business As Usual,* p. 9.

37. Statement by John D. Biggers before the House Military Affairs Committee, April 7, 1941, 210 Production–Programs–1941 File Folder, Box 958, WPB Policy Documentation File, RG 179, MMB, NA, p. 3.

38. Stone, *Business As Usual,* p. 9.

39. Ibid., p. 10. My interpretation, of course, is diametrically opposed to Stone's, though I make use of his statistics. Whereas he believes that the first full year of American preparedness (1940–1941) amounted to "smoke and mirrors," I argue that corporate liberal exertions created an economic environment and legal order indispensable to mass production of defense goods in later years. Huge percentage increases in the quantity of weapons that the United States possessed by May 1941 should not be dismissed. Instead, they indicate a pivotal transition from the "unready state" of 1939 to the "warfare state" of 1943–1944.

40. *Nation,* May 25, 1940, p. 644; June 8, 1940, pp. 708–9; *New Republic,* February 17, 1941, pp. 227–32; Wayne S. Cole, *Roosevelt and the Isolationists, 1932–1945* (Lincoln: University of Nebraska Press, 1983), pp. 403, 420.

41. Christy Borth, *Masters of Mass Production* (New York: Bobbs-Merrill, 1945), pp. 34–60; Donald M. Nelson, *Arsenal of Democracy: The Story of American War Production* (New York: Harcourt, Brace, 1946), p. 25; Thomas Ferguson, "From Normalcy to New Deal: Industrial Structure, Party Competition, and American Public Policy in the Great Depression," *International Organization* 38,

no. 1 (Winter 1984): 41–94. Although Ferguson stops short of the preparedness period, I believe many of his insights are applicable to it. In particular, I argue that the pursuit of economic stability remained a strong motivation for U.S.-based multinational corporations throughout the preparedness and war years.

42. See, for example, Smith, *The Army and Economic Mobilization,* pp. 128–39; Warren F. Kimball, *The Most Unsordid Act: Lend-Lease, 1939–1941* (Baltimore, MD: Johns Hopkins University Press, 1969), pp. 193–229.

43. Cole, *Roosevelt and the Isolationists,* p. 422.

44. John Keegan, *The Second World War* (New York: Penguin Books, 1990), pp. 215–18.

45. Ibid., p. 218. Also see George C. Herring, *Aid to Russia, 1941–1946* (New York: Columbia University Press, 1973), pp. 45–48.

46. A brief survey that notes the usual problems is Allan M. Winkler's *Home Front U.S.A.: America During World War II* (Arlington Heights, IL: Harlan Davidson, 1986), p. 6.

47. Smith, *The Army and Economic Mobilization,* p. 104.

48. *Washington Post,* August 28, 1941, p. 6.

49. John H. Martin, "Administration of Priorities," *Harvard Business Review* (Summer 1941), p. 423.

50. Nelson, *Arsenal of Democracy,* p. 128.

51. Ibid.

52. *United States Statutes at Large,* Vol. 55 (1941–1942), Part I, p. 236; Memorandum from Stettinius to William Knudsen, July 28, 1941, Priorities Division, OPM–Personnel, May–December 1941 File Folder, Box 36, WPB Policy Documentation File, RG 179, MMB, NA, p. 2.

53. Memorandum from Stettinius to Knudsen, July 28, 1941, NA, p. 2.

54. Stettinius to Knudsen and Sidney Hillman, August 26, 1941, Priorities Division, OPM–Personnel, May–December 1941 File Folder, Box 36, WPB Policy Documentation File, RG 179, MMB, NA.

55. Ibid.

56. Ibid.

57. Ibid.; Memorandum from James L. O'Neill to E. R. Stettinius Jr., July 30, 1941, Priorities Division, OPM–Personnel, May–December 1941 File Folder, Box 36, WPB Policy Documentation File, RG 179, MMB, NA.

58. *Fortune,* August 1941, p. 43.

59. Martin, "Administration of Priorities," OPM, Division of Priorities Publicity Release, March 19, 1941, Office of Production Management File Folder, Box 6, National Defense Advisory Commission, 1940–41, RG 220, Roosevelt Library, p. 419.

60. OPM, Division of Priorities Publicity Release, March 19, 1941, Roosevelt Library.

61. Ibid.; Martin, "Administration of Priorities," p. 419.

62. See, for example, *Fortune,* August 1941, p. 43.

63. *Washington Post,* August 28, 1941, p. 6.

64. Smith, *The Army and Economic Mobilization,* p. 103; Fesler, et al., *Industrial Mobilization for War,* pp. 102–3.

65. Winkler, *Home Front U.S.A.,* pp. 39–40.

66. Meg Jacobs, "How About Some Meat?": The Office of Price Administration, Consumption Politics, and State Building from the Bottom Up, 1941–1946," *Journal of American History* 84 (December 1997): 914–15.

67. Fesler et al., *Industrial Mobilization for War*, p. 104.

68. Ibid., p. 103.

69. Nelson, *Arsenal of Democracy*, p. 146.

70. Polenberg, *War and Society*, p. 7.

71. Fesler et al., *Industrial Mobilization for War*, p. 135.

72. Ibid., p. 140.

73. Stone, *Business As Usual*, p. 9.

74. *Nation*, June 8, 1940, p. 708.

75. Ibid., pp. 708–9.

76. *New Republic*, February 17, 1941, pp. 230–31.

77. Ibid., pp. 230–32.

78. Ibid., pp. 231–32.

79. Fesler et al., *Industrial Mobilization for War*, pp. 106–7.

80. Master Organizational Chart, July 15, 1941, OPM–Functional Charts File Folder, Box 19, WPB Policy Documentation File, RG 179, MMB, NA.

81. A good example of the commodity section–industry advisory committee set up involved the Plates, Shapes, Sheets, Strips, and Tin Plate Section of the Production Division and its partner, the Plate Advisory Committee. See Fuller to Biggers, June 11, 1941, 016.206 C File Folder, Box 37, WPB Policy Documentation File, RG 179, MMB, NA, pp. 2–3.

82. Fesler et al., *Industrial Mobilization for War*, p. 107.

83. Ibid., p. 109.

84. Ibid., pp. 109–10.

85. Smith, *The Army and Economic Mobilization*, p. 105.

86. Fesler et al., *Industrial Mobilization for War*, pp. 110–11.

87. Winkler, *Home Front U.S.A.*, p. 39.

88. Jacobs, "How About Some Meat?," p. 915.

89. Fesler et al., *Industrial Mobilization for War*, p. 111.

90. See, for example, Catton, *The War Lords of Washington*, pp. 71–72.

91. Thomas M. Campbell and George C. Herring, eds., *The Diaries of Edward R. Stettinius, Jr., 1943–1946* (New York: New Viewpoints, 1975), pp. xix–xx.

92. Fesler et al., *Industrial Mobilization for War*, pp. 110–11; Catton, *The War Lords of Washington*, p. 71.

93. *Current Biography*, 1941, pp. 608–10. An interesting biographical sketch of Nelson can be found in Alan Brinkley, *The End of Reform: New Deal Liberalism in Recession and War* (New York: Knopf, 1995), pp. 184–85.

94. *Current Biography*, 1941, p. 609.

95. Nelson, *Arsenal of Democracy*, p. 65.

96. *Current Biography*, 1941, pp. 609–10; Fesler et al., *Industrial Mobilization for War*, p. 20.

97. Nelson's easygoing manner, together with his conciliatory approach toward civilian agencies and the military, was often interpreted as weakness. See Polenberg, *War and Society*, p. 220; Blum, *V was for Victory*, p. 121.

98. Fesler et al., *Industrial Mobilization for War*, p. 273.

99. Smith, *The Army and Economic Mobilization*, p. 140.

100. Ibid., pp. 140–41; Polenberg, *War and Society*, p. 221.

101. Fesler et al., *Industrial Mobilization for War*, p. 273.

102. Ibid., p. 274; U.S. Senate Special Committee Investigating the National Defense Program, Hearings, 77th Congress, 1st session, 1941, Part 5, 1343–1344.

103. Cole, *Roosevelt and the Isolationists*, pp. 420–21.

104. Ibid., p. 415.

105. Ibid., p. 420.

106. Barton J. Bernstein, "The Automobile Industry and the Coming of the Second World War," *Southwestern Social Science Quarterly* 47 (June 1966): 22–25; *Wall Street Journal*, October 31, 1941, p. 6; November 26, 1941, p. 6.

107. *Nation*, June 8, 1940, p. 708; *Fortune*, January 1942, pp. 123–24.

108. *Fortune*, January 1942, p. 124.

109. Polenberg, *War and Society*, p. 221.

110. Ibid., pp. 220–24. In addition, see U.S. Senate Special Committee Investigating the National Defense Program, Hearings, 77th Congress, 1st Session, 1941, Part 5, 1336.

111. *Fortune*, November 1941, p. 150.

112. Nelson, *Arsenal of Democracy*, p. 158; *Fortune*, November 1941, p. 168.

113. *Fortune*, November 1941, p. 168.

114. Ibid.; Nelson, *Arsenal of Democracy*, p. 158.

115. *Fortune*, November 1941, p. 168.

116. Ibid.

117. Ibid., p. 150.

118. Fesler et al., *Industrial Mobilization for War*, p. 113.

119. Ibid., p. 114.

120. *Nation's Business*, February 1942, p. 18; *Fortune*, February 1942, p. 150.

121. Ibid.

122. *Courier-Journal* (Louisville), July 17, 1941, p. 2; July 30, 1942, p. 12; Norman Polmar and Thomas B. Allen, *World War II: America at War, 1941–1945* (New York: Random House, 1991), p. 881.

123. *Fortune*, February 1942, p. 150.

124. Ibid.; Nelson, *Arsenal of Democracy*, pp. 41–42.

125. Keegan, *The Second World War*, p. 218.

126. Fesler et al., *Industrial Mobilization for War*, p. 962.

127. Winkler, *Home Front U.S.A.*, pp. 25–26.

128. *Fortune*, May 1941, pp. 86–87.

129. Ibid, p. 86.

130. John Morton Blum emphasizes this point over and over again in his fine book *V was for Victory*. See, for example, pp. 5–8.

131. *Nation's Business*, January 1942, p. 30.

132. Nelson, *Arsenal for Democracy*, p. 193.

133. Smith, *The Army and Economic Mobilization*, p. 105; Winkler, *Home Front U.S.A.*, p. 6.

Epilogue

1. H. S. Dennison to Ida M. Tarbell, March 14, 1935, 1933–1934–1935 File Folder, Case 1, Henry S. Dennison Papers, Harvard University (Baker) Library, Cambridge, Massachusetts, p. 1.

2. Ibid.

3. Ibid.

4. Ibid.

5. See, for instance, Gloria Vollmers, "Industrial Home Work of the Dennison Manufacturing Company of Framingham, Massachusetts, 1912–1935," *Business History Review* 71 (Autumn 1997): 466.

6. Brian Waddell, "Economic Mobilization for World War II and the Transformation of the U.S. State," *Politics and Society* 22, no. 2 (June 1994): 165. Also see Waddell, *The War Against the New Deal: World War II and American Democracy* (DeKalb: Northern Illinois University Press, 2001).

7. Ibid. Waddell emphasizes the victory of military–state bureaucratic authority over New Deal civilian–state authority. This theme reoccurs throughout his article, and he explains that this outcome was due in part to "Roosevelt's decreasing commitment to social reform."

8. Allan M. Winkler, *Home Front U.S.A.: America during World War II* (Arlington Heights, IL: Harlan Davidson, 1986), p. 6; Geoffrey Perrett, *Days of Sadness, Years of Triumph: The American People 1939–1945* (New York: Coward, McCann & Geoghegan, 1973), p. 256.

9. Norman Polmar and Thomas B. Allen, *World War II: America at War, 1941–1945* (New York: Random House, 1991), p. 880.

10. The standard interpretation is that Nelson possessed the authority to take over military contracting and purchasing but chose not to do it. He wanted to avoid delay and believed that the military should be free to pick the weapons it wanted. See, for example, Kim McQuaid, *Big Business and Presidential Power: From FDR to Reagan* (New York: William Morrow, 1982), pp. 87–89; Richard Polenberg, *War and Society: The United States, 1941–1945* (Philadelphia: J. B. Lippincott, 1972), pp. 217–18; John Morton Blum, *V was for Victory: Politics and American Culture During World War II* (New York: Harcourt Brace Jovanovich, 1976), pp. 121–22.

11. McQuaid, *Big Business and Presidential Power*, p. 88; Winkler, *Home Front U.S.A.*, pp. 31–32.

12. McQuaid, *Big Business and Presidential Power*, p. 88.

13. Polmar and Allen, *World War II*, p. 880.

14. See, for example, Richard R. Lingeman, *Don't You Know There's a War On? The American Home Front, 1941–1945* (New York: G. P. Putham's Sons, 1970), p. 107, and Blum, *V was for Victory*, pp. 122–23.

15. Polenberg, *War and Society*, p. 220.

16. Ibid., p. 223.

17. Ibid.

18. Gregory Hooks, *Forging the Military-Industrial Complex: World War II's Battle of the Potomac* (Urbana: University of Illinois Press, 1991), p. 117; Polenberg, *War and Society*, p. 224.

19. McQuaid, *Big Business and Presidential Power,* p. 91.

20. Ibid.; Polmar and Allen, *World War II,* p. 576.

21. See Keith E. Eiler, *Mobilizing America: Robert P. Patterson and the War Effort, 1940–1945* (Ithaca, NY: Cornell University Press, 1997), pp. 332–35. I drew information from Eiler's account but disagree with him on Patterson's role in the war. Although I believe Patterson played a significant role in procurement and overall supply, I do not give him as much credit for industrial mobilization as Eiler does. Many others, such as the corporate liberals, made valuable contributions as well.

22. For a colorful account along these lines, see David M. Kennedy, *Freedom from Fear: The American People in Depression and War, 1929–1945* (New York: Oxford University Press, 1999), p. 621.

23. The standard interpretation of Donald Nelson and the War Production Board can be found in Alan Brinkley, "The New Deal and the Idea of the State," in Steve Fraser and Gary Gerstle, eds., *The Rise and Fall of the New Deal Order, 1930–1980* (Princeton, NJ: Princeton University Press, 1989), pp. 102–4; Blum, *V was for Victory,* p. 121; Winkler, *Home Front U.S.A.,* pp. 6–7; H. K. Rutherford, "Mobilizing Industry for War," *Harvard Business Review* 18 (Autumn 1939): 2.

24. Polmar and Allen, *World War II,* p. 880.

25. Winkler, *Home Front U.S.A.,* p. 22.

26. Alan S. Milward, *War, Economy and Society, 1939–1945* (Berkeley: University of California Press, 1977), p. 70.

27. Warren F. Kimball, *The Most Unsordid Act: Lend-Lease, 1939–1941* (Baltimore, MD: Johns Hopkins University Press, 1969), p. 229; Winkler, *Home Front U.S.A.,* p. 22.

28. U.S. Senate Special Committee Investigating the National Defense Program, Hearings, 77th Congress, 1st Session, 1941, Part 5, 1349–1355.

29. Meg Jacobs, "How About Some Meat?": The Office of Price Administration, Consumption Politics and State Building from the Bottom Up, 1941–1946," *Journal of American History* 84 (December 1997): 938–40.

30. J. George Frederick, *The New Deal: A People's Capitalism* (New York: Business Bourse, Publishers, 1944), p. 156.

31. John D. Biggers et al., *Human Relations in Modern Business: A Guide for Action Sponsored by American Business Leaders* (New York: Prentice-Hall, 1949), pp. 44–45.

32. Address by Walter D. Fuller Before the Meeting of County Chairmen, June 29, 1943, File Folder 4, Box 96, Marion B. Folsom Papers, University of Rochester Library, Rochester, New York, p. 5.

Bibliography

I. Primary Resources

A. Manuscript Collections

Henry S. Dennison Papers. Harvard Business Library. Cambridge, Massachusetts.

Marion Folsom Papers. University of Rochester Library. Rochester, New York.

W. Averell Harriman Papers. Library of Congress. Washington, DC.

Leon Henderson Papers. Franklin D. Roosevelt Presidential Library. Hyde Park, New York.

Herbert H. Lehman Papers. Lehman Suite. Columbia University. New York, New York.

Franklin Delano Roosevelt Papers. Franklin D. Roosevelt Presidential Library. Hyde Park, New York.

Edward R. Stettinius Jr. Papers. University of Virginia Library. Charlottesville, Virginia.

Gerard Swope Materials. Oral History Collection (Butler Library). Columbia University. New York, New York.

Robert E. Wood Papers. Herbert Hoover Presidential Library. West Branch, Iowa.

B. Archival Sources

National Archives. Civil Records Branch. Record Group 187. Central Office Records. College Park, Maryland.

National Archives. Modern Military Branch. Record Group 107. Records of the Planning Branch, Assistant Secretary of War, Office of the Secretary of War. College Park, Maryland.

National Archives. Modern Military Branch. Record Group 179. War Production Board Policy Documentation File. College Park, Maryland.

C. Government/Public Documents

Digest of Public General Bills, 76th Congress (1939–1941).

"Industrial Mobilization Plan" (Revision of 1939). Washington, DC: U.S. Government Printing Office, 1939.

United States Senate Special Committee Investigating the National Defense Program (also known as the Truman Committee), Hearings, 77th Congress, 1st Session, 1941. Washington, DC: U.S. Government Printing Office, 1941.

United States Statutes at Large, Vol. 54 (1939–1941), Vol. 55 (1941–1942).
Vital Speeches (1938–1941).

D. Newspapers
Baltimore Sun (1939–1941)
Louisville Courier-Journal (1939–1942)
New York Times (1933–1941)
New York World Telegram (1939)
Wall Street Journal (1939–1941)
Washington Post (1933–1941)

E. Periodicals
American Machinist (1939–1941)
Business Week (1933–1941)
Dun's Review (1939–1941)
Factory (1939–1941)
Fortune (1933–1941)
Iron Age (1939–1941)
The Nation (1939–1941)
Nation's Business (1932–1942)
The New Republic (1939–1941)
The New Yorker (1939–1941)
Newsweek (1933–1941)
Saturday Evening Post (1937–1945, 1955)
System, the Magazine of Business (1924–1926)
Time (1933–1941, 1986)

F. Interviews
Nathan, Robert R. Bethesda, Maryland, and Arlington, Virginia. May 20, 1992, and July 10, 1995.

II. Secondary Sources

A. Books
Abramson, Rudy. *Spanning the Century: The Life of W. Averell Harriman, 1891–1986.* New York: William Morrow, 1992.

Adams, Stephen B. *Mr. Kaiser Goes to Washington: The Rise of a Government Entrepreneur.* Chapel Hill: University of North Carolina Press, 1997.

Alchon, Guy. *The Invisible Hand of Planning: Capitalism, Social Science, and the State in the 1920s.* Princeton, NJ: Princeton University Press, 1985.

Altmeyer, Arthur. *The Formative Years of Social Security.* Madison: University of Wisconsin, Press, 1968.

Badger, Anthony J. *The New Deal: The Depression Years, 1933–1940.* New York: Hill and Wang, 1988.

Bailyn, Bernard. *The Ideological Origins of the American Revolution.* Cambridge, MA: Harvard University Press, 1967.

Bellush, Bernard. *The Failure of the NRA.* New York: W. W. Norton, 1975.

Bemis, Samuel Flagg. "The Shifting Strategy of American Defense and Diplomacy." In *Essays in History and International Relations in Honor of George Hubbard Blakeslee,* Massachusetts: Clark University, 1949.

Benjamin, Roger, and Elkin, Stephen L., eds. *The Democratic State.* Lawrence: University Press of Kansas, 1985.

Berkowitz, Edward, and McQuaid, Kim. *Creating the Welfare State: The Political Economy of Twentieth-Century Reform.* New York: Praeger, 1980.

Bernstein, Barton J., ed. "Economic Policies." In Richard S. Kirkendall, ed., *The Truman Period as a Research Field.* Columbia: University of Missouri Press, 1967.

———. *Towards a New Past: Dissenting Essays in American History.* New York: Vintage Books, 1968.

Bernstein, Irving. *The Lean Years.* Boston: Houghton Mifflin, 1960.

———. *The New Deal Collective Bargaining Policy.* Berkeley: University of California Press, 1950.

———. *Turbulent Years: A History of the American Worker, 1933–1941.* Boston: Houghton Mifflin, 1969.

Biggers, John D., et al. *Human Relations in Modern Business: A Guide for Action Sponsored by American Business Leaders.* New York: Prentice-Hall, 1949.

Blum, Albert A. "Birth and Death of the M-Day Plan." In Harold Stein, ed., *American Civil-Military Decisions: A Book of Case Studies.* Tuscaloosa: University of Alabama Press, 1963.

Blum, John Morton. *V Was for Victory: Politics and American Culture During World War II.* New York: Harcourt Brace Jovanovich, 1976.

Borth, Christy. *Masters of Mass Production.* Indianapolis, IN: Bobbs-Merrill, 1945.

Braeman, John, Bremner, Robert H., and Walters, Everett, eds. *Change and Continuity in Twentieth-Century America.* Columbus: Ohio State University Press, 1964.

Brand, Donald R. *Corporatism and the Rule of Law: A Study of the National Recovery Administration.* Ithaca, NY: Cornell University Press, 1988.

Brandes, Stuart D. *American Welfare Capitalism, 1880–1940.* Chicago: University of Chicago Press, 1976.

Brinkley, Alan. *The End of Reform: New Deal Liberalism in Recession and War.* New York: Knopf, 1995.

———. "The New Deal and the Idea of the State." In Steve Fraser and Gary Gerstle, eds., *The Rise and Fall of the New Deal Order, 1930–1980.* Princeton, NJ: Princeton University Press, 1989.

Brody, David. "The Rise and Decline of Welfare Capitalism." In John Braeman, Robert H. Bremner, and David Brody, eds., *Change and Continuity in Twentieth-Century America: The 1920s.* Columbus: Ohio State University Press, 1968.

Bruchey, Stuart. *Enterprise: The Dynamic Economy of a Free People.* Cambridge, MA: Harvard University Press, 1990.

Burk, Kathleen, ed. *War and the State: The Transformation of British Government, 1914–1919.* London: George Allen & Unwin, 1982.

Burk, Robert F. *The Corporate State and the Broker State.* Cambridge, MA: Harvard University Press, 1990.

Burner, David. *Herbert Hoover: A Public Life.* New York: Knopf, 1979.

Burns, James MacGregor. *Roosevelt: The Lion and the Fox.* New York: Harcourt, Brace and World, 1956.

————. *Roosevelt: The Soldier of Freedom.* New York: Harcourt Brace Jovanovich, 1970.

Campbell, Thomas M., and Herring, George C., eds. *The Diaries of Edward R. Stettinius, Jr., 1943–1946.* New York: New Viewpoints, 1975.

Case, Josephine Young, and Needham, Everett. *Owen D. Young and American Enterprise.* Boston: David Godine, 1982.

Catton, Bruce. *The War Lords of Washington.* New York: Harcourt, Brace and Company, 1948.

Chandler, Alfred D. *The Visible Hand.* Cambridge, MA: Belknap Press, Harvard University Press, 1977.

Cohen, Lizabeth. *Making a New Deal: Industrial Workers in Chicago, 1919–1939.* Cambridge: Cambridge University Press, 1990.

Cole, Wayne S. *America First: The Battle Against Intervention, 1940–1941.* Madison: University of Wisconsin Press, 1953.

————. *Roosevelt and the Isolationists, 1932–1945.* Lincoln: University of Nebraska Press, 1983.

Collins, Robert M. *The Business Response to Keynes, 1929–1964.* New York: Columbia University Press, 1981.

Crowther, Samuel. *John H. Patterson: Pioneer in Industrial Welfare.* Garden City, NY: Doubleday and Page, 1923.

————. *Why Men Strike.* Garden City, NY: Doubleday, Page and Company, 1920.

Cuff, Robert D. *The War Industries Board: Business Government Relations During World War I.* Baltimore, MD: Johns Hopkins University Press, 1973.

Dennison, Henry S. *Ethics and Modern Business.* Boston: Houghton Mifflin, 1932.

Dennison, James T. *Henry S. Dennison: New England Industrialist Who Served America.* New York: The Newcomen Society, 1955.

Domhoff, G. William. *The Power Elite and the State.* New York: Aldine de Gruyter, 1990.

Eiler, Keith E. *Mobilizing America: Robert P. Patterson and the War Effort, 1940–1945.* Ithaca, NY: Cornell University Press, 1997.

Eisenhower, Dwight D. *Crusade in Europe.* Garden City, NY: Doubleday & Company, 1948.

Ferrell, Robert H. *Peace in Their Time: The Origins of the Kellogg-Briand Pact.* New Haven, CT: Yale University Press, 1952.

Ferguson, Thomas. *Golden Rule: The Investment Theory of Party Competition and the Logic of Money-Driven Political Systems.* Chicago: University of Chicago Press, 1995.

Fesler, James W., et al. *Industrial Mobilization for War: History of the War Production Board and Predecessor Agencies, 1940–1945.* Washington, DC: U.S. Government Printing Office, 1947.

Finegold, Kenneth, and Skocpol, Theda. *State and Party in America's New Deal.* Madison: University of Wisconsin Press, 1995.

Finney, Burnham. *Arsenal of Democracy: How Industry Builds Our Defense.* New York: Whittlesey House, 1941.

Flanders, Ralph, Dennison, Henry S., and Filene, Lincoln. *Toward Full Employment.* New York: Whittlesey House, 1938.

Foner, Eric, ed. *The New American History.* Philadelphia: Temple University Press, 1990.

Fraser, Steven. *Labor Will Rule: Sidney Hillman and the Rise of American Labor.* New York: Free Press, 1991.

Frederick, J. George. *The New Deal: A People's Capitalism.* New York: Business Bourse, 1944.

———, ed. *The Swope Plan: Details, Criticisms, Analysis.* New York: Business Bourse, 1931.

Freeland, Richard M. *The Truman Doctrine and the Origins of McCarthyism.* New York: Knopf, 1972.

Furner, Mary O., and Supple, Barry, eds. *The State and Economic Knowledge: The American and British Experiences.* Cambridge: Cambridge University Press, 1990.

Gabel, Christopher R. *The U.S. Army GHQ Maneuvers of 1941.* Washington, DC: Center of Military History, United States Army, 1991.

Galambos, Louis. *Competition and Cooperation.* Baltimore, MD: Johns Hopkins University Press, 1966.

———. *The Public Image of Big Business in America, 1880–1940: A Quantitative Study in Social Change.* Baltimore, MD: Johns Hopkins University Press, 1975.

Galambos, Louis, and Pratt, Joseph. *The Rise of the Corporate Commonwealth: U.S. Business and Public Policy in the Twentieth Century.* New York: Basic Books, 1988.

Gerber, Larry G. *The Limits of Liberalism: Josephus Daniels, Henry Stimson, Bernard Baruch, Donald Richberg, Felix Frankfurter, and the Development of the Modern American Political Economy.* New York: New York University Press, 1983.

Goodwin, Doris Kearns. *No Ordinary Time: Franklin & Eleanor Roosevelt: The Home Front in World War II.* New York: Simon & Schuster, 1994.

Gordon, Colin. *New Deals: Business, Labor, and Politics in America, 1920–1935.* Cambridge: Cambridge University Press, 1994.

Graham, Otis L. *Toward a Planned Society: From Roosevelt to Nixon.* New York: Oxford University Press, 1976.

Hamilton, David E. *From New Day to New Deal: American Farm Policy from Hoover to Roosevelt, 1928–1933.* Chapel Hill: University of North Carolina Press, 1991.

Harris, Howell John. *The Right to Manage: Industrial Relations Policies of American Business in the 1940s.* Madison: University of Wisconsin Press, 1982.

Hawley, Ellis W. *The Great War and the Search for a Modern Order: A History of the American People and Their Institutions, 1917–1933.* New York: St. Martin's Press, 1979.

———. *The New Deal and the Problem of Monopoly.* Princeton, NJ: Princeton University Press, 1966.

Hawley, Ellis W. "The New Deal State and the Anti-Bureaucratic Tradition." In Robert Eden, ed., *The New Deal and Its Legacy: Critique and Reappraisal.* Westport, CT: Greenwood Press, 1989.

———. "A Partnership Formed, Dissolved, and in Renegotiation: Business and Government in the Franklin D. Roosevelt Era." In Joseph R. Frese, S. J., and Jacob Judd, eds., *Business and Government.* New York: Sleepy Hollow Press, 1985.

Heclo, Hugh. *Modern Social Politics in Britain and Sweden.* New Haven, CT: Yale University Press, 1974.

Heilbroner, Robert, and Singer, Aaron. *The Economic Transformation of America: 1600 to the Present,* 3rd ed. Fort Worth, TX: Harcourt Brace College Publishers, 1994.

Herring, Jr., George C. *Aid to Russia, 1941–1946.* New York: Columbia University Press, 1973.

Himmelberg, Robert F. *The Origins of the National Recovery Administration.* New York: Fordham University Press, 1976.

———, ed. *The New Deal and Corporate Power: Antitrust and Regulatory Practices during the Thirties and World War II.* New York: Garland, 1994.

———, ed. *Survival of Corporatism During the New Deal Era, 1933–1945.* New York: Garland, 1994.

Hogan, Michael J. *Informal Entente: The Private Structure of Cooperation in Anglo-American Economic Diplomacy, 1918–1928.* Columbia: University of Missouri Press, 1977.

Hooks, Gregory. *Forging the Military-Industrial Complex: World War II's Battle of the Potomac.* Urbana: University of Illinois Press, 1991.

Huntington, Samuel P. *Political Order in Changing Societies.* New Haven, CT: Yale University Press, 1968.

Ickes, Harold. *The Secret Diary of Harold L. Ickes, Vol. 2: The Inside Struggle, 1936–1939.* New York: Simon and Schuster, 1954.

———. *The Secret Diary of Harold L. Ickes, Vol. 3: The Lowering Clouds, 1939–1941.* New York: Simon and Schuster, 1954.

Jacoby, Sanford M. *Modern Manors: Welfare Capitalism Since the New Deal.* Princeton, NJ: Princeton University Press, 1997.

Janeway, Eliot. *The Struggle for Survival: A Chronicle of Economic Mobilization During World War II.* New Haven, CT: Yale University Press, 1951.

Johnson, Chalmers. *MITI and the Japanese Miracle: The Growth of Industrial Policy, 1925–1975.* Stanford, CA: Stanford University Press, 1982.

Jonas, Manfred. *Isolationism in America, 1935–1941.* Ithaca, NY: Cornell University Press, 1966.

Jones, Jesse. *Fifty Billion Dollars: My Thirteen Years with the RFC, 1932–1945.* New York: Macmillan, 1951.

Karl, Barry. *Executive Reorganization and Reform in the New Deal.* Cambridge, MA: Harvard University Press, 1963.

———. *The Uneasy State: The United States from 1915 to 1945.* Chicago: University of Chicago Press, 1983.

Keegan, John. *The Second World War.* New York: Penguin Books, 1990.

Kennedy, David M. *Freedom from Fear: The American People in Depression and War, 1929–1945.* New York: Oxford University Press, 1999.

Kimball, Warren F. *The Most Unsordid Act: Lend-Lease, 1939–1941.* Baltimore, MD: Johns Hopkins Press, 1969.

Klein, Maury. *Union Pacific: The Rebirth, 1894–1969.* Garden City, NY: Doubleday, 1987.

Koistinen, Paul A. C. *The Military-Industrial Complex: A Historical Perspective.* New York: Praeger, 1980.

———. *Planning War, Pursuing Peace: The Political Economy of American Warfare, 1920–1939.* Lawrence: University Press of Kansas, 1998.

Kolko, Gabriel. *The Triumph of Conservatism: A Reinterpretation of American History, 1900–1916.* Chicago: Quadrangle Books, 1963.

Kroos, Herman. *Executive Opinion.* Garden City, NY: Doubleday, 1970.

LaFeber, Walter, Polenberg, Richard, and Woloch, Nancy. *The American Century: A History of the United States Since the 1890s,* 4th ed. New York: McGraw-Hill, 1992.

Leff, Mark H. *The Limits of Symbolic Reform: The New Deal and Taxation, 1933–1939.* Cambridge: Cambridge University Press, 1984.

Leuchtenburg, William E. *Franklin D. Roosevelt and the New Deal, 1932–1940.* New York: Harper and Row, 1963.

———. "The New Deal and the Analogue of War." In John Braeman, Robert H. Bremner, and Everett Walters, eds., *Change and Continuity in Twentieth-Century America.* Columbus: Ohio State University Press, 1964.

———. *The Perils of Prosperity, 1914–1932.* Chicago: University of Chicago Press, 1958.

Lichtenstein, Nelson. *Labor's War at Home: The CIO in World War II.* Cambridge: Cambridge University Press, 1982.

———. *The Most Dangerous Man in Detroit.* New York: Basic Books, 1995.

Lindblom, Charles E. *Politics and Markets: The World's Political-Economic Systems.* New York: Basic Books, 1977.

Lingeman, Richard R. *Don't You Know There's a War On? The American Home Front, 1941–1945.* New York: G. P. Putnam's Sons, 1970.

Loth, David. *Swope of G.E.* New York: Simon and Schuster, 1958.

Lowi, Theodore J. *The End of Liberalism,* 2nd ed. New York: Norton, 1979.

Lustig, R. Jeffrey. *Corporate Liberalism: The Origins of Modern American Political Theory, 1890–1920.* Berkeley: University of California Press, 1982.

Martin, George. *Madam Secretary: Frances Perkins.* Boston: Houghton Mifflin, 1976.

McConnell, Grant. *Private Power and American Democracy.* New York: Vintage Books, 1966.

McJimsey, George T. *Harry Hopkins: Ally of the Poor and Defender of Democracy.* Cambridge, MA: Harvard University Press, 1987.

McQuaid, Kim. *Big Business and Presidential Power: From FDR to Reagan.* New York: William Morrow and Company, 1982.

Millis, Walter. *Arms and Men: A Study in American Military History.* New York: G. P. Putnam's Sons, 1956.

Milward, Alan S. *War, Economy and Society, 1939–1945.* Berkeley: University of California Press, 1977.

Nash, Gerald D. *The Great Depression and World War II: Organizing America, 1933–1945.* New York: St. Martin's Press, 1979.

Nelson, Daniel. *Unemployment Insurance: The American Experience, 1915–1935.* Madison: University of Wisconsin Press, 1969.

Nelson, Donald M. *Arsenal of Democracy: The Story of American War Production.* New York: Harcourt, Brace and Company, 1946.

Noble, David F. *America by Design: Science, Technology, and the Rise of Corporate Capitalism.* New York: Knopf, 1977.

Offner, Arnold A. *American Appeasement: United States Foreign Policy and Germany, 1933–1938.* Cambridge, MA: Harvard University Press, 1969.

Overy, Richard. *Why the Allies Won.* New York: Norton, 1995.

Patterson, James T. *Congressional Conservatism and the New Deal.* Lexington, Kentucky: University of Kentucky Press, 1967.

Perez, Robert C., and Willett, Edward F. *The Will to Win: A Biography of Ferdinand Eberstadt.* New York: Greenwood Press, 1989.

Perrett, Geoffrey. *Days of Sadness, Years of Triumph: The American People 1939–1945.* New York: Coward, McCann & Geoghegan, 1973.

Pike, Frederick B., and Stritch, Thomas, eds. *The New Corporatism: Social-Political Structures in the Iberian World.* Notre Dame, IN: University of Notre Dame Press, 1974.

Plotke, David. *Building a Democratic Political Order: Reshaping American Liberalism in the 1930s and 1940s.* Cambridge: Cambridge University Press, 1996.

Polenberg, Richard. *War and Society: The United States, 1941–1945.* Philadelphia: J. B. Lippincott, 1972.

Polmar, Norman, and Allen, Thomas B. *World War II: America at War, 1941–1945.* New York: Random House, 1991.

Prothro, James Warren. *The Dollar Decade: Business Ideas in the 1920s.* New York: Greenwood Press, 1969.

Radosh, Ronald, and Rothbard, Murray N. *A New History of Leviathan.* New York: E. P. Dutton, 1972.

Schlesinger, Arthur M. Jr. *The Age of Roosevelt: The Coming of the New Deal.* Boston: Houghton Mifflin, 1959.

———. *The Age of Roosevelt: The Crisis of the Old Order, 1919–1933.* Boston: Houghton Mifflin, 1957.

———. *The Age of Roosevelt: The Politics of Upheaval.* Boston: Houghton Mifflin, 1960.

Schwarz, Jordan A. *The Speculator: Bernard M. Baruch in Washington, 1917–1965.* Chapel Hill: University of North Carolina Press, 1981.

Skocpol, Theda. "Bringing the State Back In: Strategies of Analysis in Current Research." In Peter Evans, Dietrich Rueschemeyer, and Theda Skocpol, eds., *Bringing the State Back In* Cambridge: Cambridge University Press, 1985.

Skowronek, Stephen. *Building a New American State: The Expansion of National Administrative Capacities, 1877–1920.* Cambridge: Cambridge University Press, 1982.

Smith, R. Elberton. *The Army and Economic Mobilization.* Washington, DC: Office of the Chief of Military History, Department of the Army, 1959.

Sparrow, Bartholomew H. *From the Outside In: World War II and the American State.* Princeton, NJ: Princeton University Press, 1996.

Spector, Ronald H. *Eagle Against the Sun: The American War with Japan.* New York: Free Press, 1985.

Stein, Herbert. *The Fiscal Revolution in America.* Chicago: University of Chicago Press, 1969.

Stettinius, Edward R. Jr. *Lend-Lease: Weapon for Victory.* New York: Macmillan, 1944.

Stone, I. F. *Business As Usual: The First Year of Defense.* New York: Modern Age Books, 1941.

———. *The War Years, 1939–1945.* Boston: Little, Brown, 1988.

Swope, Gerard. *The Swope Plan.* New York: Business Bourse, 1931.

Timmons, Bascom. *Jesse H. Jones: The Man and the Statesman.* New York: Holt, 1956.

Tone, Andrea. *The Business of Benevolence: Industrial Paternalism in Progressive America.* Ithaca, NY: Cornell University Press, 1997.

Vander Meulen, Jacob. *The Politics of Aircraft: Building an American Military Industry.* Lawrence: University Press of Kansas, 1991.

Vatter, Harold G. *The U.S. Economy in World War II.* New York: Columbia University Press, 1985.

Waddell, Brian. *The War Against the New Deal: World War II and American Democracy.* Dekalb: Northern Illinois University Press, 2001.

Warken, Philip W. *A History of the National Resources Planning Board, 1933–1943.* New York: Garland, 1979.

Webber, Michael J. *New Deal Fat Cats: Business, Labor, and Campaign Finance in the 1936 Presidential Election.* New York: Fordham University Press, 2000.

Weigley, Russell F. *History of the United States Army.* Bloomington: Indiana University Press, 1984.

Weinstein, James. *The Corporate Ideal in the Liberal State, 1900–1918.* Boston: Beacon Press, 1969.

Wells, Wyatt. *Antitrust and the Formation of the Postwar World.* New York: Columbia University Press, 2002.

White, Gerald T. *Billions for Defense: Government Financing by the Defense Plant Corporation During World War II.* University: University of Alabama Press, 1980.

Wiebe, Robert. *Businessmen and Reform: A Study of the Progressive Movement.* Chicago: Quadrangle, 1962.

———. *The Search for Order, 1877–1920.* New York: Hill and Wang, 1967.

Wilkins, Mira. *The Maturing of Multinational Enterprise: American Business Abroad from 1914 to 1970.* Cambridge, MA: Harvard University Press, 1974.

Williams, William Appleman. *The Contours of American History.* Chicago: Quadrangle Books, 1966.

Wiltz, John E. *In Search of Peace: The Senate Munitions Inquiry, 1934–1936.* Baton Rouge: Louisiana State University Press, 1963.

Winkler, Allan M. *Home Front U.S.A.: America During World War II.* Arlington Heights, IL: Harlan Davidson, 1986.

Witte, Edwin. *The Development of the Social Security Act.* Madison: University of Wisconsin Press, 1963.

Wolfskill, George. *The Revolt of the Conservatives: A History of the American Liberty League, 1934–1940.* Boston: Houghton Mifflin, 1962.

Wood, Gordon S. *The Creation of the American Republic, 1776–1787.* Chapel Hill: University of North Carolina Press, 1969.

Zieger, Robert. *Republicans and Labor, 1919–1929.* Lexington, Kentucky: University of Kentucky Press, 1969.

B. Articles

Auerbach, Jerold S. "New Deal, Old Deal, or Raw Deal: Some Thoughts on New Left Historiography." *Journal of Southern History* 35 (February 1969): 18–30.

Berk, Gerald. "Corporate Liberalism Reconsidered: A Review Essay." *Journal of Policy History* 3, no. 1 (1991): 70–84.

Berkowitz, Edward, and McQuaid, Kim. "Businessman and Bureaucrat: The Evolution of the American Social Welfare System, 1900–1940." *Journal of Economic History* 38 (March 1978): 120–42.

Bernstein, Barton J. "The Automobile Industry and the Coming of the Second World War." *Southwestern Social Science Quarterly* 47 (June 1966): 22–33.

Collins, Robert M. "Positive Business Responses to the New Deal: The Roots of the Committee for Economic Development, 1933–1942." *Business History Review* 52 (Autumn 1978): 369–91.

Dennison, Henry S. "Stabilizing Employment in a Diversified Seasonal Industry." *The Annals of the American Academy* (September 1922).

Dennison, Henry S., and Tarbell, Ida. "The President's Industrial Conference of October 1919." *Bulletin of the Taylor Society* (April 1920).

Domhoff, G. William. "Corporate Liberal Theory and the Social Security Act: A Chapter in the Sociology of Knowledge." *Politics and Sociology* 15, no. 3 (1987): 297–330.

Ferguson, Thomas. "From Normalcy to New Deal: Industrial Structure, Party Competition, and American Public Policy in the Great Depression." *International Organization* 38 (Winter 1984): 41–94.

Gaddis, John Lewis. "The Corporatist Synthesis: A Skeptical View." *Diplomatic History* 10 (Fall 1986): 357–62.

Galambos, Louis. "The Emerging Organizational Synthesis." *Business History Review* 44 (1970): 279–90.

Gitelman, H. M. "Welfare Capitalism Reconsidered." *Labor History* 33 (1992): 5–31.

Griffith, Robert. "Dwight D. Eisenhower and the Corporate Commonwealth." *American Historical Review* 87 (February 1982): 87–122.

Hacker, Jacob S., and Pierson, Paul. "Business Power and Social Policy: Employers and the Formation of the American Welfare State." *Politics and Society* 30, no. 2 (June 2002): 277–325.

Harris, Joseph P. "The Emergency National Defense Organization." *Public Administration Review* 1 (Autumn 1940): 1–24.

Hawley, Ellis W. "The Discovery and Study of a 'Corporate Liberalism.' " *Business History Review* 52 (Autumn 1978): 309–20.

Hawley, Ellis W. "Herbert Hoover, the Commerce Secretariat, and the Vision of an 'Associative State,' 1921–1929." *Journal of American History* 61 (June 1974): 116–40.

Henderson, Leon, and Nelson, Donald M. "Prices, Profits, and Government." *Harvard Business Review* 19 (Summer 1941): 389–404.

Hogan, Michael J. "Corporatism: A Positive Appraisal." *Diplomatic History* 10 (Fall 1986): 363–72.

———. "Revival and Reform: America's Twentieth Century Search for a New Economic Order Abroad." *Diplomatic History* 8 (Fall 1984): 287–310.

Holl, Richard E. "Marion B. Folsom and the Rochester Plan of 1931." *Rochester History* 61, no. 1 (Winter 1999): 1–21.

Jacobs, Meg. "How About Some Meat?: The Office of Price Administration, Consumption Politics, and State Building from the Bottom Up, 1941–1946." *Journal of American History* 84, no. 3 (December 1997): 910–41.

Jacoby, Sanford M. "Employers and the Welfare State: The Role of Marion B. Folsom." *Journal of American History* 80, no. 2 (September 1993): 525–56.

Jeffries, John W. "The 'New' New Deal: FDR and American Liberalism, 1937–1945." *Political Science Quarterly* 105 (Fall 1990): 397–418.

Kolko, Gabriel. "American Business and Germany, 1930–1941." *Western Political Quarterly* 15 (December 1962): 713–28.

Leuchtenburg, William. "The Pertinence of Political History." *Journal of American History* 73 (December 1986): 585–600.

Martin, John H. "Administration of Priorities." *Harvard Business Review* 19 (Summer 1941): 419–28.

McCormick, Thomas J. "Drift or Mastery?: A Corporatist Synthesis for American Diplomatic History." *Reviews in American History* 10 (December 1982): 318–30.

McKelvey, Blake. "A Semi-Centennial Review of Family Service of Rochester, Inc." *Rochester History* 23, no. 2 (April 1961): 1–11.

McQuaid, Kim. "The Business Advisory Council of the Department of Commerce, 1933–1961." *Research in Economic History* 1 (1976): 171–97.

———. "Corporate Liberalism in the American Business Community, 1920–1940." *Business History Review* 52 (Autumn 1978): 342–68.

———. "Henry S. Dennison and the 'Science' of Industrial Reform, 1900–1950." *American Journal of Economics and Sociology* 36 (January 1977): 79–98.

———. "Young, Swope and 'New Capitalism': A Study in Corporate Liberalism, 1920–1933." *American Journal of Economics and Sociology* 36 (July 1977): 323–34.

Nash, Gerald D. "Experiments in Industrial Mobilization: W.I.B. and N.R.A." *Mid-America* 45 (1963): 157–74.

Rutherford, H. K. "Mobilizing Industry for War." *Harvard Business Review* 18 (Autumn 1939): 1–10.

Sklar, Martin J. "Woodrow Wilson and the Political Economy of Modern United States Liberalism." *Studies on the Left* 1 (1960): 17–47.

Skocpol, Theda. "Political Responses to Capitalist Crisis: Neo-Marxist Theories of the State and the Case of the New Deal." *Politics and Society* 10 (1980): 155–201.

Skocpol, Theda. "A Society Without a 'State'? Political Organization, Social Conflict, and Welfare Provision in the United States." *Journal of Public Policy* 7 (October–December 1987): 349–71.

Skocpol, Theda, and Finegold, Kenneth. "State Capacity and Economic Intervention in the Early New Deal." *Political Science Quarterly* 97 (1982): 255–78.

Skocpol, Theda, and Ikenberry, John. "The Political Formation of the American Welfare State in Historical and Comparative Perspective." *Comparative Social Research* 6 (1983): 87–148.

Swenson, Peter. "Arranged Alliance: Business Interests in the New Deal." *Politics and Society* 25 (March 1997): 66–116.

Vogel, David. "Why Businessmen Distrust Their State: The Political Consciousness of American Corporate Executives." *British Journal of Political Science* 8 (1978): 45–78.

Vollmers, Gloria. "Industrial Home Work of the Dennison Manufacturing Company of Framingham, Massachusetts, 1912–1935." *Business History Review* 71 (Autumn 1997): 444–70.

Waddell, Brian. "Economic Mobilization for World War II and the Transformation of the U.S. State." *Politics and Society* 22 (June 1994): 165–94.

Weir, Margaret, and Skocpol, Theda. "State Structures and Social Keynesianism." *International Journal of Comparative Sociology* 24 (January–April 1983): 4–29.

C. Encyclopedias

American National Biography, Vol. 7, 1999.

Business Leader Profiles for Students, 1999.

Current Biography (1939–1941).

Dictionary of American Biography (1946–1950).

National Cyclopaedia of American Biography (1943–1946, 1953, 1955).

D. Dissertations

Bland, Larry I. "W. Averell Harriman: Businessman and Diplomat, 1891–1945." Ph.D. dissertation, University of Wisconsin, 1972.

Brown, Linda. "Challenge and Response: The American Business Community and the New Deal, 1932–1934." Ph.D. dissertation, University of Pennsylvania, 1972.

Koistinen, Paul A. C. "The Hammer and the Sword: Labor, the Military, and Industrial Mobilization, 1920–1945." Ph.D. dissertation, University of California, Berkeley, 1964.

Metcalf, Evan B. "Economic Stabilization by American Business in the Twentieth Century." Ph.D. dissertation, University of Wisconsin, 1972.

Index